MEHER BABA, AN IRANIAN LIBERAL

Intercultural Research Series of Anthropography No. 5

MEHER BABA, AN IRANIAN LIBERAL

KEVIN SHEPHERD

Anthropographia Publications
Cambridge

First published in 1988
by Anthropographia Publications,
P.O. Box 13, Cambridge CB4 1EZ, England.

ISBN 0 9508680 5 1

Printed and bound in Great Britain by
Redwood Burn Limited, Trowbridge, Wiltshire.

CONTENTS

PREFACE

The "movement" associated with Meher Baba now has a large Indian following amongst Parsis and Hindus, and a smaller one in Western countries. This movement is highly law-abiding, and in general reflects the moral rulings of the figurehead. The devotional strains originated in Indian ranks, and have been overstated outside India. My own position has sounded ambiguous to both critics and partisans, since I respect Meher Baba (and have done since my youth), but do not choose to propagandize in any way for the movement in his name. To define whether or not Meher Baba was the literal *avatar* is beyond my range of competence, and I have seldom seen this done satisfactorily even one fraction. I must leave that subject for theologians to argue over. I do admit that Meher Baba was a powerful influence upon me from my early youth onwards. Some academic critics of Meher Baba take the attitude that it is not possible to write about him without losing caste, but I have no caste to lose, and I do in contrast take the view that there is no subject which anthropography cannot tackle in the interests of human knowledge.

The following pages consist of both appraisal and critique of diverse elements, a treatment which moves at a radical tangent to the "orthodox" perspective of the devotional movement attaching to Meher Baba. This study is primarily sociological and philosophical, though the latter term does of course include mysticism.

Many of the books on Meher Baba are very much in the idiom of personal reminiscences, and have disadvantages proportionately. There has rarely been any attempt to approach the phenomenon in terms of a more total context, and with due critical appraisal where the data requires. This is what I intend to do; Charles Purdom was formerly the only writer to have worked on these lines, though my treatment does differ from his substantially.

Though Meher Baba has sometimes been misnomered as the "Indian messiah," he was actually of pure Iranian blood. This Iranian background grants a context rather different from that often associated with him, and it is rather surprising that this context has not so far been outlined. This study is the first to do so, and in accordance with the analytical requirements of the science and philosophy of anthropography.

Kevin R.D.Shepherd

Intercultural Research Centre of Anthropography,
Cambridge

February 1986

INTRODUCTION

The analysis of sectarian movements sometimes reveals that the founder, or purported founder, is not adequately represented by the collective aftermath. It is not always possible to ascertain any such disparity in the case of some movements owing to a sparse documentation concerning origins. It is my contention that the copious documentation relating to Meher Baba furnishes proof of a dichotomy in representation and a proportionate deficit.

The relevant documentation is now prolific to the extent that it is no longer possible for casual inspection to conveniently evaluate the substance of the contention expressed above. The variety of the sources are further complicated by the span of some half a century to which they relate; the complexity of the different periods in the biography of the subject can be, and has been, offset by undue focus upon some preferred aspect or phase.

The structure and content of the present book differs radically from that of other treatments of the subject. Leaving aside diary notes and personal memoranda, several published treatments have taken the form of a combination of the author's life with that of the subject, an arrangement not always conducive to wider issues or non-personal facets of occurrence. Much of this writing is clearly of a devotional nature, and evidences a marked opting for the more easily assimilable and simplified aspects of Meher Baba's life and teaching. That he himself permitted this dilution during his lifetime is evident enough, but it cannot be taken as an accurate or comprehensive index to the subject.

The one biographer who attempted to achieve a contrasting

objectivity was Charles Purdom, who significantly detached his personal views from his factual narrative. When he did include some of his personal views at the end of his treatment, they were not all complimentary to the devotional movement that increasingly formed around Meher Baba. A critical view of the "movement" is therefore not without precedent. Had Purdom written after the subject's death, one suspects that his muted critique would have made itself more apparent in the factual section.

Another writer who expressed a notable tangent to devotional enthusiasm was Dr. William Donkin, who produced a unique monograph upon an abstruse and yet very tangible subject of sociological significance. *The Wayfarers* detailed Hindu and Muslim "saints" and other categories who had been in contact with Meher Baba over a lengthy period. Interestingly, this account was largely indigestible to Meher Baba's devotees (particularly Westerners); it was seldom read and very seldom achieved intelligent comment. Some writers who did refer to this research notably simplified it inordinately. Even Purdom failed to come to adequate grips with it.

Possibly the most surprising trend in this vein of neglect was that Meher Baba's major work *God Speaks* was often left unread by his followers. Some found it too laborious to read, and evinced an almost total lack of familiarity with the contents. It is quite true that by comparison with many other mystical works, this book is unusually complex and calls for some concentration, but the disparity between "following" some leader and being in ignorance of what he expounds should be readily apparent to the more studious.

Meher Baba's magnum opus was not only dictated via an alphabet board owing to his austere silence of mouth, but incorporates many words from the Persian-Arabic repertory of Sufism and the Sanskrit tradition of Vedanta. The supplement was substantially contributed to by a Muslim pupil, one Dr. Abdul Ghani Munsiff, who was a lifelong student of sufi subjects. Yet it is evident that Meher Baba's devotional following in the West had little or no affinity with such linguistic and philosophical channels.

This is one discernible element of the dichotomy in representation to which I draw attention.

It is an interesting fact that, statistically, the number of Muslim pupils and contacts was very low in the last years of Meher Baba's life, and much higher in earlier years. The devotional literature shows little or no awareness of statistics, but it is a fact that the prodigious increase in numbers of Meher Baba's followers from the early 1950's onwards was centred in Hindu populations primarily, and secondarily amongst Parsis and Westerners. The older Muslim element amongst his pupils did not replenish itself, and by the time that *God Speaks* was published in 1955, the Muslim component in his activity was well on the wane. Yet his major work clearly shows a working use of concepts and terminology drawn from sectors of Muslim Sufism, and in fact it emerges from a close analysis that this Sufi element is actually stronger than the Vedantic in this particular book.

Although Meher Baba was born a Parsi, there is nothing in his teaching that can be traced to orthodox Zoroastrianism. There are, however, certain strong affinities with the Kaivani philosophers of Mughal India, who are classifiable as "Zoroastrian ishraqis" in alignment with earlier trends in Iran. I have shown elsewhere, in *From Oppression to Freedom*, that Meher Baba's father Sheriar Irani fits a Kaivani pattern to a remarkable degree. None of this had ever been hinted at in the literature available on Meher Baba; his father was of little or no interest to the Meher Baba movement, and in fact it was Meher Baba's mother who disparately received most of the plaudits from devotees, since she was far more conspicuous in overt events. This kind of truncated perspective is typical of the devotee mentality which formed around the "avatar" projection which Meher Baba verbalized from 1954 onwards, though with various stylizations not commonly found in the Hindu milieu of which it was an extension.

It tends to be forgotten that Meher Baba did not project the issue of "avatarhood" in any definitive sense until the 1950's, by which time he was sixty years old. He had referred earlier to this matter, but in a much more oblique manner for the most part, and *never* publicly. Even in the late 1940's some of his more intimate Indian pupils did not regard him as anything more than a "master" in status. In the earlier years he was commonly referred to as Shri Meher Baba, while Muslims knew him as Hazrat Meher Baba. The devotional movement did not commence to use the celebrity label of Avatar until the mid–1950's, as a result of which usage it stuck to collective ideas of reverential expression. It was not Meher Baba who inaugurated this development, but his Parsi secretary Adi K.Irani, a man who was fond of styling himself as Avatar Meher Baba's "Disciple and Secretary" on his office stationery, an idiosyncrasy that passed without criticism from devotional ranks.

That Meher Baba did make high claims of prerogative is not to be denied, and it is not for me to attempt to assess matters outside my scope of competence. But this consideration does not extend to more pedestrian evaluations which are necessary. I am referring to manifestations of elitism amongst his devotional following, one of which has been pointed out above. It is necessary to be critical of popular developments within the movement under discussion in order to ascertain the precise context of various statements and events concerning the figurehead and/or the factors motivating the canonizers.

It can be remarked here that although Meher Baba can be aligned in several respects with the Kaivani tradition of Mughal India, there are also certain differences. He definitely departed from the disposition of his father Sheriar Mundegar, who by comparison was a "Junaydi," to use a term denoting esoteric caution in early sufi annals. Meher Baba was very much more in the "Hallajian" tradition of more overt communications. Lest this be thought too superficial a comparison (as such comparisons do tend to become), I hasten to add that Meher Baba also shows signs of some intrinsic Junaydi characteristics.

Even if Meher Baba's claims to prerogative are dismissed or deemed to be in need of modification, as his critics urge, his teaching was in many ways original and sophisticated. This is one of the factors that has sometimes caused critical and impartial investigators a certain amount of puzzlement. Anybody who studies his teaching sufficiently will see that it remains curiously unintegrated into devotional accounts. Critics might therefore conclude that Meher Baba had not sufficiently integrated his own teaching into his life. But to the contrary, my own conclusion is that he did integrate his philosophy into his lifestyle, but that neither his philosophy nor his methodology were understood by many of the people who claimed to represent him.

As a messianic trend, the Meher Baba movement is overdue for sociological analysis, providing that such analysis squares with the requirements of an adequate intercultural philosophy. Due attention should be given to the fact that there was both an "avataric" phase and a "pre-avataric" phase in Meher Baba's life, and that the latter phase was of a substantially longer duration. General ideas concerning Meher Baba have often been influenced by the attacks of his detractors, particularly the elaborate attack of Paul Brunton. Conversely, devotee enthusiasm frequently mars reports that do otherwise contain some relevant information.

It is rare that investigators have the opportunity to view in such detail a biography which is capable of variant interpretations. For instance, the devotional movement currently in existence sees itself as precipitating (however indirectly) the beginnings of a new religion. If this is so however, then it is also evident that a *zahiri* (externalist) interpretation has been adopted and more *batini* (esoteric) developments neglected. These neglected elements are clearly attested in the material under discussion. One wonders what the fate of heretics will be once a suitably tapered version of the inherited material has been adapted for a larger population, or populations.

The serious reader of any researched book is entitled to learn the qualifications of the researcher. What background have I in the subject of this book that merits any attention? I am not a devotee of Meher Baba and have no affiliation with the movement passing under his name. But I can claim some personal participation in, and observation of, this movement during Meher Baba's lifetime, or at least until the end of 1966. I met Charles Purdom and many other followers of Meher Baba, including several Parsis, a few Hindus, and one Muslim. I received several personal communications from Meher Baba, who was living in an almost inaccessible seclusion from the outside world. I was in my teens at that time, and knew of Meher Baba from 1962 onwards. My viewpoint did not coincide with the majoritarian view in this movement, and this led to my secession from its activities owing to the fact that my views were deemed heretical by those who assumed spokesmanship for Meher Baba. I did not however lose interest in Meher Baba himself, and afterwards wrote the first full-scale biography in four volumes (see Bibliography no. 35) as a personal project of mine. I had always felt that the record should be set straight, and in 1966 had mentioned this to Meher Baba by letter. His cabled reply was: "I am happy with your intentions, but it is not the time for you to attempt such a work." He was a better judge than me, because too few people wanted the record set straight, and also because some matters became much clearer to me with the passing of years.

In the anthropographic sense, Meher Baba is a particularly relevant point of reference in the comparative evaluation of pre-Islamic Iranian groupings and trends. He fills a sorely needed "ethnoarchaeological" niche in the necessary evaluation of vanished phenomena in the diachronic scale. Consider the following points which I have anthropographically formulated:

1). As a "guru" figure in the Indian milieu, Meher Baba was unique by virtue of his Zoroastrian birth. Hence we have here an "Irano-Aryan" ethnic counterpart to the Indo-Aryan guru figures that are more familiar to the media, a counterpart that cannot be found in Iranian Islam owing to the Arab and Turkish admixtures. The uniqueness of this juxtaposition is not imaginary, and the subject could therefore provide a singularly fruitful and valid source of comparisons if these are sufficiently ramifying.

2). There are certain aspects to Meher Baba which confer upon him significance as an extension of the Azar Kaivan trend of *ishraq* (illuminism) in an Irano-aryan form. He himself never adopted any such label of identification. He was in fact very original in respect of his verbal media and his lifestyle phases. As a consequence of this originality, it is perhaps not surprising that he has had imitators in Poona, California, and elsewhere. However, these copyist gurus of varying nationalities are so crudely cheap as to make any synchronic (or near synchronic) comparisons highly favourable to Meher Baba. Upon close inspection, Meher Baba's originality is not easy to imitate, since it employed various curbs not usually found in sectarian movements. These curbs are apparent to some extent in the Kaivani tradition, and on a more diachronic scale, are vestigially discernible in gnostic ranks of Sassanian Iran. The Mazdakite movement has recently been revealed as much more complex than was formerly thought (see my *Minds and Sociocultures*, Appendix 1), and its ascetic wing is more accurately denoted by Zardusht-i Khurragan than by Mazdak. This ascetic contingent were anti-priest but not social militants like the less tempered Mazdakites. The latter tended to non-ascetic and libertine habits, and seem to have conveniently diluted the more intrinsic nonconformist tradition that was earlier than Mazdak (a tradition which is not to be confused with institutional Manichaeism). Meher Baba fits the ascetic mould of the "Mazdakite" *dris-den* rather closely, insofar as this is now marginally discernible. He was an avowed anti-ritualist but strictly discountenanced any involvement in political affairs. His personal lifestyle was very markedly austere – his fasts are comparable to Gandhi's, his seclusions put him out of the reach of devotees for long periods at a time, while his silence became almost proverbial even amongst critics. Significantly perhaps, he would not allow devotees to become ascetics, owing to their unpreparedness; unfledged ascetics can tend to become gurus rather too quickly. The Kaivani tradition was markedly ascetic, and it is evident that devotees cannot merit the same classification as Kaivanis (Kaivanis amount to disciples proper, in a way that would render common usage of "disciple" as a completely devalued word).

3). Since we possess far more information about Meher Baba than the Sassanian Mazdakites, it seems sensible to employ the bulk of data to comprehensive advantage rather than committing it to oblivion as has so far occurred in the field of Iranist scholarship. Comparisons are not limited to the Sassanian era, despite the tendency of specialist scholars to emphasize the differences between Sassanian Iran and Islamic Iran. Meher Baba's "Hallajian" capacity for bold gnostic declaration clearly renders him distinct from his father Sheriar Mundegar, but there was no hereditary transmission claimed in this instance. This gnostic aspect was not without social consequence. The Parsi community has strongly registered Meher Baba's emphases, and in certain rural areas of Hindu India, his teachings have produced a powerful force against superstitions that would otherwise be more operative. The "Hallajian" propulsion can produce a dynamic for a change in the social system that can be beneficial or no depending upon the quality of incentive. This prompts the question as to the long-term social contribution value of such dynamic. To what extent would a Zardusht-i Khurragan have echoed the emphases of Zarathushtra Spitama of more archaic fame? To what extent does Meher Baba tally with the unorthodox tangent of the earlier Zarathushtra of the Gathas? This latter question is obviously difficult to answer, but I do not see why Meher Baba should be considered a less eligible source of comparison here than even Mani (who was also many centuries later), despite linguistic removes (which are arguably more superficial than is sometimes thought). Meher Baba may have been even closer to the intrinsic *dris-den* tradition of the Mazdakites than Mani was, though surprisingly little is known about the latter individual of the third century A.D. Those scholars who view the Zoroastrian priesthood as the direct heirs of Zarathushtra Spitama will tend to deem *dris-den* and other gnostic dissenters as irrelevant, but the argument that orthodoxy is equivalent to origins is no more convincing than the Spanish Inquisition being whitewashed as the work of Christ.

4). The possible influence exerted by Azar Kaivan (d. 1618) in Mughal affairs of state policy is tempered in the annals by the evident secrecy with which Kaivan and his associates cloaked themselves. This secrecy is partly traceable to persecution vogues from which they fled, and raises the question as to what might have been their dominant traits if persecution had been unknown to them. Sheriar Mundegar Irani had likewise known what it feels like to be a member of an afflicted social minority, but his son was reared in a very different setting. If Meher Baba had been subject to persecution, we would be unlikely to know him as, e.g., an exponent of clarified *tanasukh* (transmigration). The originality of such teaching is not easily explained away on the grounds of an inherited oral chain of transmitters. Yet it remains a possibility that a similar teaching was current amongst the Mughal era Kaivanis, one which would have found difficulty in percolating to the court even if it had been divulged. This would have been not least because orthodox Hindu ideas on the subject of the transmigration of souls were in too clear a contrast for eclectic sympathies to have brusquely imposed a new model. While the emperor Akbar and his advisers like Abu'l Fazl Allami may have realized that Kaivani teachings represented an escape route from the Muslim versus Hindu deadlock, the emperor could not in practice prevent, e.g., the premature fate of immolation reserved for Hindu wives on the funeral pyre of their husbands, owing to the conditioning of caste Hindus on such points. This situation perhaps serves to throw into extra relief the unique sociological parallel in more recent times: a Zoroastrian *baba* accomodating himself to a Hindu philosophical and devotional milieu while promulgating exceptional wujudi (irfani) sufi emphases in a way that serves to universalize their application in a neo-ishraqi context. In philosophical terms, the result effectively outstripped the Muslim versus Hindu deadlock comprised by the two major divisional factors of his environment.

In attempting to bring out useful features in the life and teaching of Meher Baba, I intend to combine anthropographic standards of critique and empathy. I will first give a summary of key biographical events before attempting a summary of his teaching. This will better enable the reader to approach the complexities in Parts Three and Four.

PART ONE

BIOGRAPHY: A PRELIMINARY TREATMENT

Meher Baba was born in Poona on 25th February, 1894. His name of birth was Merwan Sheriar Irani. His parents were Irani Zoroastrians who had emigrated to India, where they had become part of the Parsi community of Zoroastrians centred in the Bombay-Surat area. His father, Sheriar Mundegar, had been a dervish for eighteen years, travelling widely in both Iran and (later) India before adopting a sedentary life. Starting from poverty, this male parent had become a prosperous tea shop proprietor by the time of Merwan's birth. Sheriar was also a self-taught scholar in Persian and Arabic, and maintained an outlook on life that was saturated with sufi ideas and perspectives. Merwan was his second eldest son, but was his favourite son, and benefited from his father's acquaintance with Persian classical literature.

Merwan Irani was an intelligent boy and was ensured a good education by his father. He learnt English in accordance with the general Parsi vogue, but did not neglect other languages. He was not only proficient in Persian and Gujarati, but also Urdu, which is related to Persian and spoken by Indian Muslims.

After matriculating successfully from the best high school in Poona, Merwan became a university undergraduate at the Deccan College in 1911. He was the only one amongst Sheriar's sons to achieve college level, and likewise the only one to become a poet. He showed a flair for English literature, which was his academic speciality, but his main interests were in Persian and Indian literature. He was familiar with the work of Rumi and Hafiz, and modelled his own poetic style upon the latter. He wrote much poetry in

Persian and vernacular languages, some of which is distinctive.

In addition to athletic capacities at school and college, Merwan also exhibited a contemplative disposition, and spent solitary hours at the local Zoroastrian tower of silence and also Muslim cemeteries. In this he was clearly following his father's precedent; Sheriar's influence upon him seems to have been a strong one. These tendencies were not shared by his brothers, of whom there were eventually four.

During his college studies, Merwan became strongly linked to Hazrat Babajan.[1] This Muslim woman was reputed to be about a hundred years old, and then had the beginnings of what transpired to be a substantial following in the local area. Of strong sufi associations, this matriarch lived in the same cantonment zone of Poona as Merwan's family. It was in May 1913 that Merwan began to frequent her makeshift abode under the neem tree in the Char Bavadi locality. He visited her every evening, but their meetings were almost completely silent.

It was the kind of non-verbal momentum that was to become a strong personal hallmark of Meher Baba, and a factor which did not always contribute to a convenience for reporting. The most discerning eye-witness of this early period was his father Sheriar, but that worthy was not the most communicative of men when it came to matters that he regarded as important.

In January 1914 Merwan's mother Shirin was horrified to discover early one morning that he could not speak and was lying on his bed with wide open but vacuously staring eyes. He lay like this for three days to her even greater alarm. She concluded that he was critically ill. She felt some hope when he began to move about of his own volition on the fourth day, but was soon dismayed to realize that he acted like a virtual automaton. She could not even get him to eat any food. He seemed to have effectively died whilst still physically alive.

Medical treatment produced no change in Merwan's extraordinary condition. It is reliably reported that for nine months he would not eat (unless force-fed) and did not sleep. His mother thought that he had become insane, which is what the doctors assumed. He himself much later commented that his father knew that his condition was not as everyone else thought. In his own varied travels Sheriar had doubtless seen strange states of mind exhibited that were known to dervish lore, but the increasingly westernized Parsi community had no knowledge of such experiential tangents and could not credit their existence. In Shirin's eyes, her son's university career had been ruined; he had gained the opportunity of a fully qualified Western education, a passport to everlasting success and prosperity in the conventional Parsi view. To Sheriar this meant little, since he distrusted the basic assumptions of Western education. He had never bothered to learn English, instead preferring fluency in Arabic.

Shirin came to blame Babajan for her son's strange condition. According to Merwan's later report, Babajan was in fact the cause of it, but his version of causation was very different to his mother's. He said later that his inner state had *consciously* expanded; his mother assumed that he had lost consciousness.

After nine months, his condition changed to some semblance of normality. He began to eat regularly and seemed aware of what was going on around him, but remained strangely indrawn and largely aloof from human contact. But a few months later, in April 1915 he became more physicalized and began to take long walks around the city, followed by excursions to distant places. He visited several figures of sufi background: Banemiyan Baba of Aurangabad, Tippu Baba of Bombay, Tajuddin Baba of Nagpur, and Sai Baba of Shirdi. He also made contact with the Hindu sage Narayan Maharaj of Kedgaon.

All these contacts were fleeting, and his relatives had little idea of his motivations, since he was not very communicative. But there was one figure whom they all had good cause to remember in subsequent years, namely Upasni Maharaj of Sakori. This fierce Hindu guru was a highly atypical holy man,[2] and became Merwan's supervisor from now on. After their initial encounter in December 1915, Merwan visited Upasni regularly at the latter's new ashram at Sakori. This relationship lasted for six years, and occurred despite Shirin's resentment of the continued influence of non-Westernized mystical entities in her son's altered career. For he was never again to take up a university course, but was instead reduced to a role as a menial.

Shirin insisted that Merwan adopt some profession, or at the least take up some business venture. He tried to oblige her, but was unable to remain in employment owing to his acutely introverted state. He ended up working in his father's teashop, and afterwards in a newly opened toddy shop. Yet puzzling as it was to most of his relatives, young men began to be increasingly drawn to him and felt a definite reverence for him.

Finally, in mid–1921 Merwan moved from Poona to Sakori to stay with Upasni Maharaj. After several months, Upasni told some of his pupils that Merwan(ji) had gained a special prerogative. He told one of his leading disciples, a Zoroastrian named Gustadji Hansotia, that Merwanji was "the *sadguru* of this age," and that Hansotia should now serve Merwanji and not he (Upasni).

By now, Merwan displayed a completely normal demeanour and reflex, but far from reverting to college habits or taking up any profession or business, he chose to lead an ascetic existence in a small hut (*jhopdi*) on open ground at Poona. Throughout his life he was to display a personal preference for small and rudimentary huts as living quarters, bereft of the amenities deemed essential by civilization. At the Poona *jhopdi*, he was the focus for a mixed assortment of Zoroastrian, Muslim, and Hindu acquaintances and admirers who began to identify themselves as his followers. For the most part he did not impose on them any form of training or discipline however. This he began to do after journeying by foot to Bombay in May 1922; there he accomodated over forty men in the urban dwelling known as the Manzil-e-Meem, and presided over a rigorous and distinctive routine in which he asserted his prerogative as the instructor and "master" of the pupils. But he would not align himself with any particular religious or spiritual tradition, not Zoroastrian, Vedantic, or even Sufi. His teaching was already distinctive even at this very early period. Extant details reveal him as a psychologist of no small ability.

He was now known as Meher Baba ("compassionate father") to his pupils. Though he was very easygoing towards women, he was an iron disciplinarian with males, and those in his close proximity soon found that it was not easy to maintain his standards. Many of the men with him found a welcome respite from discipline when he closed the Manzil and departed with only a few selected individuals on a gruelling and unpredictable series of journeys that took him as far afield as the Afghan and Nepalese borderlines. Meher Baba (whom I shall hereafter also refer to as Baba) was no softpedaller, and never opted for any easy course as he could very conveniently have done. Instead he commenced his characteristic programme of prolonged fasting in addition to non-luxury travelling and general austere living standards.

The ascetic personal characteristics of Meher Baba received their most well known manifestation in his adoption of complete silence of mouth, commenced in July 1925. He never spoke a single word until his death forty-four years later. This notable personal aloofness from human intercourse was mitigated to some extent by his aura of humour which he managed to mutely project, but the concentrative aspect of his personality was often unduly minimized in devotee reports. In January 1927 he gave up writing, save for his signature, and thereafter employed an (English) alphabet board for purposes of communication. But this meant that he was often dependent upon the verbal clarifications of others to an extent that should not be ignored.

It is perhaps not entirely surprising that in a man of Meher Baba's introspective capacity, there were increasing references to his "inner work." Yet some of these statements sound blatantly fantastic even to people who are disposed to concede that there are forms of extra-sensory activity. This feature remains the most problematic one in respect of evaluating him. It has been imitated since his death with much less finesse. In the interests of clarification, it should be pointed out that there are recorded instances of his having made an exotic prediction which he afterwards made clear to those concerned as representing a contrived exaggeration which they should have been able to see behind. That literalists often took him for granted is no reflection upon the fact that he himself was a non-literalist by his own admission. Meher Baba's case does differ from other recent cases of "non-literalism" in that he continually stressed that a fundamental integrity can never be dispensed with in effective matters. He even stressed that there is a serious karmic punishment for a lack of integrity in those who pose as gurus and related entities. There is no proof that any teacher who merely repeats this is a fount of integrity, but in Meher Baba's case this represents a more sophisticated teaching than that convenient to Hesse-type siddhartas who find that "to let go" is the easiest path to the stars.

A few months before commencing his silence, Baba sedentarized himself again at a site near Ahmednagar which became known as Meherabad. Initially a small ashram, he now quickly developed it into a sizeable colony of some four hundred inhabitants. The daily and overall emphasis was unusually practical. It was not a "let go" project of the currently fashionable "esoteric" type, but one of pronounced disciplinarian and humanitarian dimensions that involved a great deal of sweat. This was another aspect of Meher Baba that his imitators have not found to their liking, with due deletions. Not only did he undertake personal supervision of the local village untouchables, but he also maintained a (secular) school for boys, fed the poor, and tended lepers with his own hands. This humanitarian penchant was to continue through various phases for many years.

Though the Meherabad colony flourished and began to acquire a very favourable reputation in the Deccan, Baba unaccountably closed it down completely at the end of 1926, and even left the site temporarily. He said that his "work" no longer required the colony, and hence the latter had to go. He had already curtailed the inflow of visitors very substantially, and was clearly not intent upon accumulating a greater public fame, a course which he could very easily have taken.

A much less popular, though undeniably exceptional, undertaking was actualized at Meherabad the following year when Baba returned to the site. He kept himself aloof from any public limelight and commenced a punishing fast during which he subsisted on liquid only for six months, at the end of which he could not immediately walk properly. During this fast, he confined himself in a small hut, a characteristic aspect of his repeated seclusions. Yet he managed throughout to supervise an educational institution that was perhaps unique of its kind in India at that time. This was the Meher Ashram, which lasted from 1927 to 1929. It numbered over a hundred boys on an inter-religious basis, providing them with free boarding school services. The inmates notably included both Sunni and Shi'i Muslims in addition to Hindus and Parsi and Irani Zoroastrians. In addition to a secular curriculum, these boys were given a non-sectarian tuition in mystical and philosophical subjects, and Baba himself strongly contributed to this latter facility.

Part of this school developed into a specialized faculty known as the Prem Ashram. This was for selected boys who effectively became pupils of Baba and not merely pupils of the secular course. Most of these boys were in their early or mid teens. A contemplative capacity bcame a pronounced hallmark of these selected individuals, but the two most exceptional instances were two Muslim youths from Iran. Chota Baba Hazrat Abdulla and Aga Ali ibn Haji Muhammad are monograph subjects in their own right, and repay close attention from anyone interested in sufi states of mind.

Even this institution was not permitted to last however, and Baba almost completely closed it down. Amongst other things, it had effectively demonstrated his affinity with Iran, and in 1929 he undertook a visit to the country of his forbears. He went to several cities in Iran, including his ancestral Yazd where he gained a surprisingly strong recognition from Babis and Bahais. But his reception as a whole was very favourable, and the sympathy of the new Pahlavi government for the pre-Islamic Iranian heritage seems to have contributed to this enthusiasm. It is surprising to some that Meher Baba did not exploit this situation more; it is a fact that he desired privacy on this visit and declined offers to arrange a meeting with Reza Shah.

Returning to India, Baba switched his headquarters from

Meherabad to Nasik, a city in the same zone of Western India. Yet his movements were fluidic on the whole, and there were many sporadic journeys to other places. It is worth pointing out that a great many of his travels in India were strictly *incognito*, and that it caused a certain amount of puzzlement as to why he moved about in such secrecy. His devotees were not exempt from such feelings, and often felt frustrated at not being able to see him more often.

Meher Baba's personal routine at his ashrams was invariably and perennially strict. He was a vegetarian and teetotaller, and maintained a firm disciplinary environment for the pupils resident with him. They were even forbidden to smoke tobacco, and alcohol was taboo. The men and women were segregated. The men were largely occupied in routine chores and manual labour. All were vegetarian (though he permitted pupils outside the ashram to eat meat). The ashram routine did not involve any relinquishment of former religious affiliations: Muslims remained Muslims, and Hindus remained Hindus. This was his express wish, and he never at any time in his life formulated any sectarian identity for his followers.

His ashram community were referred to as *mandali*, from the Marathi word *mandal*, meaning a group, or by extension, the members of a family. This word was not in ashram usage elsewhere. The inmates wore no distinguishing uniform, and there was a marked absence of ritual observance such as was common in Indian ashrams. He did allow his Hindu followers a certain latitude in respect of ceremonial, though restrained by comparison with orthodox norms. He was totally opposed to Zoroastrian ritual observance. His emphases were consistently egalitarian and anti-ritualist.

Probably the most exceptional Zoroastrian member of the *mandali* was Gustadji Hansotia (d. 1957), a former pupil of both Upasni Maharaj and the redoubtable Sai Baba of Shirdi. Gustadji was the only male pupil whom Baba instructed to observe a permanent silence of mouth, which he did from 1927 onwards until his death thirty years later. Like many (though not all) of the *mandali*, Gustadji was a lifelong celibate.

One of the influential entities who acknowledged Meher

Baba's calibre was Hazrat Babajan of Poona, the sufi matriarch who had a strong Muslim core following. Apart from numerous references heard by a wide selection of people, proof of her affinity with him is afforded by two very rare excursions which she made at the end of her life to his Meherabad ashram. The second of these special visits occurred very shortly before her death in September 1931.

It is undeniable that Meher Baba successfully maintained the simple lifestyle that characterized his two main teachers: Babajan and Upasni Maharaj. All his ashrams were notable for their rustic features. There was an uncompromising absence of luxuries; he retained primitive kerosene lamps even while other ashrams were switching to electricity. Only at the end of his life did he allow the women *mandali* an increased degree of comfort in their surroundings; the men never did receive any concessions.

Even while on tour, Baba's accomodation remained for the most part extremely simple. Apart from such venues as the Aga Khan's bungalow at Mahabaleshwar (which ensured quiet), the only flambuoyant environments in which he moved were some of those included on his visits to Europe and America. The irony of his two brief sojourns in Hollywood was their extreme contrast with his more characteristic environments, plus the fact that the first of these was advertised by Westerners in a manner that gave outsiders the mistaken impression that this *eclat* was his staple diet.

His first voyage to the West occurred in September 1931, and his initial destination was England. At that date he had gained only a few Western pupils, who had sought him out in India, but from now on a more extensive Western following accumulated, comprising some very varying dispositions. One of the points which most puzzled some of his new followers was that he was quite evidently not bent upon gaining vast numbers of adherents. Certain of them had considerable difficulty in adjusting themselves to this and other atypical dispositions of their "master," to use the standard parlance. Further, even some of the Indian "mandali" were surprised to find that he gave much of his time in Europe to a rather superficial group of middle and upper class women. Men like Kaka Baria could not see this contingent lasting five minutes in an ashram setting.

The amount of time Baba spent in the West was actually very minimal. By the end of 1934 he had made eight visits, but all of them were brief and fast-moving in their change of scenery. Most of these visits were explicitly private. Only three times did he venture from Europe to America. The greater part of this phase was spent in comparative seclusion at the Nasik and Meherabad ashrams. At one point he invited a small group of Western women to India, and they came; he sent them back to Europe after only a few weeks, and much to their surprise, which alerted press men eager for a scoop, some of whom typically misreported.

Charles Purdom, Baba's early British biographer, was one of those who were aghast at Baba's indifferent attitude to newspaper coverages. Before it was sufficiently grasped by most Westerners that Baba did not intend any publicity drive, reporters were not discouraged by certain of the women. As a consequence, insensitive and unintelligent persons gave their own versions of what was supposed to be happening. Some newspapers in England accordingly discovered the "Indian messiah." Purdom's own published version of Baba at that time reads acutely differently. He was the editor of *Everyman*, a respectable magazine for the British reading public, who were still frequently unsure that they wished to lose their Empire assets.

Purdom was one of those who were to feel permanently sore on the point of the extent to which Baba allowed enthusiastic devotees to do more or less as they wanted in the field of public communications. It is a fact that Baba would very rarely interfere with the way in which people wished to project his image – though he would sometimes indicate *in retrospect* that an error had been made. It might be said that he seemed to regard this open-handedness as "everybody's opportunity," which was one way they learnt entry to greater opportunities, providing that their understanding increased.

A number of the Western women (some of whom were nicknamed "Kimco") at first regarded Baba's visits to Europe as a kind of glorified holiday opportunity. He at first tended to humour this disposition, but afterwards made it clear that their ideas had been mistaken. Some of the Indians were puzzled that he continued to give these women conspicuous attention; he appeared to regard it as an important task to integrate them into a much less superficial setting than that to which they were accustomed.

The critics will perhaps interpose that the objective was to cream off funds from the gullible. But this I know to be untrue; it was not easy to gift Meher Baba with funds, and any monies accruing from the group in question were not equivalent to more than paying the excess on the menus for those who could not accustom to the simple tastes of the *mandali*.

Even when this coterie developed more discerning attitudes, they tended for long to retain elements of their former *joie de vivre* and bourgeois habits. Though Baba did not prevent the aura of greatness that gradually adhered to them (owing to their association with him), the published material makes it quite evident that Kimco and others strangely eschewed (or found indigestible) the 1933 publication of *Shri Meher Baba: his Philosophy and Teachings*, prepared by a Muslim pupil Ramju Abdulla. Even the more assimilable *Sayings of Shri Meher Baba* prepared the same year by Will Backett (an English pupil) is not very well integrated into the pages of Kimco. One might perhaps conclude that in affirming such well known Advaitic perspectives as “All those who experience the gross world as real are asleep,”[3] Meher Baba had resigned himself to the eventuality of a lengthy awakening on the part of the slumberers.

A much more original message was that given by Baba to the jet set of Hollywood, where he stayed for six days only to the accompaniment of newspaper headlines in May 1932. In this communication he mentioned with disapproval corrupt politicians who accepted bribes, the increase of crime, the exploitation of the masses by groups seeking personal gain, the destruction of large quantities of food in order to maintain market prices, the shelving of useful inventions, and the hoarding of large sums of gold which required to be redistributed for the benefit of the world.[4] Not everybody in

Hollywood liked him, and not merely because he referred to "avatars" (in the plural) who observed silence with the intention of ridding the world of self-interest.

The film stars and commercialists were not the only ones to exhibit superficial sophistication. The Kimco group and other female admirers had interpreted his references to "breaking silence" in their usual demonstrative manner. Certain individuals were very fond of expensive attire, and had specially procured "God-realization dresses" which they intended to wear on the anticipated occasion of Baba's forthcoming speech at the Hollywood Bowl. Perhaps he considered that his tangibly public and verbal critique of capitalism was sufficient cause to leave the country quickly. The fact is that he afterwards poked fun at those admirers concerned for their rendition of the "Hollywood Bowl" event.

It is quite evident that finer points were lost upon some of his followers. Yet the focus upon the more extroverted mentalities is misleading, since there were many other developments less salient in the phase of these early visits to the West. This comparative obscurity is well illustrated by the case of a woman who met Baba as early as any of the other English followers in 1931, and who remained the closest friend of the two pupils in England who received the most regular postal communications from Baba, but who was completely unknown even via hearsay to the large New York group of devotees at the end of her life.[5] Ann Powell, or "Welsh Ann" as she was sometimes known, was of humble social background, but was nevertheless a regular contact of Baba on his visits to England, and was virtually inseparable from the activities of Will and Mary Backett, who were the chief medium of Baba's contact with English followers and interested parties until their deaths in 1962–3. None of these three people could boast of such social distinctions as were possessed by followers like Princess Norina Matchabelli; unlike some others, they did not trumpet their elect status in the more spiritual field of eminence.

For nearly two years, during 1935–6, Baba stopped his global travels and intensified his seclusion tendencies, which were rarely in complete abeyance. Companioned only by the silent Gustadji and one other pupil, he spent six weeks in a cave at Mount Abu in Rajasthan, fasting on milk only, during June-July 1935. To thwart interruption, he disguised himself as one of the *mandali*. Afterwards, he continued the seclusion in a small hut on Meherabad Hill, and also maintained a severe fasting programme on liquid only that was memorable even by his exacting standards. Yet it is remarkable how little coverage this and similar phases of his life subsequently received in general devotional memory.

When he returned to Europe for a few days only in November 1936, some of the Westerners continued to cultivate an erroneous impression of their importance in his "work," since he arranged for a group of fifteen Western pupils to stay with him in India. Even a casual inspection of the facts is sufficient to dispel this myth of importance in those cases concerned, a myth which nevertheless lingered. However, it is also evident that this development did have its own significance, though not perhaps the one that was most fluently accepted by a section of the inhabitants of the new Nasik ashram.

The Western visitors were installed in specially adapted quarters at Nasik, which accordingly gained the reputation of a "luxury ashram" amongst the Indians. The allowances for comfort confirmed the doubts of some of the *mandali* that the less ascetic Westerners would sufficiently adjust to both Baba and India. Meher Baba did not live at this ashram, but at Meherabad and Rahuri. In fact he visited Nasik very infrequently, and for much of the time the Westerners only had their own company and a few of the *mandali* who superintended them. Eastern estimation of the visitors did not vastly improve in respect of some individuals,[6] and after a few months Baba terminated the project.

Details of the "luxury ashram" are of considerable psychological interest. There were four men and eleven women, including Princess Norina Matchabelli, Countess Nadine Tolstoy, and the remaining components of "Kimco." Frictions between the diverse individuals abounded, and for once realism is assured in the annals of aspiration to higher honours. Realism is often neglected in devotional reports, and in other reports which varnish "spiritual" situations.

In disbanding the Nasik contingent, Baba visited Europe once more in the summer of 1937, spending an unusually long period in one place, namely Cannes, where he lived in a villa apart from the Westerners. When he returned to India in October 1937, it was the end of his appearances in the West for fifteen years, and never again were his visits to be so frequent. Further, he took back with him to India only three of the Westerners (all women). He subsequently called several more Western women to India, but they were firmly integrated into the secluded group of Eastern women *mandali* and remained a nonsalient appendage to his activities. Only one Western woman, Rano Gayley, remained permanently with the women *mandali*.

The group of Indian women *mandali* were small in number, in contrast to the males. Parsis and Hindus comprised it, though the former came to predominate. This group had been started at Meherabad during the "colony" phase of the mid–1920's. It was moved to Meherabad Hill in 1934, where it came to be referred to as the "women's ashram." Though smaller than the male counterpart, it was not regarded as inferior. The simplicity of this women's ashram was not at first congenial to Western women, though this was not the only reason why Princess Matchabelli and others were jealous of the regard which Baba expressed for Mehera, one of the Parsi inmates.[7]

The women's ashram on Meherabad Hill might be described as a Parsi version of the group of nuns formed at Sakori by Upasni Maharaj and which subsequently continued under the leadership of Godavri Mai (Mata). There were differences however, including the absence of traditional rites. The women in Meher Baba's ashram never wore distinguishing garb, and there were no vows of any kind. Discipline was strict however, particularly in the Meherabad phase. For a long time, Mehera was never allowed to see any man except Baba. The low profile of this group lessened in much later years, as a consequence of which four of the Indian women became well known in the "movement" at large. Others connected with them reaped comparative obscurity, including Mehera's mother Daulatmai[8] and a distinctive Parsi disciple of Upasni Maharaj known as Gulmai.[9]

Meanwhile, in 1936 Meher Baba had commenced a

specialist aspect of his activities which can legitimately be described as unique in known annals. He established an ashram at Rahuri for a substantial number of indigent madmen and other socially alienated types. He tended them personally, and it was this project which absorbed more of his attention than the "luxury ashram" at Nasik. It was not easy to assist him, and most of the *mandali* were not direct participants. The Westerners showed a confused appraisal of this project, and the subsequent development of the Rahuri phase met with a marked non-comprehension even from Parsi members of the *mandali*.

Amongst the inmates of the Rahuri ashram were a few whom Baba called "God-mad," meaning persons who had become mentally unbalanced as a result of an uneven concentration upon spiritual matters; their form of insanity was quite different to that of the mad in general, and could be greatly helped and relieved by sympathetic care of a special kind. The Westerners at first confused these with another category whom Baba specified: the *masts* or "God-intoxicated." Though some Westerners found it very difficult to understand, these *masts* were explained by Baba as being in genuinely advanced states of mind that could be mistaken even in the East for insanity. Some *masts* were revered as local saints. An important feature of Baba's explanation was that *masts* are *only* to be found in the East, and never in the Western world. He was singularly specific on the subject of *masts*, and even pinpointed the parts of the globe where they are to be found: Egypt, Arabia, Iran, Tibet, and China, though most of them exist in India and Pakistan. It is important therefore to clearly understand that Meher Baba's version of *masti* is in terms of an Eastern phenomenon only, and not to be confused with clinical conditions that can be found in the West.

For thirteen years (1936–49), Meher Baba's activities were centred upon the *mast* phenomenon in India and Pakistan, and even after that period the phenomenon was not neglected. It is impossible to do justice to it in a few pages, and so I will content myself here with isolating several relevant points which should first be assimilated:

1). *Masts* are known in Muslim sufi and Hindu lore, but the subject is not clearly classified in those channels. Meher Baba's classifications and explanations do agree with the basics of sufi tradition in Islamic countries, and hence it is not in keeping to sweepingly jettison implications as many Westerners are apt to do in matters unrelated to them.

2). Meher Baba was intimately familiar with cases of madness as known in the West, but he quite definitively distinguished these from the *"God-mad"* and *mast* categories. It may be that he was far more scientific here than some conventional medics in the East, who have been heavily conditioned by modern medical science as relevant to the West.

3). Meher Baba gave precise rankings for many of the *masts* he contacted in India and Pakistan, an interesting feature of his explanations. Some of these were famous saints, but by no means all of them. These *masts* bear no relation to the commonly accepted gurus who proffer teaching and instruction. *Masts* do *not* teach or prescribe "exercises." Unlike the God-mad category, the *masts* do not constitute any kind of arrested development, even though they may display highly eccentric characteristics. According to Meher Baba, they should never be molested, nor their daily habits interfered with. A substantial number of them show an extraordinary affinity with animals.

4). In addition to the *mast* and God-mad categories, Meher Baba also contacted a large number of individuals whom he described as "*salik*-like pilgrims," meaning persons also in alignment with advanced states of mind but who do not become so absorbed in these states owing to a different evolutionary orientation. These *salik*-like pilgrims vary greatly in the level of their advancement; some are virtual beginners, while others are much more mature in experiential terms. This category do sometimes teach and instruct, and with results proportionate to their degree of maturity or capacity.

5). The period of thirteen years work abovementioned was well documented in a lengthy presentation by a qualified British medic. *The Wayfarers* was published in 1948, and its author Dr. William Donkin was a firsthand witness of much that achieved record in those pages.[10] The sub-title perhaps belied its relevance to medical interest in stipulating its description of "the God-intoxicated, and also . . . Advanced Souls, Sadhus, and the Poor." It does effectively reveal that Meher Baba was not concerned merely with private seclusion or his distinctive ashram contingents. His ministrations to both the poor and the clinically mad were not common, but his ministrations to *masts* are not traceable in other biographies. Nor does his practice of locating and contacting and donoring other categories have much correlation in other extant reports of mystical personalities. He did not deem the majority of the sadhus he contacted as anything exceptional, but rather treated them as a needy population sector, an extension of the even more prodigious number of beggars.

6). Relevant is the fact that Meher Baba's work with *masts* and related categories was unpublicized prior to the publication of Donkin's book, and afterwards continued without the slightest press coverage or local fanfares.

7). The *masts* and "*salik*-like pilgrims" were a Muslim and Hindu phenomenon. Donkin rarely specified whether the subject was a Hindu or a Muslim, and in some instances it is impossible to gain any indication of such religious background. My own analysis of such background features emerged with the conclusion that approximately seventy-five per cent of the *masts* contacted were Muslims by birth, which represents a substantial number of individuals when it is taken into account that there were about seven hundred *masts* involved in this project at conservative estimate. The ratio is almost reversed with regard to "*salik*-like pilgrims" however; in this department Hindus emerge as comprising approximately sixty-five per cent of the contacts. The number of *salik*-like pilgrims was considerably less than the *mast* total however, amounting to over two hundred and fifty persons.[11] If these figures are at all accurate, then the subject is overdue for investigation by Muslim researchers.

8). The overall number of contacts made by Meher Baba during the 1940's are very much higher when it is remembered that there were about 16,000 destitutes and roughly 13,000 sadhus (and faqirs) included. Yet the much more specialized activity of locating *masts* and *saliks* is remarkable when it is realized that a thousand or more Muslims and

Hindus of unusual characteristics were laboriously tracked down throughout almost every area of the Indian subcontinent, from Kashmir to South India. Prior to the population turmoil which marked the division between India and Pakistan in 1947, Meher Baba was notably active in territory that is now part of Pakistan, where a sizeable number of contacts were made.

9). The primary reasons for this "*mast* work," as it is usually referred to, are difficult to elucidate. The fact is that this activity gained Baba absolutely nothing in the sense of publicity or income, the two major motivations of the commercial variety of so-called "spiritual masters." On the contrary, the activity was unsung and he himself was the source of charity. In a philanthropic guise he made numerous arduous and *incognito* journeys that were sufficient to tax the strength of the strongest men who accompanied him, men who had to be specially selected for their stamina. It was he who gifted his contacts, and not *vice versa*.

10). Percentage estimates of religious background in relation to *masts* become more complex when it is taken into account that some *masts* were contacted more than once, and that a few gained a distinct favouritism. The "five favourites" was Donkin's term of reference for those five individuals who gained the lion's share of Meher Baba's attention; of these, four were Muslims and one a Hindu (the latter having been named "Mohammed" by Muslims). Chatti Baba, Karim Baba, Ali Shah, and Nur Ali Shah Pathan (alias Chacha) were distinctive individuals whom it is not easy to describe in a few lines. Mohammed, ambivalently of Hindu background, was the only *mast* to permanently reside at Meherabad ashram. Meher Baba defined Chacha as a *majzub*, which means something more than a *mast* in the very precise clarification of Arabic, Persian, and Sanskrit terminology which the former expounded on his English alphabet board. All these five, together with a number of others, became closely associated with a memorable aspect of the "*mast* work": the establishment of special ashrams on a temporary basis for the specific purpose of an intensive interaction with selected *masts*. To the best of my knowledge, these "*mast* ashrams" were unique. It was, significantly, *masts* who were selected as inmates, and not *salik*-like pilgrims.

The first *mast* ashram was formed at Ajmer, a Chishti centre of pilgrimage, in February 1939 during the "Blue Bus tour." It is perhaps appropriate that the shrine of Khwaja Muinuddin Chishti (d. 1236) became directly associated with this ashram, since the sufi overtones and undertones of the *mast* work were by no means inconsiderable. In the precincts of this famous shrine lived an old Pathan nicknamed Chacha who was revered by locals, and who unaccountably (to onlookers) accompanied a Hindu pupil (Kaka Baria) of Meher Baba to the latter's abode. According to Baba, this old Sunni Muslim was more advanced than any of the *masts* he contacted. Chacha might have stepped straight out of the Mughal era; there was not the slightest vestige of Westernization in his squalid hovel and unearthly appearance.

Ten years later, a Muslim pupil contributed a notable chapter to *The Wayfarers* on the "usefulness of *masts* to humanity." By that time, Abdul Karim Abdulla (alias Ramju) had witnessed seven *mast* ashrams and had long since ceased to feel any slight from such queries as that expressed by the Chishti spokesman Hasan Nizami in the early 1920's – Nizami had asked why Ramju, who had been reared in an environment of strict Sunni orthodoxy, had become a pupil of a "clean-shaven Zoroastrian."

By the time Chacha made an unprecedented journey from Ajmer all the way to Satara in the summer of 1947, to become the focus of the seventh (and last) *mast* ashram, a very large number of saints, *masts*, and *salik* types had been personally contacted by Baba and a few of the men *mandali* (though largely unknown to the *mandali* as a whole). The vast majority of these contacts were never centred in an ashram, and in fact there were only two *mast* ashrams to punctuate the continual journeys involved in the *mast* work from 1941 onwards.

It is worth noting that Meher Baba was never particularly accessible during this whole period. Many of the *mandali* were not directly involved in his major work schedule. His Indian followers at large often had to wait years even to catch a brief glimpse of him. The Western followers were entirely dependent upon news-sheets and letters.

During 1939–40 there were five *mast* ashrams inaugurated and disbanded, the two most long-lived being sited at Bangalore and Meherabad. Subsequently there were six years of what Donkin called the "great *mast* tours" (1941–46), during which Baba moved his headquarters continually to numerous places throughout India (and Pakistan). There was a particularly long sojourn at Lahore in 1943 and another at Hyderabad (Deccan) in 1945. Both these cities were strong Islamic milieux, a factor reflected in the contacts made.

What was probably the most important contact of all during these richly documented years was one with Upasni Maharaj at Dahigaon in October 1941. This was Meher Baba's only meeting with his former teacher since 1923. It was typically unpublicized, and occurred in an isolated rural situation. Only a few pupils were allowed to be present, and even they were not allowed entry to the hut where the encounter actually took place. Upasni died only two months later, and his comments on the meeting escaped reporting. Meher Baba often mentioned the event in later years, but in an oblique manner.

* * * * *

Baba's communications on the alphabet board varied greatly; a basic distinction has to be drawn between (a) his explanations of psychological and metaphysical subjects (b) his instructions and specific remarks to different pupils and devotees, and (c) his disclosures concerning his "work." An example of (a) was his discourses given on a monthly basis during the years 1938–42 at the request of the editors of a periodical devoted to him. These *Discourses* were written up by Dr. C.D. Deshmukh of Nagpur University, and later appeared in variant editions; they are very clear in style, and have undoubtedly provided material for pirates on the guru media.

An example of (c) was his private statement made in 1948 which affirmed that he had worked seven years with men, seven years with boys, seven years with women, and was now concentrating upon his "universal work," one aspect of which concerned *masts*, advanced souls, the God-mad, and the poor. As was frequent, there was no supporting clarification, and the audience had to make what they could of this disclosure.[12] A literal tripartite period of twenty-one years can only fit the period 1918–38, and does feasibly pinpoint to 1918–24 as being focussed upon men, 1925–31 as being focussed primarily upon boys, and 1932–38 as being focussed primarily upon women (though the last two trends are simplistic if treated too rigorously).[13] A strong case can be made for an increasingly "impersonal" tone from 1939 onwards, though it is apparent that many had difficulty in adjusting to this.

The phase nature of Meher Baba's activities is particularly striking, and not at all common. It was to continue after 1948, though it is strongly arguable that memories were often short.

It was during the period of the "great *mast* tours" that Baba moved his ashram base from Meherabad to Pimpalgaon, though he was very often absent. The Nasik quarters had long ago been dispensed with, and these two sites in the Ahmednagar area of the Deccan were the ones principally associated with him. Meherabad was prone to chronic drought, and had been gifted to him not least because it was an unproductive piece of land. In 1944, he moved some of the *mandali* to a property near the village of Pimpalgaon, in a valley that was much greener than the Meherabad locale. Only a distance of some eighteen miles separated the two ashrams; Meherabad was retained, but never again became Baba's personal abode. Those of the women who were involved in the move gained much more commodious quarters at the new site, which became known as Meherazad. The men remained in extremely simple accommodation that did not depart from the austere standards of Meherabad. Baba's ascetic aspect continued, and included a seclusion on Tembi Hill (overlooking Meherazad) that notably incorporated a *mast*. For twelve days in December 1947, Baba lived in a cabin on the summit of this hill, with another hut on a lower slope being reserved for Ali Shah, one of the "five favourites," a *mast* of Ahmednagar. For three hours daily,

Baba would go down to the lower hut and "work" with Ali Shah in erstwhile silence. Since this "work" was not verbal, it is perhaps logical enough that it was not readily explicable in passing references. Ali Shah himself was almost as taciturn as Baba; his only concession to westernization was a cardigan and jacket worn for extra warmth in colder weather. His beturbanned outfit, long wispy beard, and timeless personality might have made it seem to anyone reflective that time had stopped since the days of Aurangzeb.

In 1949 Baba gave permission for electric lighting to be installed at Meherazad. But before this could be done, he had literally disposed of both his ashrams in an extraordinary demonstration of the relinquishment of private property.

The intensive *mast* work continued up to the time of the "Great Seclusion" of forty days lasting from 22nd June until 31st July 1949, during which the recluse environment was the stationary body of the blue bus formerly used on some tours, now preserved near the men's quarters at Meherazad. Afterwards the *mast* work receded, and there occurred the phase known as the New Life, which some have viewed as the most distinctive of all the varied phases comprising Baba's life pattern.

He stressed that his "Old Life" would have to end. The *mandali* were to be disbanded. Those who wished to stay with him during the "New Life" could do so as "companions" providing they were prepared to meet the stipulations enjoined. Both of his ashrams were to be relinquished, along with all their effects (to date these were legally his property). Nothing was to remain in his name except his tomb premises on Meherabad Hill (where his future tomb had already been constructed).

All this came as a deep shock to the *mandali* and devotees. Some felt that it was too great a step to take, and that perhaps he would modify it. He proved decisively that he meant what he said.

The two ashrams were legally made over to certain capable businessmen amongst his pupils. He advised them to resell their new investments. The proceeds of the sale of these ashrams were used to provide for the immediate needs of his dependants, including families whose fortunes had now become inextricably interconnected with his own. His will in favour of the *mandali* was duly torn up, as were those wills which had been made in his favour by various members of the *mandali*. The small publishing venture known as Meher Publications was dissolved.

It was agreed that he himself would decide which of the women *mandali* would accompany him as "companions," but that each of the men would have to make their own choice as to their future. The New Life, he said, would entail rigorous mendicancy and a complete lack of responsibility on his part for any of his companions. He emphasized that the coming phase would not be easy; those involved would have to be prepared to regard themselves as already dead. The companions had to discard "all fads, fancies, notions and vagueness, particularly in respect of spiritual leanings and beliefs."[14]

Baba selected only four women to accompany him in the New Life, and was careful to limit the potential number of men, since he allowed only thirty-two male pupils to make the crucial choice. Perhaps more significant was the fact that only sixteen of these latter chose to become companions.

Had he decided that his personal entourage had become too large and superfluous? Had the patterns and associations of the Old Life now outlived their usefulness? If so, then particular attention should be given to the manner in which later associations accumulated.

On 16th October 1949, he commenced the New Life with his twenty companions, walking from Ahmednagar in heavy rain. They stayed a few weeks at Belgaum, where features of the new phase crystallized to some extent. One of his companions wanted to return home, and was permitted to do so. Others also found it difficult to adjust. It was not merely that they were not allowed to read newspapers or talk politics (prohibitions which had a precedent as far back as the Manzil-e-Meem), nor was it merely the physical labour which was to precede begging. Rather, it seems to have been the extreme uncertainty of events that caused friction. Baba typically changed his plans. Adi K. Irani heatedly affirmed that he had his doubts about Baba's intentions.

It was not permitted for anyone from the "Old Life" to contact Baba's travelling party. All spectators were strictly discouraged. Not only was Baba *incognito* as usual during travels, but he seemed bent upon erasing his superior identity within the group of companions as much as possible. He likewise accomplished physical labour. "I am on the same level with you," was his refrain, though prompt obedience was expected.

When the party arrived by rail at Benares, the begging stipulations came into force, Baba himself initially participating. After a week of this, they moved to nearby Sarnath, of Buddhist fame, where a special prayer was offered in the Buddhist ruins one morning by the males, who wore loincloths despite the cold weather. Prior to the New Life, Baba had never been known to participate in such prayers of supplication, but this is what he now did.

There followed a laborious mendicant journey to Hardwar, sacred city of the Hindus, with the men proceeding by foot and the women travelling more comfortably in a caravan drawn by bullocks. They arrived in January 1950, but their ultimate destination transpired to be the village of Manjri Mafi near Dehra Dun. Here the number of men in the party decreased; Adi K. Irani, Dr. Abdul Ghani Munsiff, and two others chose to opt out of the direct line of fire and to lead the New Life at their own homes. One other pupil later dropped out of this demanding phase (which was much harder for the men than for the women) by late May, when the remaining ten made a firm renewal of their decision. Gustadji and Dr. Donkin were amongst them. An additional pupil, Kaikobad Dastur, was an eleventh participant here; his case is complex in that he had for long been under special disciplinary rules, and was acknowledged by Baba as having experienced advanced states of mind.

Several thousand sadhus and saints were contacted by Baba in the Hardwar locale, but he explained that these contacts were different from those made in the "Old Life"; from this new perspective, no distinctions were made between such categories as *masts*, mad, sadhus, and other types.

The events and implications of the New Life were never fully assimilated by his followers at large, and arguably not even by some of those involved. Many of Baba's explanations of it were oblique, but there is an absence of ambiguity in his statement that it was endless and would be kept alive after his death by those who lived "the life of complete renunciation of falsehood" and other shortcomings, who "do not seek material possessions, or power, who accept no homage," and who "give no importance to caste, creed, and religious ceremonies."[15]

This last message was given in September 1950, by which time he had moved back to Western India from the north, staying at Mahabaleshwar. A little later, he characterized his stance in the New Life as that of the "servant of God" and "the seeker," indicating that he had radically altered his orientation. This was confirmed the following year, when at Hyderabad (Deccan) in June, he said that he would undertake special work which would enable him "to attain to the Old Life Meher Baba state" and to "manifest universally."

It is clear that he intended his New Life as an enactment of some kind that demonstrated the ideal for the seeker of truth. This much was grasped by his followers, but other explicit indications were overlooked. When, for instance, he stated in the new year of 1952 that he had regained his "Old Life Meher Baba state," he also said that he retained his "New Life ordinary state" – along with the ignorance, weaknesses and humility of the latter. There was no specification that this juxtaposition ended with the Free Life, the name by which the next phase came to be known.

The New Life caused much puzzlement amongst his followers. The main point to grasp here is that the tone of outer events appeared to indicate that Baba reverted to his Old Life. The majority assumed that there was a continuation between the subsequent avatar-figure and the Old Life, and the New Life was accordingly viewed as a strange but comparatively brief interim that no longer required close attention. On the contrary, the indications of a close analysis reveal that the element of continuation was marginal and indirect in terms of external manifestation; the *avatar* projection bears traces of a humiliation imposed by the weaknesses and ignorance of his following. It may be that it was not only the world at large, but also his following who could not live "the life of complete renunciation of falsehood."

The special work which was the medium for regaining the Old Life state was referred to by Baba as *manonash* ("annihilation of mind"). It was seclusion "work," and hence not readily amenable to day-by-day scrutiny. This spanned a period of four months ending on 16th February, 1952. There were two principal venues: first Khojaguda Hill near Hyderabad (Deccan), a site noted for the tomb of Hazrat Baba Fakhruddin, of sufi associations. A laborious journey to Meherazad followed with a few companions. This was the first time Baba had returned to the ashram, now officially owned by Nariman Dadachanji, a wealthy Parsi devotee. Baba insisted that his group should pay the owner fifty rupees a month for rent. The other tenants saw very little of him, owing to his intense absorption in his "work," which occurred in a secluded hut.

When the *manonash* seclusion was over, Baba's resumption of Old Life characteristics included a resettling at Meherazad without having to pay rent. The *mandali* regrouped there, but not in the same strength of numbers as before. It is important to observe that new recruits for the *mandali* were not made, as might have been expected; most members of the *mandali* were now well advanced in years, and Baba's policy was clearly conservative in letting his old group die off one by one while making only very few additions insuffficent to maintain the numbers. In fact, it is quite obvious that he was not specifically "teaching" the *mandali* thereafter; they performed routine chores and were subject to his personal instructions, though these instructions were frequently not intensive. One exception is the case of Kaikobad Dastur, who was an advanced *salik*-like pilgrim according to the indications. Baba acknowledged this elderly Zoroastrian's "inner experiences," though to the other *mandali* he tended to downgrade such experience in general. There are clear reasons for this, since large numbers of enthusiasts always desire and assume experiences for which they are not prepared, and can rarely distinguish between incipient and advanced forms of experience. Some of the *mandali* took this perspective to extremes however, notably Adi K. Irani, who lived in Ahmednagar and acted as Baba's secretary. As a consequence, much of the "inside" aspect of Baba's activity was squashed into a devotional straitjacket suiting the aptitude of the more vocal followers who gained the limelight.

Baba's personal routine did not change very noticeably from pre-New Life days, though there was a slight relaxation upon austerity in that he now regularly used a room in the main house at Meherazad which was reserved for the women; this building was far more comfortable than the men's quarters and was equipped with basic electricity. Formerly he had spent much of his life in huts and cabins, often very cramped, and lacking in all amenities. His penchant for seclusion and fasting continued however; practically all of his time at the ashram was spent in "semi-seclusion," i.e., accessible only to the *mandali*, since no visitors were allowed, save occasionally in very restricted numbers. None of his ashrams after 1926 were of the "open" variety, that is, a place where anybody can visit at any time.

One aspect of Meher Baba that did change increasingly after the New Life phase ws his general leniency in communications. It is discernible that his attitude towards his following grew much more lenient than in the old days. He had always been more easygoing with persons who had not committed themselves to obeying his personal instructions, but aside from this consideration, there was nevertheless an increase in open-handedness. There were also many more followers than in earlier years. Further, there is the important consideration that he was much more lenient with the *mandali* than hitherto, and particularly the women.

While Baba's following mushroomed in the post-New Life phases, there was not the slightest attempt to develop the ashram or to make any innovations to accomodate outside parties on more than a fleeting basis. These features are so untypical of ashram life in India that it is necessary to view Baba as distinct from his following, as a virtual recluse who consistently kept a majority at arm's length.

The period immediately following *manonash* was referred to by Baba as his Complicated Free Life, in which bindings would dominate freedom; this would change after 10th July into the Full Free Life, in which freedom would dominate bindings; afterwards would commence on 15th November his Fiery Free Life, in which he would share the truth of his realization with those who sought it. This tripartite Free Life received an even more vague assessment than its predecessor.

The Complicated Free Life was marked by a visit to America. It was his first visit to the West for fifteen years. He spent most of his time at Myrtle Beach in South Carolina, where a large tract of land had been made into the Meher Center-on-the-Lakes by one of his wealthy American devotees. It was later said that he thought a great deal of this centre and its originators, but the fact is that he spent very little time there in comparison to expectations. He told Elizabeth Patterson that this centre should be modelled upon an outline he had given for an earlier and unfinished project at Byramangala; this suggestion was not furthered, however.[16] It would admittedly have required a very high standard of leadership for such objectives to be achieved. Simplified devotional emphases are not conducive to "solitary quarters for meditation" or "an abode of the saints" to use two of Baba's abbreviated expressions. It may be more accurate to state that Baba highly rated the potential of this centre; beautiful scenery is not in itself an achievement of supramundane significance.

It was nothing of a publicity tour. He allowed only one open day at Myrtle Beach, when a wide variety of people came to see him. There followed in late May a motor journey to California, but en route Baba met with a serious accident in Oklahoma. He suffered a fractured arm and leg, and members of his travelling party were also hurt in the collision with another car that was driving on the wrong side of the road. He had previously predicted that he would shed blood on American soil.

After partially recuperating at Myrtle Beach, he left for New York in mid-July. There he gave many private interviews, though still in pain and demobilized. At this juncture he gave time to the "American Sufi" group led by Ivy Oneita Duce, who wanted to place her own movement under his direction. He indicated that they would have to change their emphases; this group retained an organizational form that was in contrast to the devotional movement at large, and became known as Sufism Reoriented.

A visit to Europe followed soon after. Staying in London for six days, he then moved on to Switzerland, where he was sufficiently on the mend to start using crutches. He took a plane back to India in August, and it was several weeks before he could begin to move about without any support. But by November 1st at Meherazad, he launched into the preliminary "rhythm for the Fiery Life," attending regular meetings of pupils at Meherabad, and finalizing arrangements for intensive travel in India. In some respects this preliminary to the Fiery Free Life was similar to the New Life approach, but there were also pronounced differences, including an emphasis upon his transcendence of all religions and their practices. He maintained a sort of running commentary on the lives and teachings of past exemplars like Guru Nanak, Bayazid Bistami, Khwaja Muinuddin Chishti, Baba Farid Shakar Ganj, Eknath, and Sai Baba of Shirdi.

It was Ramju Abdulla who recorded that, on the second day of the Fiery Free Life, Baba said: "All *masts*, wherever they are, are helping in the inner crusade . . ."[17] Baba does not appear to have defined the nature of this "inner crusade," but it is deducible that it was connected with an event to which he constantly referred at this time, if obscurely – an unprecedented disaster was soon to befall mankind. This did not necessarily mean that the disaster would occur in an unmodified form, but such statements and underlying trends tended to be neglected in the general appraisal of this phase.

The abovementioned statement was made in Bombay on

16th November 1952, at the start of a widespread and complex touring programme that included contacts with *masts* and *salik*-like pilgrims, mass *darshans* for the public, and ministerings to the poor. Contrary to his former practise, he now gave "open" *darshan* (meeting) to the masses. The saliency of the *mast* work reappeared, but accompanied by Baba's public exposure such as he had frowned upon during the pre-New Life years. The contrast is striking, and was quite deliberate, though his public appearances were not unsolicited; upon his return from America, he had been requested by numerous Indian devotees to extend his company to them also.

Darshan is a Hindu event, and is a common form of showing veneration for saints and teachers, often accompanied by the hope of blessing. The supplicant touches his or her head to the feet of the revered entity. Baba had formerly made concessions to this national habit, though many of the relevant occasions were attended by his specific followers only. But "open" *darshan* meant his accessibility to the public, including many simple people who were illiterate. He now seemed to want specific contact with this sector, though the personal overtones were slight – the vast majority of *darshan* recipients gained only a fleeting contact with him that amounted to seconds.

That this open *darshan* trend was specifically related to a Hindu audience is underlined by the response from two salient geographical areas: Hamirpur and Andhra Pradesh. Hamirpur was a backward district in North India; many poor and low class rural Hindus flocked to Baba when he came to give *darshan*, and many of them counted themselves as his followers from then on. A similar phenomenon, though on a larger scale, occurred in Andhra in East India. Devotees from these two areas came to form the greater percentage of his Indian following, vastly outnumbering Parsi devotees and eclipsing the diminishing Muslim element.

In Andhra, educationalists and government ministers also became enthusiastic over Baba's appearances. It seems that the egalitarian aspect of his teaching particularly appealed to them, in addition to other factors, at a time when the Hindu intelligentsia were struggling to clear the backlog of caste prejudice and underdevelopment in the new surge of national reconstitution. In Andhra occurred the phenomenon of entire village populations becoming followers of "Avatar Meher Baba." There was no such equivalent in the Western devotional movement, or even in heavily urbanized Eastern foci such as Bombay, and hence comparisons with Andhra (and Hamirpur) devotionalism are unfair to the latter, where conditions, lifestyles, and aptitudes were radically different.

Baba had been repeatedly invited to visit Andhra since 1947, but he had not so far responded. He had visited the area on his incognito *mast* tours, and over the past decade a few devotees had been extremely successful in spreading news of his existence in this large region, with the result that he was in some demand from an interested public. Andhra now became an autonomous state separate from Madras State, and incorporated the Hyderabad locale formerly ruled by the Muslim Nizam. It was a Telegu-speaking zone, a language that was not spoken by any of the *mandali*, and some of the latter expressed surprise at the public response when they witnessed it.

By contrast, Baba had been reluctant to visit Delhi, and only agreed to do so under the pressure of entreaties. Yet he had a success here at the Camp College (Punjab University) in New Delhi, a Sikh institution where some three thousand undergraduates asembled to meet him. He was observed to be particularly happy on this occasion of December 2nd, 1952. By the time of the New Life he had gained a small contingent of Sikh pupils, who were free to follow their religious norms in consonance with Baba's Kaivani-style disposition; this contingent came to include an eminent Sikh member of Parliament, namely Amar Singh Saigal. Yet Baba's emphases were not at all politically based, any more than they were sectarian. To one group of students at the Camp College, he gave a message which significantly deaccentuated the stress on national freedom which had recently been in much vogue on the media. "Enough has been done to make people food-minded," he stated, and urged that to make them God-minded was now imperative;

spiritual freedom should be the preoccupation, and not national freedom.[18] His emphasis here was perhaps the only viable route to regain the broad intercultural view of Mahatma Gandhi, while yet offsetting the tendencies to Westernization that replaced colonialism. His aversion to the political front was conceivably the reason for his reluctance to visit the capital on a mass *darshan* tour. The day after the Sikh event, he gave a message at Delhi University, but it was brief and very spiritualized.

The curious fact emerges that prior to the Fiery Free Life, Baba had never been in the habit of entering the shrines of saints and masters, which were numerous in India and frequently emerged in his itineraries. He himself would remain outside while sending his pupils inside any such shrine to pay their respects. But this procedure changed when he visited the tombs of his own masters Upasni Maharaj and Hazrat Babajan at Sakori and Poona respectively, together with the tomb of Sai Baba at Shirdi. This occurred at the commencement of the Fiery Free Life. The new trend was confirmed at Khuldabad, where he visited a number of local sufi shrines in this historic vicinity near the Ellora Caves. One of these tombs was that of Hazrat Zarzarizarbaksha, the medieval sufi shaikh whom Baba had formerly emphasized as the master of Sai Baba of Shirdi in a previous incarnation. It seems apt enough that in this new concession to the sanctity of shrines, he was acknowledging his own spiritual genealogy and its antecedents – which were of Sufi and Vedantic componency, and notably the former.

The touring ended on January 31st, 1953. These two and a half months of travel were then followed by a lengthy period of comparative obscurity at Dehra Dun. Save for a couple of *darshans* intended for local people, he went out of public focus for a year, and after a few months sent out word that all letters to him should cease. He expressed a particular distaste for anyone wanting to see him for *darshan*. He was more interested in contacting *masts*, though the details were for long submerged in the devotional literature.

By the end of this period of withdrawal, he had begun to refer to his followers as "lovers," in consonance with his stress on divine love (a well known Hallajian topic) that marked the Fiery Free Life. But the end of the Fiery Free Life was not clearly demarcated, at least in the circulars sent out to his followers. Like the New Life, it became submerged by *darshan* adjuncts in the minds of his devotees. Baba had initially characterized the Fiery Free Life as a phase in which both freedom and bindings would be consumed in the "fire of divine love."

In a message known as "Baba's Declaration," dictated at Dehra Dun on 21st March 1953, he referred to future events in his career that were subsequently to arouse much speculation amongst his followers, though a simplified version eventually gained common acceptance. He said that prior to his death he would have to face "universal humiliation, apparent universal defeat and violent death." The violence endured by his physical body would ultimately cause his death. The physical violence would precede a glorification in the "victory of divine truth." He also mentioned the "manifestation of the divine truth" which would accompany the breaking of his silence.[19] He made further reference to these events in later messages, making some additions and using variant descriptions. The breaking of his silence was already a familiar theme, but the other topics were new. However, there was a strong precedent for the "violent death," since at the Manzil-e-Meem in the early 1920's he had predicted that he would be murdered by Zoroastrians.

Less open to misinterpretation, but equally prone to being forgotten, was his emphasis in the same message of March 1953 that people generally entertained a "very superficial understanding of what is actually meant" by surrender to a master (i.e., a Perfect Master in Baba's terminology, indicative of superlative achievement which is extremely and inconveniently rare). "The complacent belief of a disciple that he has completely surrendered to a master is due to ignorance and hypocrisy." Doubtless anyone in such error would have denied it. In general Baba stressed obedience as a requirement for serious pupils, though he defined obedience as an inferior stage to "surrender." From the early 1950's onward, obedience became a slogan for some, though this too arguably became to some extent a complacent belief in personal qualifications.

Significantly perhaps, Baba's favoured post-New Life appellation for his followers, i.e., "lovers," equates with his specification of a preliminary quality to obedience. Love was inferior to obedience in his training schema; it denoted an attitude that had not yet become sufficiently one-pointed to achieve more profound results in the orientation and development of those concerned. This love of devotees should not, however, be confused with divine love, which is an attribute of saints and others who have undergone the condition of surrender.

According to Charles Purdom, the Fiery Free Life reached its culmination in September 1953, and at that time Baba dictated "The Highest of the High," an unusual communication in which he referred to the *avatar* theme but scrupulously avoided identifying himself blatantly as *avatar*. "If I am the Highest of the High" was instead the leitmotif. He was evidently concerned to point out various errors in devotional approach, e.g., to approach the adept with the expectation of supernatural aid for the gratification of mundane desires. In this respect he distinguished himself from "the sadhus, saints, yogis, walis and such others who are on the *via media*," categories who did perform miraculous feats to satisfy transient material needs. "It is for me to awaken you from time to time throughout the ages" was the extent of his affirmation.[20]

In this message Baba did specify that Zarathushtra was an earlier *avatar* than Rama, Krishna, and Buddha. This was a different format to conventional Hindu *avatar* lore therefore, much as the addition of Jesus and Muhammad was. Also, from this time onwards, he frequently distinguished his approach from that of gurus and yogi types, of whom he said that there were only a limited number of genuine entities. His approach was distinctive by comparison with popular guruism even in the post-New Life phases. Critics of the *avatar* theme are led to wonder if he was obliged to compete with Hindu gurus in winning the loyalty of some sections of his following – since otherwise his projection would have been unpopular. His attitude to the miracle mentality was consistently a tough one in these later years. He not merely dissociated himself from miracles, but also played down occult matters in general, indicating that "powers" and "experiences" could be a major source of delusion. Such emphases now became much more marked than in the 1920's, and leads one to conclude that a large audience required different control to that of a smaller one of different componency. Ironically for critics therefore, while gradually shaping his own *avatar* image, Meher Baba hit at a major media of commercialism; he himself could have thoroughly exploited this latter avenue, but he did not.

Meher Baba's statements frequently exhibit a rare candour. He was well aware that avatars are as common as mud in India, and was known to remark that they exist in every other village. To the best of my knowledge, a Zoroastrian *avatar* on Indian soil is unique, and in many respects a refreshing change from those specimens of bogus who specialize diversely in over-eating and in being reincarnations of the local celebrity who died only the year before. Straight-faced readers are urged to remember that the *avatar* concept is a very elastic one, and as accurate in definition as the person who uses or exploits it.

In February 1954 Baba undertook a sequel to the mass *darshan* tours of Hamirpur and Andhra. This was in response to insistent request. The sequel was brief but concentrated; he was never again to repeat his visit to either area. The same surge of mass response was again evident. At Mahewa in Hamirpur district, the entire local population maintained a vigil in front of Baba's mud hut on February 12th. He is said to have openly declared himself to be the *avatar* on this occasion, though exactly what he said has never appeared in print. The fact remains that, whatever comments he may have made on this tentative subject in the past, he had never once made any public declaration. More palpable is his affirmation in Hamirpur that he would incarnate again after seven hundred years. This at least makes it impossible for bandwagon avatars to reveal themselves as his reincarnation shortly after his death, as has happened in the case of Sai Baba of Shirdi.

Typical of his forthright remarks was that concerning the

various messages on metaphysical themes which he dictated for circulation in Hamirpur and Andhra: "In the spiritual path, these messages and addresses mean nothing. Without actual *experience*, all philosophical statements are idle talk."[21] It follows from this, therefore, that merely to repeat his messages is useless unless they are a fact of one's own knowledge; devotees were relying totally upon *his* statements in their derivative broadcasts. If, for instance, Meher Baba filled a unique role as an *avatar*, it is difficult to see how anybody else but the elect would be in a position to corroborate it.

An interesting message entitled "The Word of Words" clearly explained that the breaking of his silence would not involve an outpouring of verbosity, but rather the "Word of Words" that would impart to those prepared the gnosis of *"Ana'l Haqq"* (I am the Truth). This Word would go from him to the world "as from God, not as from a philosopher." Despite this clarification in gnostic terms, his devotees continued to believe that the "breaking of silence" would involve physical speech, i.e., as from a philosopher. This belief was also current among the *mandali*, though varying perhaps in the extent of literalism.[22]

The second Andhra mass *darshan* tour lasted just under a fortnight. The most outstanding and instructive episode was the "Workers' Meeting" held at Rajahmundry on 1st March, 1954. The workers concerned were those involved in the arrangements for the tour, which was now very nearly over. This meeting was marked by his unusually forthright attitude with a large assembly of devotees; he took a very firm line against various attitudes and behaviour patterns they were establishing. His words on this occasion were afterwards given the title of "What Baba means by Real Work." This broadside stands out as the most important post-New Life statement he ever gave to his followers insofar as their own activities were concerned. He started by saying (or rather dictating) that the addresses he had been presented with, the messages he had given, the chanting of *arati*, the performance of his *puja* (worship), garlanding him, and bowing down to him for *darshan* – all this meant "absolutely nothing."

He went on to remark that "somehow I feel that something is very wrong deep down," here referring to the way that devotees were spreading his "message of love" as it was coming to be called. Not only were there competitions and jealousies in this venture, but where was the necessity for *him* to have "entanglements of organizations and centres and directives through messages and mass *darshan* programmes?" He could do his work himself, and in silence. He did not need "workers," though he gave opportunities to share in his work. But these opportunities were only effective if undertaken according to the standards of his "universal work."

He referred in particular to the collection of money in his name "without true basis." Such activity should be stopped immediately. One of the "workers" then asked: "Without money, how is propaganda possible?" Baba's answer to this human-headed mule was appropriate enough: "I have not understood what work you are doing for me." He did not want propaganda or publicity, he reiterated. His work needed no money. When money had come into vogue in human affairs, Judas had sold his avatar for that form of exchange.

Accordingly, he now wished that the Andhra committee of workers should cease what they called work, and instead begin to live "the life of sacrifice, love and honesty." Not only were these workers to stop functioning as a committee, but all Baba centres in Andhra were to be dissolved at his wish. He would have nothing to do with any "literature on Baba," and he wanted the new publications venture dissolved. Instead, he wanted each individual to be "Baba's 'Centre' personified." His "message of love" could only consist of living the life of sacrifice, love and honesty. His (verbal) message was that *God alone is real and everything else is unreal*, and this was what he wanted to be conveyed to others (i.e., not shallow devotionalism or misrepresentations). Such transmitters were his true workers.

Laboriously, he reiterated that his work did not require any centres, offices, or accounts. "Henceforth, you will be responsible for your own actions," he warned, and there is evidence enough that he really meant it. "I mean to stop sending messages to you all from henceforth, and I will stop all correspondence. I will now do the work of my personal programme." The clear indication was that he would no longer be concerned with, or responsible for, the programmes of others, even if they misrepresented such programmes as part of his own work.

In a continuation of this meeting held the following morning (March 2nd), he reiterated firmly the points he had made, adding: "Now if on your own, you establish centres in cities, in towns, in villages, and in your own homes, that is your own concern and not mine." Any complications they encountered in dissolving the various existing centres and offices could be referred to his secretary Adi K. Irani and other members of the *mandali*. But "not one word of the letters you write to them should be brought to my ears." Yet he was concerned to emphasize that nobody should take the advice of the *mandali* as Baba's advice. The *mandali* would not purposely mislead, but "the *mandali* are not Baba," and hence due reflection should be given to their advice before acting upon any of it. One devotee then implored: "Give us help through Adi." Very patiently, Baba pointed out that Adi's experience in office work for the past twenty years did not mean an incapacity for error. "Advice you can have from Adi, but not as from Baba through Adi."

Such cautioning references to the *mandali* were significant. The fact is that devotees *did* tend to regard the *mandali*, and particularly the more vocal individuals amongst them, as infallible mouthpieces. But Baba was obviously at pains in these sessions to affirm that they were not. The subservience to authority figures can become an associational habit blind to distinctions and finer points.

Towards the end of this session, someone asked him if devotees would be informed of the time and place of his breaking silence. With some amusement, Baba replied: "If this is what is meant by breaking silence, it would be better that I don't break it." He reiterated that those who connected themselves with the "powerhouse" inherent in his work would be proportionately enlightened, and quite independently of external broadcasts. He must have known that the number who were capable of integrating with this powerhouse effect was very small, since many were preoccupied with externals.

The "Workers' Meeting" made an impact upon his Indian devotees at the time, but as the years passed it was unfortunately forgotten. Baba was rarely one to reiterate important pronouncements relating to people, as distinct from inner "work" occurrences. After defining the weaknesses and ineptitude of devotee performance, he closed the subject and disowned it, leaving his recorded words as testimony.[23] Devotees were not subsequently prevented from doing what they wished to do – it was their choice, even if retrogressive. This was a characteristic of his approach, which distinguished the inner from the outer for those who were capable of accomodating to the former. If people could only scratch the surface, he could not *make* them dig deep; this creates too much pressure in those lacking the psychological muscle.

True to his word, Baba afterwards withdrew from the devotional circuit, and commenced a much stricter aloofness from incoming letters than ever before. He never again undertook mass *darshan* tours. In future, it was usually only possible to reach him via a telegram or cable in emergency, and even this recourse did not guarantee a reply from Baba personally.

In September 1954 he gave his "last mass *darshan*" to the public, the venue being Wadia Park in Ahmednagar. For this occasion he had dictated "Meher Baba's Call," which formally affirmed his identity as *avatar*.[24] Like many of his messages, it was not typical of the guru idiom; by comparison with the Rajahmundry manifesto however, it is a set piece.

The first "official" reference amongst the *mandali* to "Avatar Meher Baba" came from Adi K. Irani in a circular issued in June 1954. Two years later, in February 1956, the same spokesman commenced to style himself as "Disciple and Secretary – Avatar Meher Baba."[25] Insofar as I was able to discover, this was not at Baba's request but solely at the discretion of the secretary. In a circular of November 1954, Adi K. Irani first used Baba's designation of "lovers" to refer to devotees.[26] Whatever one may think of the secretary's stylizations, his circulars were otherwise extremely impersonal in their format and kept to basic events or messages. A much more high-flown stylistic idiom of expression was evolved by Mani, Baba's sister, who had been a cloistered member of the women's ashram since her early teens. In 1954 she was given permission (by Baba) to take over the correspondence with certain long-established devotees in America (including Princess Matchabelli). Two years later she commenced a regular newsletter to the Western followers at large, which continued until Baba's death. Her communications mark a clear tangent to earlier news-sheets, and also concurrent ones. The "Mani style" as it might here be termed, was too sentimental for critical tastes, but it is important to mention simply because it became to an extraordinary extent the *lingua franca* of the devotional movement which burgeoned from this time onwards. It was a very feminine style, which is understandable enough, but it was widely copied not merely by women but also by men. This style chose to refer to Baba as the "Beloved," and further established the fashion of referring to his followers as "lovers."[27] Poetic moderation was not the norm. More puzzling perhaps was the veneration which Mani began to receive from the inception of these newsletters; indeed, she tended to overshadow even Mehera in some minds, though one suspects that the focus would have been different had the letters been written by another hand. A notable feature of the Mani style was that it did not keep to basic events and messages, but devoted much space to the description of nature, birthday celebrations, and other extraneous devotee activities, including "Baba Centres." There is in fact discernible a strange reversal of the priorities insisted upon by Baba at Rajahmundry. What exactly was occurring?

The salient fact which emerges is that Baba was in seclusion from 1954 until the end of his life, though his withdrawal increased from 1964. This seclusion was broken intermittently, but never for long. There were no more tours in India, though he did make two more (brief) visits to the West during the 1950's. There was no further "phase" saliency such as marked the years up to the Free Life; the major characteristic was an increased withdrawal from external events. Concurrently, there occurred a gradual but steady growth in the devotional movement which acknowledged him as their leader, though there is the well-documented twist of his having repudiated this movement and allowing it to persist virtually on sufferance in accordance with the possibilities of an evolution. The evidence discloses that this movement sank into retrogression at the very end of his life (in the late 1960's), though not all of his followers can be included in such a generalization.

By comparison with the Mani style, it is refreshing to read the account by Purdom and Schloss of their three week sojourn on Meherabad Hill in September 1954.[28] Seventeen men from the West responded to Baba's invitation to spend this period at the ashram; in contrast to *darshan*, this kind of specific contact with a small-scale group was referred to as *sahavas* (intimacy). The diary of explanations given by Baba on diverse subjects includes some highly original clarifications of sufi topics which are not easily to be found elsewhere.

He dictated a message known as "The Final Declaration" which was read out at the end of that month to over nine hundred male Indian followers who assembled briefly at Meherabad. This message caused much speculation and some alarm amongst devotees at large. Accordingly, he followed up with a clarification that certain of the statements he had made employed his "own language alone," and hence were not easily open to interpretation. But other matters had been expressed in straightforward language, e.g., the humiliation that he would suffer. Critics might well ask why he should make some statements in an ambiguous vein when it is clear that much of what he said was straightforward English. But messages relating to his personal "work" had always been complex. One answer is that he wanted to make people think hard, or even intuit, rather than opt for the easiest way to association with him by forming superfluous centres, vaunting their own persona, acquiring capital from his name, and by committing other deficiencies.

"After this final meeting Baba seemed to withdraw more

and more within himself," wrote Purdom.[29] As if to punctuate the end of a span of communicativeness, on October 7th 1954 Baba relinquished the use of his alphabet board. He thereafter reduced all communication to a gesture language that was unique to himself. Only a few of the *mandali* were at first proficient in interpreting this new language, though he was nevertheless able to convey his meanings in some detail, and messages did not stop. Just prior to relinquishing the alphabet board, he had dictated in English *God Speaks*, a book which was published in America in 1955. Despite its technical content, this work received few reviews, though some readers were offput by the devotional introduction which was written by an American and included a misrepresentation of the title.

A crucial event transpired on 2nd December 1956, when Baba suffered a second motor accident, this time near Satara. His injuries were much more serious than in the first accident of 1952. His right hip was damaged, a fracture occurring in the upper rim of the acetabulum. He refused an operation, and continued to be in great pain for a while. He moved to Poona, where good medical facilities were available. The doctors said that he would never be able to walk as formerly, and indeed for a year or so he was very hampered in his movements. He later improved somewhat and was able to walk unaided, though with a heavy gait and a detectable limp. He was never again the same in a physical sense; the contrast was acute with his earlier mobility of body. His facial mobility and animated gesture language remained the same, however.

The accident effectively sedentarized him. With few exceptions, his travel agenda thereafter was confined to moving backwards and forwards between Poona and Meherazad. He and the *mandali* would spend the summer of each year at Poona in atypically comfortable surroundings, and the remaining nine months or so at the ashram. The new Poona venue was the palatial bungalow of the Maharani Shantadevi, a devotee who made available this late Victorian/Edwardian dwelling for his use. Here amidst Victorian statues and mock-Grecian columns, Baba lived out the more convivial aspect of his final years. This ornate bungalow, which became locally known as "Guruprasad," was the scene of several *sahavas* sessions of varying size and duration. But at Meherazad there was an austere privacy, and very few visitors gained access to him there.

After the crucial accident, Baba did once venture far afield to America and Australia in 1958. This is proof enough that he could have maintained long range travel if he had really wanted to. But he did not.

The last visit to America is notable for its specific cast as a *sahavas* programme, in accordance with Baba's wish, thereby excluding casual parties and other interferences such as the "close disciples" in the West were likely to introduce. (In 1956 they had pressed upon him a television engagement which he does not seem to have viewed with enthusiasm). It was at request that he undertook the trip, for which purpose the Americans and Australians had to raise the money for his travelling expenses and for the *sahavas* expenses. All participants had to undertake to spend the full time at the venue selected, to make no other visits elsewhere during the period, and to leave on the precise dates given them. There was to be no publicity whatsoever. These stipulations were evidently made to curtail the tourist tendencies that were particularly noticeable in Westerners.

The American *sahavas* took place at the Myrtle Beach Centre-on-the-Lakes and lasted ten days from 20th–30th May, 1958. There were 225 people in attendance, and he gave numerous off-the-cuff explanations in addition to previously dictated material.[30] Whether he seriously viewed such a large gathering as a teaching event is open to question; at any rate, some of those present were evidently restless by the end of the *sahavas*, since they insisted upon giving "entertainments" one afternoon, and even roped in Charles Purdom to tell a sedate joke. Baba was observed to look quite unusually strained at the end of these amusements, although this was attributed to his "inner work." Baba himself expressed his typical humour at the *sahavas*, but it is arguable that he knew the difference between a lightness of spirit and an incapacity to concentrate for very long.

It may or may not be coincidence that Baba never

returned to the West. "Entertainments" subsequently became a major vogue amongst some Western followers, particularly amongst the new generation of the 1960's. But it is a fact that Baba made it very difficult for any Westerner to visit him in India save on one occasion only during these fading years. He seemed to regard the congregations of his Indian devotees as quite separate events; a very few Westerners occasionally gained special permission to attend some function or other at Guruprasad, but literally in ones, twos, and threes.

Shortly before leaving India for the American *sahavas*, Baba had sent a message to his Western following in which he remarked that "this period of my *sahavas* will fall within the orbit of my universal suffering and helplessness." Exactly what was meant by "universal suffering" was not defined, but he did mention a hint given to the *mandali* reminding them of his affirmation that his glorification would follow his humiliation.[31] It is apparent that he was indicating that the phase of humiliation was then in progress. Yet it is a fact that such hints were overlooked; until his dying day both the *mandali* and devotees at large anticipated his "humiliation" as a future event, if one very imminent. Some were much more vague on this point than others, but there was no firmly drawn conclusion expressed that his humiliation was a current and continuing event.[32] It is easy to see why this anomalous perspective on such matters was maintained, since otherwise more people would have had to acknowledge that all was not well with the status quo of the movement. It would not have been easy to advertise a humiliated *avatar*, most of whose followers did not understand his "passion" statements.

It seems that in Baba's perspective, his second accident was a concrete manifestation of his "humiliation." But it is apparent that the attendant helplessness went somewhat deeper than the factor of physical disablement.

He was not at all helpless, however, when it came to refusing offers of property. When he arrived in Australia to spend a week there in June 1958, it was to find that several acres of property on Kiel Mountain in Queensland had been purchased and nominated as his property. He would not consent to this, and maintained that he owned no goods or property. He gave instructions that each of those who had contributed money for the purchase of the property should have their portion returned.[33] To the best of my knowledge, he never compromised his aversion to ownership.

The only opportunity that Westerners thereafter gained to visit him in numbers was in November 1962 at the meeting which became known as the East-West Gathering. This occurred at Poona, and was attended by about three thousand Eastern followers from India, Pakistan, and Iran, and by 144 Westerners. Purdom was one of those present, and reports:

"To meet Baba again after more than four years was to find him greatly changed. He was now more than ever a suffering man. His expression was as bright, his eyes as keen as ever, and his alertness seemed not to have diminished, but he was withdrawn, and for much of the time looked far away, as though not belonging to the world. He constantly smiled and was ready to joke, and his humour had not deserted him, but there was a certain indifference that I had not noticed before. Above all there was an immense sadness that moved me strangely. When he walked one saw that he went heavily."[34]

The East-West Gathering lasted four days. He gave *darshan* to the Easterners in the afternoons, while there was a *sahavas* in the mornings for the Westerners. On the third day a message he had dictated was read out to the gathering. It was entitled "My Dear Workers," and is remarkable for its forthrightness; it links up in tone with his comments made at Rajahmundry eight years before. "Despite much talk about a 'Baba-family,' there is more a semblance than a reality of kinship among you," he stated, which made a change from Mani's customary attribution of a family identity in her newsletters. He remarked upon how his devotees had been publishing literature, organizing meetings, building centres, and even having statues made of him (this latter development occurred in Andhra). He expressed a doubt as to how much of his "message of love and truth" was actually represented in these activities, particularly in view of the lack of "brotherly feeling in your hearts." Pointed was his insistence that "I have been patient and indulgent over the way you have been doing these things, because you have been very young children . . . and children must have some sort of games to play." This was not at all flattering to the image that some held of themselves as close disciples (in which various rivalries had been involved). He indicated that what he really wanted was "the same work done in a different way . . . the way of effacement." It is obvious that he did not mean erecting statues of him in an effacing manner, owing to numerous other anti-externalist emphases. "My work is your opportunity," he reiterated, though he must have been fully aware that even in impressing an avatar identity upon the post-New Life period, this was not sufficient to make enthusiasts live the New Life before becoming presumed experts on the Free Life. "Most of you do things which I do not like you doing" seems to have been interpreted by many people as referring to someone else.[35]

The following summer at Poona was the last in the intermittent series of *sahavas* extended to the Indian followers. Thereafter, for the last six years of his life, Baba's seclusion rendered him much more inaccessible even while staying annually at the Maharani's commodious bungalow. Even local Poona devotees found it difficult to see him, and some even began to complain that they were being excluded on account of their social background.

He made a concession to the desire of the Indian followers to see him when, in May 1965, for six days at Poona he gave *darshan* to a few thousand devotees from India and Pakistan (and a small group from Iran). But he was in acute pain from a new source of affliction; a critical condition in the cervical spine had developed, giving him considerable pain centred in the nape of the neck and extending down to his shoulders. A leading neurosurgeon was unable to remedy this aggravation, and expressed surprise at its persistence. The patient had to be fitted with a surgical collar. He even resorted to use of the alphabet board again, since the movement involved in his gesture language increased the pain considerably. His injured hip was still a problem also, and as a consequence of this dual pressure he was reduced once more to a wheelchair. The doctors were of the unanimous opinion that he should not give the *darshan*, but he did so, and at considerable strain to himself.

There were no further concessions. There had been five Westerners present at the May *darshan* (though two of these were doctors), and Baba said that he would give a separate *darshan* for the Western followers by the end of the year. But this event was postponed, and never in fact occurred. The occasional visitor from the West did manage to slip through the cordon as a result of special permission, and it is evident that Baba could have given a *sahavas* if he had wanted to. But he did not do so. He was also more than ever strict about correspondence, maintaining that he wished to remain undisturbed.

From the summer of 1965 onwards, his American following began to substantially increase. The new influx was largely comprised of young people, some of whom were in the vanguard of the "hippy" boom which erupted by 1967. This influx also became evident in England, though on a much smaller scale. Some of these new followers had a background of experimentation with drugs, and it is apparent that at least a few of them had difficulty in extricating themselves from their addiction to counterfeit afflatus. Baba's main response to this new influx was to give a firm anti-drug message, which he indicated should be circulated and supported for the benefit of the many victims. In several statements he explained why LSD and other drugs should never be used save in extreme medical cases of professional diagnosis. This was of course an elementary point, but the mentality of Western youth was suitably infantile. Meher Baba firmly opposed the Leary bandwagon; none of his followers had the slightest excuse for any drug lifestyle.

The new influx of Western admirers coinciding with the hippy fads of the late 1960's created a deterioration in the verbal media of the "movement" associated with him. His philosophy became reduced to the banality of "Don't worry, be happy," a statement which devotees lifted from his sayings and made into a simplistic slogan convenient for postage stamp mentalities. Several "hip" phrases were coined by hangers-on in the new game to replace Leary's antics; "Baba's umbrella" and "Baba's love-game" are examples of this genre, which was worse than the sentimental Mani style.

The best one can say about these Western stylisms is that they were soporifically harmless by comparison with the "esoteric" drug cults that were then mushrooming. Baba had for long been known for his opposition to drug gurus, whom he seemed to regard as a particularly malignant pest. In1962 he had told the Westerners who went to Poona that there were many yogis all over the world who became drug addicts; there were many fakes who duped people by advertising their "experiences," which were in reality hallucinations caused by drug use.[36]

The great majority of the new wave of Western devotees did not gain any personal contact with Baba, not even through correspondence. He remained in seclusion, leading a very simple routine that many Western sensationalists would doubtless have found acutely boring.

An unprecedented event in Baba's life occurred on July 30th, 1968, when he stated to the *mandali*: "My work is done. It is completed one hundred per cent to my satisfaction." Though more cryptic remarks were attendant upon this disclosure, it was a very definitive announcement. Never had he said anything like this before. It was an unexpected affirmation.

Six months later he was dead.

His decease occurred at Meherazad, where for some weeks previously his health had worsened. For two months he had been afflicted with severe muscular spasms. His condition puzzled the doctors in attendance upon him. According to blood checks he should have been in a coma, but he showed no sign of mental disturbance and evidently retained total physical consciousness to the very end.

At 12.15 p.m. on January 31st 1969, he expired suddenly and silently while sitting on his surgical bed, immediately after an unusually severe spasm. The *mandali* could not at first believe that he had died, but medics confirmed the fact.

His body was buried in the tomb long since prepared for the purpose on Meherabad Hill. The architectural design of this inexpensive but solid tomb, complete with a dome, is strongly reminiscent of Muslim tombs in India that follow Central Asian precedents.

Some curious events and interpretations followed. For instance, many devotees were confused at the obviously literal fact that Baba had not spoken, not even with a single syllable of the tongue. Some of them even went to the extent of expressing theories which vaguely posited that the event, whatever it was, was yet to happen.

Possibly more strange than this was the event which was called the "last darshan." The *mandali* interpreted certain of Baba's statements to mean that the anticipated *darshan* he had referred to should be enacted as though he were still alive. Accordingly, thousands of devotees treated the summer months of 1969 as a literal "last darshan" opportunity and converged upon the Maharani's bungalow at Poona as if Baba was present there. Many young Westerners participated in this. The general literalist mentality thereafter stamped the movement.

The surviving *mandali* stayed on at the two ashrams near Ahmednagar, and showed pilgrims the tomb and the various relics associated with Baba. The words and views of the *mandali* were now regarded as infallible; it was assumed by the majority that the *mandali* were all paragons owing to the fact that they had been in Baba's physical proximity for so long.

The *mandali* stressed Baba's unique identity, and exhorted devotees to follow "only the Avatar" and to ignore all other teachers. For them there was no possible sequel to Meher Baba. The atmosphere in this respect was strangely similar to the events at Shirdi when Sai Baba had died fifty years earlier.

Prominent in this zealous trend of buttressing the ranks of the flock against all possible rivals was Adi K. Irani. He was regarded virtually as a new St. Paul, and received much adulation prior to his death some ten years later. He might be said to have betrayed the intuition factor however, since his outlook was so pronouncedly *zahiri* (literalist) as to overlook numerous *batini* (esoteric) features characteristic of Meher Baba.

It was Parsis who dominated the interpretations of Meher Baba current after his death. The Muslim element in the *mandali* was now practically extinct (save for one Iranian Muslim), and the minority of Hindus did not fill the roles of eminence. There was a marked absence of references to Baba's words uttered at the Manzil-e-Meem (at a time when he was still using his tongue), when he had said that he would meet a "violent death" at the hands of Zoroastrians.[37] This may be regarded as a *batini* reference to externalist dispositions and distortion. If much of what Meher Baba said is of significance, then this statement deserves equal attention to other selected fragments preferred by a majority.

PART TWO

TEACHING

The first version of Meher Baba's philosophy to appear in print was prepared by a Muslim pupil.[38] Apart from any significance of religious affiliation here, the very title of this early publication implies that Meher Baba requires consideration as a philosopher. Yet critics might have it that this classification is inaccurate for a person who was such an obvious mystic. This leads to a contrived question to which I shall attempt to formulate a concise answer:

Gnostic or Philosopher?

It should first be understood that Meher Baba's teaching is anything but orthodox Zoroastrian. He escaped completely from doctrinal confines. To study his more abstract teaching is like finding a purified Neoplatonism, but one must be careful of anachronistic terms here.

Though he explicitly disowned identity with any particular ism, there are two traditions clearly salient in his magnum opus entitled *God Speaks: The Theme of Creation and Its Purpose*. These two traditions are Sufism and Vedanta. Only a cretin would deny this, in view of the terminology employed, which is of sufficient density to deter casual readers. But it is not "orthodox" Sufism that he expounds, but a sophisticated "high Sufism." Nor is it "orthodox" Vedanta that he expounds, but an ingenious variant, a kind of extra-advaita that does not digress into the jejune fields sometimes patronized by unperceptive pundits.

We have, therefore, a very distinctive eclectic orientation in this teaching, which is highly original in certain of its conceptions. I hope to show the more precise background to this distinctive presentation in Part Three, but for purposes of the present section, it is sufficient to examine the components of the presentation under broad headings of philosophical analysis.

The preceding paragraphs may help to explain why the subject cannot be accused of borrowing from any Western philosopher (including Plotinus). His thesis is altogether too original within the convergent parameters of two major Eastern trends of thought and experience. Vedanta is commonly described in terms of a philosophy, while Sufism is often classified as mysticism – though many scholars have been dealing with "popular Sufism," and not its more philosophical extensions, which are still largely unknown and inadequately analyzed.

The magnum opus of Meher Baba exhibits a notably systematic form of expression. It does not rely upon any poetic or metaphorical appeal, but on the contrary, makes demanding reading which is facilitated by a knowledge of three or four languages (English, Sanskrit, Persian, Arabic). Its style is analytical and descriptive, sometimes tending to repetition in its concern with the regularity of process in the evolutionist spectrum. But the material escapes dryness or any system of forced logical proofs of the type which afflicts some Vedantic treatises, even those of Shankara the advaitin.

There is another aspect to Meher Baba's teaching that does not surface in his magnum opus (nor in numerous of his discourses). This is the more personal, aphoristic mode of expression which can be found in a wide variety of sayings and messages. A proportion of these communications (hardly any of them spoken) exhibit characteristics which can perhaps best be described as gnostic, and which attest personal experiences, claims, and predictions. An investigation of these permits a classification in terms of *hululi* traits and idioms, i.e., the expression of the "infusion" (*hulul*) or indwelling of the Absolute (= the divine essence, God, Brahman) in the creature. Meher Baba himself never seems to have used the Arabic word *hulul*, though this is perhaps the most apt abbreviation for one category of his communications. It is a term of sufi associations, of heretical overtones, and more specifically, is linked to ancient pre-Islamic Iranian traditions of gnostic idiom.[39]

The most controversial ingredient of his gnostic communications is that relating to the *avatar* concept, an ingredient which has received differing interpretations.[40] On close inspection, his definitions of this concept actually comprise a revision of related Hindu doctrines. The Sanskrit word *avatar* means "descent," i.e. of divinity into matter, and is generally interpreted in the sense of a special incarnation. However, the mythological content of Hindu *avatar* doctrines is very substantial, and the Puranic references to, e.g., a fish *avatar* and a boar *avatar*, obviously represent a pronounced degree of popularization. If Meher Baba is construed literally, then his human sequence is very much more logical and expansive than orthodox variants, but it seems impossible for anyone less than an *avatar* to dogmatically and definitively pronounce upon such matters. I am content to report a phenomenon with a hopeful sense of accuracy, which I certainly have not found in some of the literature devoted to Meher Baba.

Shock statements of gnosis have long been a recourse in Iranian sufi circles. "I am Moses, I am Jesus, I am Muhammad" was standard *qalandar* repertory in medieval and post-medieval Iran, and hence Meher Baba has a notable pedigree in this respect. But numerous of Meher Baba's statements are both more sophisticated and more definitive than this fashionable esotericism. Like the qalandars before him, he disliked clericalism, though it was not the Shi'ite mujtahids with whom he was confronted, but the Zoroastrian dasturs and brahmin priests. He definitely did specify a lofty function for himself, howsoever one defines this function; for instance, he said that the manifestation of Jesus was but three-quarters that of his own. This would not seem to unduly violate basic laws of supercession, though in theological arenas it causes consternation. Philosophically, it seems a very marginal concern – there was two thousand years in between, and each generation had its saints and adepts, most of them obscure and many doubtless totally unknown. Exclusive claims of deification seem excessive, and could very well do with updating more frequently. Meher Baba's version of *qalandar* tactics does not seem unreasonable by comparison with rigid orthodoxies. The fact of a Zoroastrian *imam* (leader) of *batini* type who assimilated a Hindu majority into his following seems a tolerable addition to all-Semitic pedigrees of prophetology. Even if one acknowledges the Muslim tradition of "There will be no prophet after me," as valid for the Semitic lineage, one is disposed to believe that the "Seal of the Saints" vindicated by Ibn al-Arabi has a longer-standing survival value that will outlast all clerical punctuation marks.

Meher Baba himself acknowledged the sufi exponent Muhiyuddin ibn al-Arabi (d. 1240) as a *qutub*,[41] the term for the highest rank in the "hierarchy of saints" that figures in sufi lore. In Meher Baba's English terminology, this rank is described as that of a "perfect master," meaning one who has reached the ultimate grade of adeptship in contrast to masters of lesser grades of adeptship. (The Sanskrit equivalent is *sadguru*, which he frequently employed). Ibn al-Arabi, a Spanish Arab, still holds a heretical reputation in some Islamic countries, and his writings have recently been banned in one sector. Ibn al-Arabi used a highly involved and intricate style in his Arabic treatises, which are not always easy to interpret, though it has been deduced by specialist scholars that he regarded himself as the "Seal of the Saints." This concept can be traced back to Hakim Tirmizi (d.*c.* 908), a Central Asian sufi writer whose treatise *Khatm al-awliya (Seal of the Saints)* elaborates upon the subject of the different grades of saints.[42] Ibn al-Arabi gave this theme an apparently new twist by relating it more concretely to the concept of prophetology. He conceded that Muhammad was superior to all other prophets by virtue of his office as *Khatm al-anbiya* (Seal of the Prophets), but maintained that the Seal of the Saints was the perfect manifestation of the "Spirit (Reality) of Muhammad," a gnostic concept which was indigestible to orthodox Muslims of pedantic tendency. This attempt to update the backwardness of reliance upon long-dead authority figures, i.e. to take notice of living teachers instead of dead ones, was accompanied by an ingenious classification which affirmed that all prophets are also saints – and that the saintly aspect of each prophet is higher than his prophetic aspect.[43]

Meher Baba seems to have wanted to ensure that there could be no confusion of priorities in his case, since he designated himself as *saheb-i-zaman* (master of a cycle) in contradistinction to the *qutub* or *saheb-i-waqt* (master of an age). This strategy seems a particularly bold variant of the *khatm al-awliya* prerogative. Ibn al-Arabi's pantheistic philosophy was nipped in the bud insofar as a thoroughgoing cultural influence was concerned. It remains to be seen whether the pantheistic philosophy of Meher Baba will be similarly eclipsed by other doctrinaire trends.

There are several conceptual links between Meher Baba and the *wujudi* (pantheistic monist) tradition of sufi gnosis which is associated with Ibn al-Arabi and which took strong root in India during late medieval and Mughal times. This gnosis of *wahdat al-wujud* (Unity of Being) is discernible in at least two of Meher Baba's "masters," namely Hazrat Babajan[44] and Hazrat Sai Baba, both of whom were in the habit of making highly unorthodox and revelatory disclosures. The latter made a statement that seems to have been a variant of the ancient sufi claim of being the *hujjat-Allah*, the "Proof of Allah,"[45] a phrase sometimes associated with the Ismailis but actually used earlier by Sahl Tustari (d. 896), the sufi gnostic[46] and teacher of Hallaj (d. 922), who was executed on account of his gnostic philosophy of *hulul*.[47] The teaching of Hallaj is sometimes categorized as *al-ittihad al-muin*, the identity of the individual soul with the Absolute, and has been deemed by scholars to be distinct from *al-ittihad al-amm al-mutlaq*, "the absolute union of divinity and the universe" which is associated with Hindu pantheists, i.e. advaitins like Shankara. This distinction is arbitrary, since the teaching of Hallaj is extant only in fragments, and monotheistic bias customarily militates against Hindus and pantheism.[48] In Meher Baba's teaching, these two variants of *ittihad* are fused in a consistent measure. His magnum opus identifies Shankara (d.*c.* 720) as a *sadguru* (= *qutub*),[49] which at least proves a non-insular perspective in matters of authority. In Meher Baba's eclectic strategy, there is at last an opportunity to investigate a tangible instance of the "Indian" influence upon Sufism that has been inaccurately mooted in orientalist scholarship,[50] though the opportunity has to date been ignored by those concerned. Empirical matters are rarely conceded in much theoretical scholarship it would seem, and hence I take the opportunity to anthropographize upon a solid historical foundation.

Being a Zoroastrian by birth, Meher Baba was outside the Muslim versus Hindu dichotomy that is customarily imposed upon the relevant studies of mysticism and philosophy. His version of "high Sufism" attests that the Perso-Arabic components of his teaching are second to none in their juxtaposition with the equally valuable Vedantic refinements that are distilled from the best in the Hindu philosophical heritage. The experiential dimensions of his "theme of creation" do not permit a victory of either camp, since experientially they are not opposed, the conflict being only in dogmatic and scholastic matters which are unrelated to any viable philosophy of realization of the truth.

It is worthwhile to point out that the clarity of exposition in *God Speaks* substantially excels that found in the intricate and highly allusive Arabic treatises of Ibn al-Arabi. The latter's famous *Futuhat al-Makkiya* (*Meccan Revelations*)[51] and *Fusus al-Hikam* (*Bezels of Wisdom*)[52] have frequently been a subject for scholarly complaint in their non-straightforward mode of exposition, a constraint largely imposed by the uncongenial environment in which they were composed. There is nothing like an ordered sequence of evolutionist explanation that is found in Meher Baba's chief work. In a less demanding format, the latter's *Discourses*, dictated during 1938–42, likewise bear a very favourable comparison with the extant discourses of Jalaluddin Rumi (d. 1273), the Iranian sufi domiciled in Qonya whom Meher Baba also defined as a *qutub* (he affirmed the existence of five of these entities at any one time, dispensing with the traditional distinction between the *qutub* and the four *awtad* or "supports"). Rumi's *Fihi Ma Fihi* (*In it what is in it*) consists of discourses,[53] or rather conversations, which reflect an unusual insight into sufi matters and the foibles of orthodox myopia, though at the same time constrained to talk in many conventional stylisms which prevented a systematically expressed psychology. It is only fair to add that Rumi's magnum opus was the *Mathnavi*,[54] a lengthy Persian work in rhyming couplets that is replete with sufi lore and illustrative material, but from which it is notoriously difficult to extrapolate a systematic philosophy.

Turning to the Sanskrit treatises of Shankara,[55] one finds a more logically weighted format of exposition than in many works of sufi idiom, though there are also disadvantages in the concessions to caste thinking that can be found in some Advaita classics. There is a distinct tendency to dryness and "forced argument" in the commentaries of Shankara on texts like the *Brihadaranyaka Upanishad*,[56] and some readers prefer the more compact and "mystical" treatises such as the famous *Vivekachudamani*[57] and *Upadeshasahasri* (*Thousand Teachings*).[58] But in these latter, the aphoristic nature of the contents frequently interrupts continuities favourable to evolutionist criteria, and hence there are drawbacks from both an "Aristotelian" and "Neoplatonist" point of view. Meher Baba's version of Vedanta dispenses with the logic-chopping, and brings out the evolutionist and gnostic ingredients in an effectively well-rounded whole, and without making the slightest concession to any caste framework, to which he was totally opposed both in theory and in practice.

The above comments do not exhaust the inventory of correspondences and differences with traditional Sufi and Vedantic works, but are sufficient to indicate an answer to the question commencing this section: Meher Baba was very much a gnostic type, but was also the formulator of a systematic philosophy that compares well with its known precedents.

Works of Advaita Vedanta noticeably do not dwell upon the *avatar* theme, but are content to draw rein at the situation of a *jivanmukta* (liberated soul) in human incarnation. The context is a markedly ascetic one. The *avatar* theme is found mainly in the popular scriptures known as the Puranas, but which link in their contents with Vedantic and other philosophical leitmotifs. Vedanta is only one of the traditional philosophical heritages of India, though it came to be regarded as the most classical expression of Indian philosophy. It is sometimes associated with conservative dispositions owing to its usage amongst the priestly caste of pundits, a stigma which cannot be aimed at the more devotional

Puranic milieu which extended to the Hindu masses irrespective of tuition in linguistic finesse.

It is a fact that Meher Baba very rarely specified any sequence of avatars to back up his more expansive gnostic claims. One might be forgiven for thinking that he was averse to doing so. The main specification was in a message given in 1953,[59] but it was not repeated. He named only Zoroaster, Rama, Krishna, Buddha, Jesus, and Muhammad. This list is inter-racial, and save for Buddha, reflects the denominational affiliations of his audience. It is a fundamentally different schema to the Semitic prophetology or the traditional Hindu series of divine incarnations. With the exception of Rama, all of the entities named have been allotted historical tangibility by scholars of religion, though in varying degrees. This whole matter of avataric entities is specified so little in Baba's communications that it merits no further mention in this book. As the *imam* (leader) of an inter-religious community which mushroomed into a substantial devotional following, his claims were not nearly so sensational as is often assumed by critics. Many of his more gnostic statements admit of more than one interpretation.

The conventional dichotomy between gnosis/mysticism and philosophy frequently breaks down beyond the purely analytical vogues of the latter. The term philosophy is often meant in the sense of a systematic exposition, though it should be obvious that a love of wisdom does not necessarily amount to a love of system, which is rather frequently the domain of sophistry. Mystical philosophers are not lessened in their significances by the mere accusation of mysticism from logicians who may be at fault in holistic aptitudes.

It is possible to investigate the philosophy of Meher Baba in terms of components which fit five broad headings: ethics, cosmology, evolutionism, psychology, sociology. I propose to duly analyze these components in that order.

Ethics

The ethical content in Meher Baba's teachings is very high. He can also be said to have lived what he preached, unlike some other recent "gurus." His personal example was incontestably one of discipline and denial, sometimes to an extreme extent as in the case of his lengthy fasts and seclusions. Though he freely allowed his followers to marry, he himself lived a strict celibate existence. At the time of Gandhi's ascendancy, he concurred in the avoidance of contraceptives as a spiritual ideal,[60] though he did not implement this as a rigid and inflexible rule, which Gandhi tended to do.

Meher Baba's unorthodox role in the mystical sphere never involved the ridicule of former religious leaders and figureheads, only criticisms of crystallized religious doctrines and ecclesiastical hierarchies. Unlike the perverse "gnostics" of various traditions, he did not in any way undermine morality. On the contrary, it would be difficult to find a more exacting moral guide in twentieth century mysticism. In his view, morality was a preliminary necessity for the spiritual path.

Some analysts might find indication of the influence of Zoroastrian ethical precepts in his attitude. If there is any truth in this, then it must be said that he added substantially to the basic Zoroastrian principle of "good thoughts, good words, good deeds" which is an emphasis in the Gathas of Zarathushtra.[61] The Gathas arguably contain gnostic extensions of ethical premises, the context much obliterated by the uncertain linguistic connotations of the ancient Avestan texts comprising these scriptural "hymns." In Meher Baba's teaching, the ethical principles do not acquire dogmatic proportions, but are a natural appendage to matters of greater and much more complex import.

He appears to have dispensed with the principle of *taqiyya* (precautionary dissembling) that was so much a part of gnostic approaches in Shi'ite and sufi circles of past centuries. British India was not a milieu of persecution; the British merely ignored "native" views, and did not interfere with these unless there was a political edge to the views expressed. Meher Baba's stress upon personal integrity led him to stipulate to his pupils that even a "white lie" was unpermissible. *Taqiyya* frequently opted for expressions of religious bias, but in Meher Baba there is none of this.

He was a staunch upholder of *ahimsa* (non-violence)

principles, and unlike his fiery teacher Upasni Maharaj, he was rarely explosive, particularly after his commencement of silence in 1925 (though he could be extremely exacting in cases of lapse from his rules of training). He was a vegetarian in diet, and would not eat eggs, though he did not enforce vegetarianism upon his followers, many of whom ate meat. Though there is an obvious comparison with Gandhi in respect of *ahimsa*, Meher Baba would not be drawn into any political issue,and repeatedly affirmed that he had no part in politics. However, he quite frequently indicated his sympathy for Gandhi, whom he said was genuinely a *mahatma* ("great soul").

Baba's ethical standpoint achieved a degree of public exposure in America at the very end of his life. This was in relation to the issue of drug-taking, particularly the ingestion of LSD which became such a fad from the mid-1960's onwards. Unlike permissive gurus, he did not favour the free-and-easy habits that dominated the hippy boom, though when he dictated his anti-drug statements, the hippy boom had scarcely begun as a widespread movement. He was opposed to the use of all drugs, having long been in opposition to the hemp-smoking *samadhi* of the mediocre sadhus who were so common in India. But he was particularly concerned to point out the dangers involved in LSD, and in a manner very different to the criticisms of those in the medical and psychiatric professions who refused to patronize the "danger drug." According to him, LSD is extremely harmful physically, mentally, and spiritually. It can damage the brain permanently, though this can be avoided in cases of medical aid using a controlled dosage. He was not repudiating the possible medical application in extreme cases able to benefit from this drug, but he was very strongly making his point against the wave of experimenters who imagined that ASC's induced by drugs were spiritually elevating and the equivalent of the enlightenment they had heard about in Eastern mysticism. He reiterated from late 1965 onwards that there was no short cut to the goal, and that repeated (non-medical) use of LSD leads to insanity, which may prove incurable even with expert medical assistance using LSD as a counter-factor.

Use of this drug can even cause death, he emphasized. He explained that ASC's produced by LSD and other drugs are only a semblance of "spiritual experiences," and more technically, that in some cases LSD induced experiences of the "shadows of the subtle plane," i.e., a distorted reflection of the subtle world existing "inside" matter. These shadow-experiences have nothing whatsoever to do with spiritual advancement, he insisted.

Some researchers and one or two well known pop stars took notice of him, but in general the hippy boom went its own way of Occidental tangent to ancient Eastern knowledge. Sensation is customarily confused with something ultimate by those with a crass apparatus of consciousness which is unprepared for any finer intake.

It is because so many people nominally interested in spiritual experiences are in reality totally unsuited to the attainment of these that ethical premises are essential for persons who wish to put at least one foot in a forward direction instead of moving backwards. It frequently happens that honours are assumed by those who fashionably ignore ethics, but the shortcomings are usually all too evident to anyone with a sense of discrimination.

Cosmology

A disciplined life and a disciplined way of thinking are the main criteria of usefulness when envisaging or discussing matters of universal import. The subject of cosmology could be called theology if the latter term is understood with sufficient elasticity (a hallmark of refined discipline). A theology was implied in the *Metaphysics* of Aristotle, whose "First Philosophy," i.e. metaphysics, was very much broader in scope than the reduced pastures of modern analytical philosophy.

It is possible for the scientifically-minded to see in Meher Baba's cosmology a rationale of complex profundities without express association with any one religious system.[62] His magnum opus is one of the very few cosmological treatises of note produced in either a Sufi/ishraqi or a Vedantic milieu since the time of Dara Shikoh's eclectic *Confluence of the*

Two Seas (*Majma al-Bahrain*) in the mid-seventeenth century.[63] It has no equivalent in modern Western philosophy from Descartes onwards, and no competition from influential twentieth century contemporaries like Wittgenstein or Bertrand Russell. An academic student of philosophy once told me that he could not get past the first few pages of *God Speaks* owing to all the "foreign" words in it, which effectively describes the adventurousness in this department of timid wisdom and language games with an ethnocentric slant.

Those who are still doubting the "concept of mind" in deference to sceptics like Gilbert Ryle are unlikely to be able to come to terms with the Eastern experience of mind. The old bogey of Cartesian dualism achieves such disparate attention from theorists because the Western categories of entity are customarily miscast. Church dogma, rationalist speculation, and empirical extroversion of the Darwinist variety are a sour mixture for the distillation of theoretical wisdom.[64] The resultant soporific state of knowledge has inevitably left room for the biased version of cosmology and evolution essayed by Teilhard De Chardin, whose Christian context belittles the contributions of "ancient religions," which are deemed to be in process of irreversible disintegration in the face of the march to progress of the true anointed.[65] In other words, very little advance has been made upon Descartes in the Western arena of speculation, and in many cases a reversal has occurred by comparison with the analytical flourishes of the gentlemanly amateur of the early seventeenth century.

It is a strangely appropriate fact that certain of the "ancient religions" made a philosophically coherent appearance in print the very same year (1955) that De Chardin's more famous thesis was published in the original French. Though one is very much better known than the other, it is arguable that the more neglected book has the greater claim to comprehensiveness and catholicity of approach. Meher Baba's magnum opus does not criticize Christianity or any other religion; in fact, it makes no criticism of any rival whatsoever, but merely states its propositions and themes without distraction.

The peculiarly deep-rooted Christian theological bias exhibited by many Western logical minds was evident even in the commentary of Baba's major contemporary biographer. Charles B. Purdom was a convinced Christian, as he is at pains to tell his reader, though this did not interfere with his wholehearted acceptance of Meher Baba as his teacher and guide. But it did interfere with his report of the content of *God Speaks: The Theme of Creation and Its Purpose*, published in 1955. The book gained its distinctive title owing to the act of creation being likened to a speech act, emblematized by the well known syllable *Om* (*Aum*) which figures in Hindu lore. Purdom ought to have known better than to assume (with some other devotees of a lesser logical acumen) that the title indicated the status of the author, but more serious was his distorted account of the evolutionism outlined in this book. Purdom's assertion that *God Speaks* "should be regarded as a symbolic work not a philosophical treatise"[66] was a consequence of his Christian conditioning, and graphically testifies to his reluctance to accept the version of transmigration expounded by Meher Baba. "The cosmology is not to be dismissed as 'pantheistic,'"[67] is another statement revealing a monotheistic bias, though in a sophisticated variant. Purdom could accept the theme of reincarnation amongst the human species, but was unable to digest the explicit theme that a reincarnating entity also applies to subhuman species.[68] Many Westerners are in the same ideological position, and are hence unable to give any causal explanation for pre-human forms of life other than a vague Darwinian reflection which conveniently and pathetically reduces cosmology to a robotic sequence of accidents – which is what all Darwinists thrive upon as an excuse for not thinking deeply enough.

One begins to wonder how many explicit philosophies have been misinterpreted by their contemporary partisans. This instance was not, of course, the first time, but it can be regarded as a particularly instructive instance in view of the tangible proof of misinterpretation in published form. Those who are apt to believe that oral records of past eras were somehow faultless owing to a prodigious mnemonic capacity must be daydreaming, it would seem.

In case it might seem surprising to some readers that Meher Baba's published teaching was misrepresented during his lifetime by a partisan, it should be interposed that Meher Baba consistently demonstrated a remarkable indifference to published views concerning him. Purdom himself was one of those who made a point of stressing this factor of indifference, though he was evidently unaware of his own misrepresentation.

Suffice it to say here that Meher Baba's magnum opus is notable for its non-symbolic and non-allegorical content. He was at considerable pains to operationalize his terminology to meet an exacting standard of definition, one of the reasons why sloppy thinkers have found it difficult to appreciate the relevant book. Purdom did appreciate *God Speaks*, but may have been confusing it with the more poetic expository style of De Chardin's *The Phenomenon of Man* (a work he is known to have liked), though there is little or no comparison between the expository styles of these respective treatises.

Purdom evidences an impatience with the terminologies of Sufism and Vedanta that are so copiously represented in *God Speaks*. He was not hostile to either of these traditions, but at the same time, he was not greatly familiar with them in any detail. He was well read in Western philosophy and Christian theology and mysticism, and also European literature in general, but his acquaintance with Eastern mystical trends did not surpass the level of writers like Aldous Huxley. Literary celebrities were seldom able to back up their pet theories on Eastern mysticism with any convincing degree of scholarship, and Purdom followed suit in this respect.

While certain of Meher Baba's off-the-cuff sayings and aphorisms can legitimately be interpreted as being intended in a symbolic idiom, e.g., his varying references to his "speaking the Word of Words," this kind of interpretation is not at all applicable in the case of the contents of *God Speaks*, which was dictated in a very unambiguous and demanding mode of verbal etiquette, as the *mandali* were well aware. The main text (Parts 1 to 8) were the product of his direct dictation from the alphabet board and via gestures, which involved the use of English, Gujerati, Marathi, and Persian, with some Arabic and Sanskrit terms. His Parsi amanuensis Eruch Jessawala was instructed to render this complex multi-linguistic text into appropriate English, though retaining the technical terminology of Sufism and Vedanta. Part 9 is a summary of the text written by Eruch in elaboration of notes dictated to him, while Part 10 is a very brief conclusion that does not fail to make its point. The subsequent American editors very largely confined themselves to grammatical considerations, and avoided tampering with the complex sentence structure of the text. The extensive Supplement consisted of notes dictated to the Muslim pupil Dr. Abdul Ghani Munsiff, who was particularly familiar with sufi vocabulary. This supplement was more radically edited by an American pupil owing to its "disjointed and disorganized" condition, and subsequently revised in a very exacting manner by Baba, who meticulously specified even the components of words (i.e. letters of the English alphabet) in communicating via his new repertory of gestures.[69] The second edition, published after his death, included minor additions and a useful glossary.

While all commentators are entitled to their own interpretations perhaps, the description of methodically ordered expository text as symbolism is a serious flaw. It is comparable in the scientific field to Darwin being caricatured as symbolical in his intentions while writing *On the Origin of Species*. Churchmen might have felt better able to relax if such an interpretation had been unanimously accepted, but any careful inspection of the text would have dispelled this illusion of convenience.

It might be instructive to focus upon the parallels with other texts as mentioned by Purdom. He likened Parts 1–8 of *God Speaks* to a commentary upon the *Brahma-Sutras*, taking account of Shankara and Ramanuja. He was also reminded of the *Enneads* of Plotinus, and the writings of Dionysius Areopagiticus, "and always with great advantage" of Meister Eckhart. Part 9 on the "Ten States of God" he found "somewhat reminiscent of the ten spheres of the divine manifestation in the *Kabbalah*," concerning which he duly observed that an ancient Persian origin had been posited by some scholars.[70] I will focus upon these suggested parallels in turn.

The *Brahma-Sutras*, also known as the *Vedanta-Sutras*, are a prized collection of over five hundred aphorisms attributed to the ancient Indian sage Badarayana. This canonical collection is generally regarded as an attempt to systematize the philosophy of the Upanishads, which represent the core of Vedantic thought. The Upanishadic texts[71] are of differing age and complexion, and do not express any consistent system of thought, being highly aphoristic in nature. The *Brahma-Sutras* do not resolve the problem of finding a consistent system of thought in these texts, not least because of their brevity. Some sutras of Badarayana are even capable of conveying opposite meanings according to the grammatical setting. The *Brahma-Sutras* do not specify which texts are under discussion, and as a consequence different commentators have opted for different texts as the basis, so that quite different topics are considered to be under examination. Further, these enigmatic Sutras frequently do not reflect any independent decision, but merely report the views of different Vedantins. When one learns that there have been very numerous commentators on the *Brahma-Sutras*, many of them subscribing to different interpretations, the prospect of consistency evaporates. This situation is to some extent redeemed by the fact that the five best known commentators of classical stature "more or less agree on certain points," e.g., that *Brahman* (the Absolute) is the cause of this world and that knowledge of *Brahman* leads to the endpoint of liberation from the world. But they differ as to the nature of *Brahman*, the nature of the causality involved, the relation of the individual soul (*jiva*) to *Brahman*, and the condition of the *jiva* in the state of liberation (*moksha*).[72]

These five Vedantic commentators are Shankara, the exponent of Advaita (non-dualism); Ramanuja, the exponent of Vishishtadvaita (qualified non-dualism); Nimbarka, the exponent of Bhedabhedavada (difference and non-difference); Madhva, the exponent of Dvaita (dualism); Vallabha, the exponent of Shuddhadvaita ("pure" non-dualism). Only the first two are at all well known outside India, though Ramanuja (d. 1137) is very seldom read by Westerners. Shankara's lengthy commentary known as the

Brahma-Sutra-bhashya[73] is not easy reading for the uninitiated, despite its English translations. The main difference between he and Ramanuja is often described (at risk of simplicity) in terms of the advaitic *Brahman* being attributeless (*nirguna*) pure intelligence and the advaitic *jiva* (soul) being in reality all-pervading and identical with *Brahman*; by contrast, the vishishtadvaitic *Brahman* is essentially a Personal God (Ishvara) with attributes (*saguna*), and the *jiva* is duly conceived as an "atomic" particle of the Lord. The other three commentators admit varying degrees of dualism.

Meher Baba does not outrightly repudiate either Shankara or Ramanuja in *God Speaks*, since he does not refer to either of them. He is much nearer to Shankara's pantheism fundamentally, though his framework of details leaves room for a "Personal God" up to a certain point of individual experience, particularly since he admits the necessary and advanced phase of *bhakti* (love), or rather *para-bhakti* (supreme love), on the spiritual path. He strikes a complete tangent to all of the classical Vedantic commentators in his complete avoidance of citing scriptural authority. The brahmanical punditry here becomes irrelevant, since his exposition is self-contained and well-integrated within an explanatory circuit that does not utilize proofs as bulwarks to argument. He does not in fact argue, he merely states and describes, and does so in a coherent manner that explains a great deal in a surprisingly compact form. His Vedantic terminology does not always fit any standard school of interpretation, Advaita included, and what he does is to effectively regularize the meaning of various terms in the context of his worldview. The result is a singularly uncluttered and original version of Vedantic significations, in addition to striking semantic plus factors associated with the philosophical tradition of Sufism.

The *Enneads* of Plotinus (d. 270) also evidence the tendency to assert "scriptural" authority, in this case Plato. Plotinus did of course expand the extant thought of Plato, to the extent that he is still criticized by orthodox Platonists even today. Though Plotinus wrote in a methodical manner on metaphysical subjects, Meher Baba compares very well with his treatises, and brings out numerous themes which are vague or altogether missing in the *Enneads*. Indeed, the Iranian is not infrequently more "Greek" than Plotinus in his consistent and consecutive cosmology and evolutionism. In Meher Baba there is none of the astrological lore which some analysts have found disconcerting in Plotinus, who did take recourse to the symbolism of his era. Meher Baba was definitely not one of those writers (or rather dictaters) who plagiarize the *Enneads*, and Plotinus would have found him a formidable philosophical rival on the other side of the Hellespont in an (imaginary) encounter between "platonists" and "gnostics." Though Plotinus is well known for having criticized persons who claimed *gnosis* after the fashion of his time, he could hardly have accused our Iranian of immorality and talismanic superstition, since both of these latter deficiencies were conspicuously absent in the life and thought of the author of *God Speaks*. If there was any Hermeticism in Meher Baba, it was of the transcendent variety which distinguished the ishraqi (illuminist) tradition of medieval Iran.

Plotinus is much more poetic in his idioms than Meher Baba. For instance, he refers to the soul (psyche) in the feminine tense, in contrast to the masculine tense he sometimes applies to "the One," i.e the ultimate reality. This feminine tense reappeared in Christian mysticism, contrary to the impersonal spirit of Vedanta and other Indian philosophies. The famous "trinity" of the *Enneads* – the One, *Nous* (mind), and Soul – is not directly analogous to the distinctive cosmology of Meher Baba, particularly since Plotinus gives no detailed explanation of how the universe came into being, and of precisely what processes are involved in the juxtaposition of hypostases.[74] The Christian mystics were unable to improve upon Plotinus, not even John Scottus Eriugena, the Irish philosopher of the ninth century whose "Christian Neoplatonism" was heretical to his sluggish Latin contemporaries. Eriugena's notable work *Periphyseon* has been discerned as one of the literary sources for thinkers among the Cathars of a later period in France, a work which was proscribed by the Papacy.[75]

One of the sources for Eriugena was the corpus of

Dionysius Areopagiticus, whose obscure background has been the subject of much speculation. He was an Asiatic who probably lived *c.* 500 A.D., possibly as a Syrian monk. HIs real name is unknown, since Dionysius is a pseudonym, and for long caused him to be mistakenly regarded by Christians as the literal friend of St. Paul. Some scholars have considered him a Neoplatonist in disguise, and a pupil of Proclus (d. 485), the Neoplatonist sage of Athens. Whatever the nature of his identity, and though his writings have certain affinities with Plotinus, he does not express any similar philosophical system. He is most famous for his references to the Godhead as the "divine dark," and advocated the method of "unknowing" as the means for achieving mystical union.[76] Though his writings had much influence upon Christian mystics and theologians throughout the medieval era, in the spectrum ranging from the heretical Eriugena to the dogmatic Aquinas, it is a diluted Neoplatonism that is expressed. There is very little in the corpus of Pseudo-Dionysius to justify a comparison with *God Speaks*, and in fact such a comparison goes a long way towards proving the differences between general mystical themes and detailed cosmology and evolutionism. Even the more systematic *Elements of Theology*,[77] a major work of Proclus, does not convey anything of the detailed sequence in *God Speaks*. Purdom's feeling that it was a great advantage to be reminded of Meister Eckhart (d.*c.* 1328) is puzzling, though he had evidently confused the content of Meher Baba's book in his preoccupation with the mystical symbolism found elsewhere. This is meant with no disrespect to Eckhart, who was perhaps one of the bolder Christian mystics of later medieval Europe,[78] but it is of much greater advantage to refer to the Iranian gnostic and philosophical tradition of which Meher Baba was an appropriate heir. Purdom made no reference in this context to such names as Abdul Karim Jili, Aziz Nasafi, Sohravardi Maqtul, and others too numerous to glibly mention.

Turning now to the question of similarities with Jewish Qabbalah, there is the salient factor to take into account that "no agreed canonical definition exists," to quote Scholem on the complex lore relating to the ten *Sefirot*, which are often taken to represent metaphysical principles of an emanationist type. The *Sefirot* are first traceable in extant texts to the *Sefer Yezirah* (*Book of Creation*), an enigmatic Hebrew treatise which exists in two versions, which may date back, in part at least, to the period between the third and sixth centuries A.D. The tradition of Qabbalah developed during the twelfth century in southern France, but the early Qabbalists described the *Sefirot* in an obscure manner, doubtless intentionally, which led to very differing interpretations. This ambiguity is true of early Qabbalistic texts like the *Sefer ha-Bahir* and the *Zohar*. The literary tradition of Qabbalah was heir to a gnostic heritage of allusive type which was likewise subject to a diversity of interpretations. Scholem describes the language of the Qabbalah as "figurative and symbolic," and hence resistant to analytical treatment. The precise nature of the *Sefirot* came to be "a widely disputed subject" amongst the later medieval Jewish Qabbalists. From the fourteenth century onwards, the *Sefirot* came to be depicted in the form of a diagram listing the basic symbols associated with each *Sefirah* (plural: *Sefirot*), an arrangement referred to as "the tree of the *Sefirot*" or "the tree of emanation."[79] This Qabbalistic tree of knowledge was subsequently much reduced in dimensions, and otherwise altered, by the Christian appropriation of the subject, which limped on into the nineteenth century in the caricatures afforded by modern occultism. Fortunately for our present study, there is no resemblance between these latter and the cosmology of Meher Baba, though whether there was any equivalence in the original Jewish symbolism is best left to the intuition. Suffice it to say here that the "ten principal states of God" as outlined by Meher Baba bear no explicit correlation with the *Sefirot*, which seems to relate to an entirely different context, whatever the reminiscences occurring to a former commentator. Since it is important to grasp the explicit formulations of the Iranian mystic in this respect, I give here a very brief resume of his "Ten States" for the convenience of the reader, though at risk of some compression:

I. God in the Beyond-Beyond State. This is ingeniously

related to II, and is the explanation for the ultimate origin of the universe. The emphasis is made that it cannot be adequately described, though Meher Baba does clarify it in a logical manner as an ultimate cause that is "neither conscious nor unconscious" of itself as Reality, a state of "God-Is" comparable to a vacuum in which the whim (*lahar*) to know itself *consciously* surges to produce the structure of the universe that comprises innumerable microcosms that are each related to the original vacuum-state of "God-Is" by virtue of a potential capacity to bridge the apparent gap imposed by the phenomenal world, a capacity that is actualized in the extension of consciousness which at its maximum passes into II.

II. God in the Beyond State. This is the original vacuum state of "God-Is" transformed into a total consciousness of Itself, realizable by all human beings after an extremely lengthy process of adaptation to maximal potentials. This state involves the consciousness of the infinite power, knowledge, and bliss, a consciousness which is the objective of the entire cosmological process. This consciousness is infinite because it transcends the phenomenal world of matter, owing to the inherent linkage in the microcosm with the original infinite vacuum-state of existence. Hence this "Beyond State" is simultaneously microcosmic and macrocosmic, since consciousness is what comprises it, and not any other unit of measurement.

III. God as Emanator, Sustainer, and Dissolver. This is expressly equated with the Vedantic trinity of Brahma-Vishnu-Shiva, and also with the less well known Sufi synonyms of Afridgar-Parvardigar-Fanakar. The context is more logically convincing than the expressions of textbook Vedanta, since the alignment of states I and II explains contradictions that are usually left in an awkward neglect. It is important to understand that state II includes the ultimate achievement in consciousness, and also lesser dimensions of that achievement. State III is an aspect of II, since state II can be said to begin at the very inception of the cosmological sequence. In state II occurs the scope of manifestation of all that is latent in the infinity of state I, and hence states III-X are effectively variations upon the range of state II, variations in terms of consciousness and perspective of the manifesting infinitude of state I. A significant feature of the Emanator theme is the description in terms of the Creation occurring as the projection of the infinite unconsciousness of state I. Though Creation is an infinite attribute, it is inevitably attended by infinite imperfections, which can only be transcended by the infinite consciousness evolved via the cosmological process. Imperfection is necessarily attended by dissolution in whatever range of time is involved for the sustaining of what is created.

IV. God as Embodied Soul. It is through the experience of apparent separateness that souls consciously realize their identity with the Oversoul (*Paramatman*), which gives rise to the experience of the infinite power-knowledge-bliss (*sat-chit-ananda*). This theme reflects a Vedantic one, but is stated with a thoroughness and attention to detail that is not found in classical treatises. Meher Baba elaborates upon the subject of *sanskaras* (impressions), which affords a notable logic to this topic.

V. God as Soul in the State of Evolution. The evolutionist teaching of Meher Baba is thoroughly panpsychist, and charts a rigorously defined sequence of transmigration which encompasses all the different levels of nature from gaseous substances to humans. It amounts to a clarification of transmigration, since it does not admit the mythological distortions to which this subject has been prone throughout the centuries, both in the ancient Mediterranean world and in India and adjoining Far Eastern countries. There is no retrograde evolution, i.e. humans reincarnating as animals. The sequence is only forward, from lower to higher species. There is no difficulty here in accepting the bare bones of the Darwinist contention that man evolved from the ape, but the context is very much bigger and more complex than the materialist theory defines or concedes. In short, the meat is missing from Darwinian evolution, which is by comparison seriously misleading in its compression of cosmology.

VI. God as Human Soul in the State of Reincarnation. Contrary to some modern theories, Meher Baba affirms that there is no need for more complex physical forms than the human in which to evolve consciousness. The problem is that most humans are not conscious of reality, but only of mundane events and their bodily needs and wants. The mental impressions (*sanskaras*) which condition their incentive and blunt their consciousness have to be dislodged and refined by a process that is acutely realistic in its specified duration of thousands of human incarnations. This will be unwelcome to those who think they are entitled to heaven or oblivion after one life-span, but convenience is not an ingredient of Meher Baba's philosophy. Vast time cycles are instead the rule. It might be said that it is the only framework of evolution that is logically realistic on an egalitarian basis of equal chances for maximal development. Other theories incur an element of peculiar favouritism or disorderly chance.

VII. God in the State of Spiritually Advanced Souls. This refers to the process of *involution* occurring in the cycle of consciousness, i.e., the transit from the tedious evolutionary pattern of the expenditure of *sanskaras* to an increasingly indrawn and finer angle of consciousness that eventually results in maximal achievements. This also relates to the thesis that consciousness becomes geared to the "subtle sphere" and the "mental sphere," which are finer-than-physical layers of existence which mediate the acceleration in consciousness that actualizes the depths of state II. Notable is the emphasis upon the unfledged nature of the experiences of many "spiritually advanced souls," particularly those negotiating the subtle sphere. These entities undergo constant delusions of grandeur, and are subject to numerous distractions that can hinder their development and that of others. The markedly realistic tone of this theme sets it apart from many other versions of the "spiritual path."

VIII. God as the Divinely Absorbed (*Majzub*). This signifies the end of the reincarnation process, when the process of sansakaric "unwinding" results in an unimpeded realization of the ultimate truth. This state of "God-realization" is not always reconnected with body-consciousness, and such instances are here classified by the Sufi term *majzub*. The Vedantic equivalent is given as *brahmi-bhut*. The Arabic term of *majzub* has often been popularly used to designate general categories of "overpowered" mystics, but Meher

Baba's use of the term is much more specific and operational. In his terminology, this word signifies a very rare condition of consciousness, that in which the original vacuum-state (state I) is consciously known by a human entity.

IX. God as Liberated Incarnate Soul. This is a refinement of VIII. The consciousness of the ultimate reality is identical, but the capacity to link this with awareness of the three spheres (i.e. physical, subtle, and mental) imparts a very different axis in consciousness. The Sufi term *azad-i-mutlaq* is used to designate this state, the Vedantic equivalent for which is *jivanmukta.* The clarification with regard to the nature of consciousness does not appear in Vedantic textbooks, and is found only very obscurely in Sufi treatises.

X. God as "Man-God." This is a further refinement of IX. It amounts to a clarification of the Sufi term *qutub* (pole, central pivot), traditionally applied to the leader of the "invisible (i.e. non-formal, unorthodox) hierarchy." According to Meher Baba, there are five of these entities in incarnation at any one time, filling distinct offices that are perpetually renewed. A *qutub* gains full control of the process linking "God-realization" with extended consciousness of the universe. As a consequence, he (or she) not only experiences the infinite attributes of states I–II, but is also able to use these attributes for the emancipation of other souls who are ignorant of reality. The equivalent Vedantic term is *sadguru* (highly qualified guru), but it should be emphasized that extant Vedantic lore is lacking in the specifics applied by Meher Baba. Even the traditional Sufi version, though much more detailed than the Vedantic on this point, does not clarify the subject to the same extent.

An extension of the *qutub* concept is the qualification of "God-man" (*rasul, avatar*), here stated to be a cyclic phenomenon, an office with greater powers that occurs only once in centuries. The denominator is here firmly inter-ethnic, contrasting with other versions of the "prophet" and "avatar" concepts. Nowhere in *God Speaks* does the author refer to himself; there is an entire absence of the first person tense, and instead a methodical series of impersonal categorizations and explanations that are surprisingly consistent and comprehensive.

It is not easy to find parallels between Meher Baba's cosmology and traditional versions in view of the fact that his is much more technical and interpenetrating in its components. If more was known to scholars about the ideology of Zurvanism, then stronger parallels might be forthcoming. Zurvanism was an ancient Iranian tradition of "theology" that was somehow assimilated to Zoroastrian orthodoxy by the Sassanian era. To be more accurate, it shows traces of having been a gnostic teaching prior to that era, and continued in variants in gnostic usage. Zurvan was considered to be a remote first cause who engendered both Ahura Mazda and Angra Mainyu (Ahriman), the "Lord of Light" and the "Hostile Spirit" respectively. Ahuramazda became the Creator god. This theme seems strongly reflected in the general gnostic ideas on "theology" prevalent in the Mediterranean world during the early Christian era, i.e., the Creator was reviled by ascetic gnostics who favoured the "Unknown God," who neither created nor governed the universe, which was the work of lower and derivative powers. This "alien" God was hidden from all creatures and unknowable by intellectual concepts, but accessible to an advanced form of psychological illumination.

Whether or not Iranian gnosticism had any influence upon early Jewish gnosticism, as has been mooted by specialist scholars,[80] there might well be an instructive point of comparison between Meher Baba's Beyond-Beyond God and the remote first cause referred to by the ancient Iranian and Near Eastern mystics. The transition from Beyond-Beyond God to the Beyond God involves a more refined dualism than that customarily envisaged for gnosticism, bearing in mind the symbolic nature of nearly all ancient gnostic texts. In Meher Baba's version there is not only a conflict between the opposite forces in nature (e.g. pleasure and pain), but also a more subtle distinction between the latent infinite consciousness and the latent infinite unconsciousness of the Beyond-Beyond God which are manifested simultaneously in the (original) Beyond state of God.

One of the Sufi terms applied by Meher Baba to the

Beyond-Beyond state of God is *Ghaib ul-Ghaib*,[81] an Arabic phrase which has elsewhere been translated as "the Mystery of Mysteries." It was a term favoured by the Ismailis, and has been considered to parallel "the Unknowable God" of the Clementine Homilies, "the Unnameable God" of Carpocrates, "the Ineffable and the Abyss" of Valentinus, and "the Unengendered One" of Basilides.[82] Nowhere in any of these versions is there any context of specifics such as Meher Baba elaborates.

The more well known Aristotelian concept of the Prime Mover was adapted many times into different theologies, with varying degrees of success. Aristotle conceived of an "eternal time" which annoyed subsequent creationists, but there is no guarantee that he was any more sophisticated than some of the Zurvanites (or proto-Zurvanites) of the Achaemenid era of Iran. The Avestan word *zurvan* came to have the meaning of "time," though there is much that is obscure as to various significations owing to the late date of the available sources.[83] Even the much later philosophy of Abu Bakr Muhammad ibn Zakariya al-Razi, alias Rhazes (d.*c.* 925) is imperfectly known owing to its fragmentary survival, but there are discernible features of this which can be described as "Zurvanite." Razi believed in *tanasukh* (transmigration), and was much closer to Meher Baba's cosmology than to orthodox Islam. Razi was an Iranian who is linked in the *Kashf al-Mahjub* with Hallaj (d. 922), his possible teacher.[84] The background of Hallaj is likewise Iranian in part, particularly since he is known to have been on close terms with representatives of the scribal class of Iran, who were the descendants of the Sassanian literati and only partly Islamized. The writings of Hallaj survive only in fragments, and represent an allusive gnostic style. His treatise *Ta Sin al-Azal* is incomplete, but has been described as giving an account of the Creation, "correcting those made by previous Shi'ite gnostics," adds Massignon.[85] The style is not comparable to *God Speaks*, and affords no systematic description, but rather symbolism, dwelling on the fall of Satan (Iblis).

Less aphoristic is the mystical commentary (*tafsir*) on the *Quran* attributed to Sahl Tustari (d. 896), the sufi teacher of

Hallaj. There are strong gnostic ingredients in this commentary,[86] which may reflect a much older Iranian cosmological teaching. However, the format is preoccupied with the interpretation of scripture, and hence is limited in scope by comparison with Meher Baba's formulation of the ultimate origin and the ultimate endpoint of human existence.

Less aphoristic also is the major work of another mystical philosopher of Iranian ancestry, namely Abdul Karim Jili (fl. 1400), whose *Al-Insan al-kamil* (*The Completed Human*) fits the wujudi (pantheist) tradition of Ibn al-Arabi.[87] Jili is not so complex as Arabi, and is more lucid. He was careful to guard himself against accusations of *hulul* or *ittihad*, but pressed to notable lengths the theme of the "perfect man," i.e. the realized gnostic, for which the prototype had become Muhammad.[88] This theme was sometimes referred to in the wujudi tradition as *An-Nur al-Muhammadi*, the Light of Muhammad, the "pre-creation light" from which everything was created, and which became incarnate in the prophets and the *aqtab* (singular: *qutub*). It is discernible long before Arabi and Jili in the formulations of Sahl Tustari, and has been credited as one of the earliest Shi'ite *ghulat* perspectives, i.e., a component of Iranian gnosis in its transit from Mazdakite antecedents. This is sometimes referred to by scholars as a logos doctrine, though the variations of meaning implicit in the word *logos* include much vagueness. Even Jili's logicalized version of *wahdat al-wujud* is very often metaphorical in the extensive use of visionary symbolism, and hence a systematic compression is long overdue, or was until very recently.

Like Arabi, Jili also made concessions to orthodoxy, and in a more obvious manner. In this respect, Meher Baba is unimpeded, since he nowhere makes concessions to orthodox dogmas in his own magnum opus, escaping the imposition which is even evident in the treatises of the less constrained Vedantic milieu. The tenuous nature of Arabi's *Fusus al-Hikam* has led to an ingenious comparison of *wahdat al-wujud* with Taoism,[89] though it is as difficult to find systematic themes in Taoist literature as it is in

Arabi's writings. This was no doubt one way of avoiding the Confucian prescriptions of custom, but the absence of an explicitly detailed cosmology has other disadvantages.

It is well known that one of the most systematic of the ancient authors on metaphysics, namely Aristotle, criticized the Pythagoreans and the Platonists for their usage of metaphorical language in the description of cosmic processes. Yet in his *Metaphysics*, Aristotle (or his pupils) was compelled in the last analysis to resort to this same expedient in describing the ultimate cause of the universe, hence lessening the weight of his "mechanical" explanation. It is relevant to compare this tactic with Meher Baba's version, which is highly distinctive.

According to *God Speaks*, the cause of creation was the "latent original infinite whim" surging in the infinitude of the Beyond-Beyond God. Since this infinitude was entirely independent, it was a natural and spontaneous event for the whim (*lahar*) to arise. "To exercise a whim is always the mark of an independent nature,"[90] is the basic perspective here. It was this *lahar* which created the first forms of limited existence in the universe, and hence the first consciousness of separateness, which produced impressions (*sanskaras*), thereafter a process which perpetuates itself according to the momentum of cause and effect within myriadal patterns of *sanskaras*. The term *lahar* is a Hindi (and Marathi) word which means ripple, wave, fancy, whim. In modern English, Meher Baba manages to give a surprisingly technical explanation of a "theological" event which is not intended metaphorically, and nor admitting of a "mechanical" interpretation in the materialist sense. It is a logical concept in the context of its own terms of reference. It is to be noted that the *lahar* causes the manifestation of God the Creator, and not vice versa. The "Personal God" is here a strictly functional entity operating in illusion (= the universe) only, and not of the same order of reality as the Beyond God, who transcends illusion in the ultimate consciousness of Oneness.

In the supplement to *God Speaks*, Dr. Ghani's (reworked) notes report the Sufi theme that God, in the state of *Wara-ul-Wara* (Beyond-Beyond God), was a hidden treasure and wanted to be known. In expressing the desire to know itself, this state gained the awareness of itself as Light (*nur*), or rather *Nur-i Muhammadi*,[91] to use another symbolic term. The Sufi theme lacks the causal arrows given to it by Meher Baba. Though the term *lahar* is of Vedantic affiliation, there is no such precise context afforded the term in any traditional literature known to the present author. It is worth adding that Meher Baba referred to the "creation point" or "Om-point" as the dividing line between the Beyond-Beyond state of God and the phenomenal universe (=*maya*), and elsewhere described this in terms of a "primal sound" or wave of vibration which crystallized in the physical sphere. Sphere is here the operative word, since Meher Baba defined more than one of these in his cosmology. This lends extra-dimensions to the modern concept of the "Big Bang" which has developed in physics, an important event which is by no means definitive in materialist science.

According to Meher Baba, there are five interpenetrating spheres of existence, four of which belong to the universe in its total context. These are the physical, the subtle, the mental, the composite, and the real or ultimate sphere. Each one is dependent upon the next in sequence for its sustained life, e.g. the physical is dependent upon the subtle, and the subtle upon the mental. The subtle sphere can be epitomized as the domain of energy, known in Hindu philosophy as *prana*; the equivalent phrase in Persian is *alam-i malakut*. The mental sphere is described in terms of "the very abode of mind, individual, collective, and universal," and also as including "everything relating to intellect, intuition, insight and illumination." The Vedantic equivalent is *mano-bhuvan*, and *alam-i jabrut* in Sufi terminology. The composite sphere is the more difficult to grasp, since it acts as a sort of cushioning envelope interposed in sub-spheres between the other four major spheres. A relevant point here is that the sub-spheres in between the mental sphere and the ultimate reality are the last to dissolve in the universal phenomenon known in Sanskrit as *mahapralaya* (and aligned with *qiyamat*), i.e. the end of a cosmic cycle when the creation recedes into the "unmanifested seed-form" in accordance with the inevitable principle of dissolution. Yet in the "very next moment of eternity,"[92] the spheres are again projected from the unmanifest, in due order of sequence from higher to lower.[93]

This cyclic theme is now fairly well known in simplified formats, but the version of Meher Baba, as usual, includes sophisticated extensions which it is difficult to find elsewhere. The Sufi version is obscure, while the Hindu versions have been much popularized and distorted. It is possible to view the *mahapralaya* (great absorption) in terms of the "Big Crunch" currently theorized by physicists and astronomers, but if the Eastern versions are correct (even approximately), then the various puzzles raised in modern science are the inevitable consequence of missing components in the framework theorized. For instance, if matter is the concretization of a more subtle vibratory level, the problem of what came from where beggars description in terms of atomic and sub-atomic physical particles.

Our Iranian cosmologist exhibits an uncommon sense of mathematical precision in his definition of what fundamentally underlies the *mahapralaya*. This definition stipulates the process of cancelling out cosmic impressions (*sanskaras*) through the alternation of the opposite forces underlying all manifestation,[94] e.g. pleasure and pain, day and night, heat and cold, expansion and contraction, to specify some of the most obvious. This is not a theme for nutshell simplicities (of which Meher Baba is not guilty), and so I will extend it into an area that has been reduced to a simplicity in Western lore.

The Jungian psychological theory of the unconscious has gained cosmological proportions in its unquestioning acceptance by many fans of "soft" psychology. Briefly, it was assumed by Jung that the "collective unconscious" can only be beneficial in its influence, an extremely optimistic assumption that has lent fuel to much commercial activity of occult fads, which are deemed to be of value no matter what they comprise. I have elsewhere pointed out that this modern Western assumption contradicts certain trends of "idealist" philosophy in the East, most particularly the *alayavijnana* concept of the Indian Buddhist philosopher Asanga (fl.*c.* 400 A.D.), which is much more realistic than that of Jung. Asanga was an exponent of what became known as the Yogachara school of Mahayana Buddhism. In the *Mahayanasamgraha*, he developed the theme of the "storehouse consciousness" (*alayavijnana*), which signifies a cosmic repository of impressions created by thoughts and actions. This repository itself is not conscious, and hence a parallel might be drawn with the "collective unconscious." But there is a crucial difference from Jungian conceptions, since the Buddhist precedent specifies that both tainted and untainted impressions are fed into the "storehouse consciousness" by individual minds. This is important because the *alayavijnana* can exert a causal influence upon individual minds who are susceptible to it. Furthermore, only perfect enlightenment has the capacity to purify certain tainted components of the "storehouse consciousness."[95]

It should be apparent that the factor of opposite forces expressed in the accumulation and expenditure of *sanskaras* cannot be simplistically narrowed down to only beneficient influences if it is accuracy that is sought after. Yet make-believe will attempt the banal. Both health and disease are aspects of the "unconscious," on whatever scale this is envisaged.

Meher Baba does not specify the *alayavijnana* in the same way that Asanga does, but he expresses certain related themes. What he calls the "universal mind" is achievable in the ultimate *baqa*; the "universal mind" comprises the thoughtstream of all minds, whose contents are imprinted or reflected in the mental sphere. The realized soul who gains this conscious extension of intelligence is in control of the collective thoughtstream,[96] and not at its mercy. But explicit in Meher Baba's mental infrastructure here is the factor of an instability upon lesser wavelengths, particularly in relation to the danger-zone of developmental transition between the subtle sphere and the mental sphere, personified in a certain type of semi-advanced soul who is at risk of misusing the attributes of this danger-zone. He emphasizes in no uncertain manner the gravity of error possible in these instances, to a quite exceptional extent in fact. The lethal forces that can be activated in such instances make for realistic reading by comparison with the "varnish and treacle" of pop-psychology, where all is beautiful to eyes that effectively lack sight.

Evolutionism

In part nine of *God Speaks*, Eruch Jessawala writes: "Meher Baba has told us that there is no Creation in the literal sense of the word,"[97] though it was here added that the universe is not to be denied, existing in its own field of illusion. This illusion is called *maya* in Vedantic parlance, and Meher Baba does strongly emerge as an advaitin (non-dualist) in this respect. There has been much written about the concept of *maya*, and a great deal of misunderstanding has occurred as a result. The term *maya* is often very glibly used, and one suspects that in representing the principle of ignorance, it is often used in ignorance. One of the best definitions I have seen in print is Baba's: "All false values and false beliefs are due to the grip of *maya*." But he did not intend any catchphrase, since "the enigma of *maya* solves itself only after Self-realization."[98]

Meher Baba tended to treat the universe as transitory rather than as sheer illusion. It is obvious from biographical details that he took his environment seriously, and with a sense of humanitarian endeavour that was well above average by comparison with most Indian gurus. Most advaitins have not denied the existence of the universe, though this has been one erroneous interpretation of their meaning. Some critics have also implied that Shankara was advocating the ideal of non-action, but it seems more accurate to say that he advocated the denial of the hold of *maya* upon the consciousness, in order to ensure that the underlying reality behind phenomena was grasped. The most extreme advaitin emphasis was expressed by Shankara's predecessor Gaudapada (of uncertain date), who affirmed: "There is no destruction, no creation, none in bondage, none endeavouring, none desirous of liberation, none liberated." Gaudapada meant this in terms of the absolute truth, not as a vapid generalization. His commentary (*karika*) on the *Mandukya Upanishad* has posed textual problems, and some scholars have considered it to comprise more than one treatise, one of which has a pronouncedly Buddhist flavour, and which has duly been considered to harmonize the more "negative" approach of the Buddhist Madhyamika school with the Upanishads. It is also possible to see in it a link with the Yogachara philosophy of Asanga,[99] a factor which throws into relief the prospect of differingly verbalized "idealist" philosophies of the East as having the same experiential infrastructure. The fact remains that this infrastructure gains considerably varying degrees of exposure and clarity in verbalized form, and here even critics are obliged to concede that Meher Baba was much more explicit on evolutionist points than numerous predecessors were. He is in fact unique, insofar as the present author is aware, for his thorough attempt to explicate and outline a regular evolutionist sequence which clarifies mythological accretions and distortions.

The Yogachara perspective was, fundamentally, that expanded consciousness only is real, but that one has to act in the world as if appearances are real; for instance, although suffering (*dukkha*) is part of the ephemeral external world, one should act as if the suffering is real and assist sufferers accordingly.[100] This can be described as Meher Baba's basic perspective, and hence his concern to make the numerous specifications relevant to evolution in his magnum opus.

Materialist arguments conventionally scoff at transmigrationist teachings owing to the modern belief that nothing can survive death, and "even if it does, we do not know what." This may well amount to a confession of ignorance, and cannot prove that transmigration is non-existent. The brain versus mind dichotomy which is currently insisted upon, and which I have elsewhere negotiated in terms of the onus of effective action in consciousness,[101] is no barrier to transmigration or panpsychism, since it is neither brain nor mind that is the fundamental denominator here, but the much more elusive factor of the essential self or soul, dormant in consciousness until a mature point is reached in individual evolution.

Meher Baba's panpsychist perspective on evolution has

the advantage of encompassing all evolutionary data relating to the diverse species in one consistent paradigm comprehensive of ultimate cosmological abstractions. This is not easy to equal for other paradigms, whether of the materialist or religious varieties. Meher Baba's rationale can compete with Darwinism in its forward momentum of the evolution of forms, and has the advantage over Darwinism in providing an endpoint that gives meaning and purpose to the origin of species, which Darwin failed to do. The Iranian philosopher has the advantage over those religious systems which fail to account for sub-human species, and those other religio-philosophical systems which confuse the contours of consciousness relevant to different species. This last is a very important point that has been seriously blurred since at least the time of the early Pythagoreans (and doubtless very much earlier), owing to a process of distortion discernible in popularized versions of mythological and symbolic lore associated with transmigration. Such distorted popularization is not limited to any particular ethnic frontier; it has occurred in Europe, the Near East, the Middle East, India, Tibet, and China, a list which is not exhaustive. The theme of transmigration is nowadays primarily associated with Hinduism and Buddhism, but historically, this represents a substantial contraction. It was variously interpreted, supported, and resisted in circles of philosophers and mystics in the classical world of Greece and Rome, and in the Islamic world. It is discernible in pre-Islamic gnostic teachings of Iran, including both the Mazdakite and Manichaean traditions. It was emphasized in Jewish Qabbalah, and some scholars think that it was present in minority Jewish beliefs as early as the time of Josephus and Philo, if not before. Some circles in the early Christian church accepted an obscure form of it, which was subsequently officially proscribed by ecclesiastics.

Classical advaitin texts uphold transmigration, but not in any systematic form such as would satisfy the requirement of modern evolutionists. This is aptly brought out in a commentary on Shankara by the German orientalist Paul Deussen. From this, the reader learns that Shankara uses much metaphor relating to "the seven hells of Yama (the god of death)," and the "heaven of the moon." Those humans who perform wicked deeds create a place for themselves in the hells of Yama, whereas those humans who perform meritorious deeds enjoy communion with the gods in the heaven of the moon. But this latter reward lasts only for as long as the effects of the deeds concerned, and another portion of effects is left over, to find recompense in the next birth. The logic of all this is that some humans are born again in one of the three higher castes (of Hindu society), whereas others, owing to bad conduct, enter the bodies of *chandalas* (untouchables) and even animals. Deussen remarks that "a reduction of these statements to a consistent whole . . . is not made in the work of Shankara."[102] This seems an understatement of the caste bias here. It is very difficult to be certain of the authenticity of some Shankara texts, but it is apparent from at least one of the major texts definitively conceded to him that Shankara's commentary was closely tied to the words of the scripture under elucidation – in accordance with the laborious formalities of punditry. Hence, the lengthy *Brihadaranyaka Upanishad* is found to contain the statement that those who do not know the way of meditation and nor the way of rites "become insects and moths, and biting things (i.e. gnats and mosquitoes)." This reference to pest is made in a highly allusive passage using archaic Vedic metaphor, and there is no certainty that any of it was intended literally. Shankara's commentary is concerned with constructing a standardized interpretation in which the way of rites is revealed to be inferior to the way of meditation (*jnana*). The latter enables liberation from the wheel of rebirth, while the former ties the soul to this wheel. Those who were lower in the scale than ritualists are haplessly consigned to the metaphorical fate of "tiny creatures," which was in general accepted as a literal event in brahmanical society. However, there is no reference in this commentarial passage to rebirth as an untouchable.[103]

Turning to Meher Baba's version of transmigration, one finds an entirely different form of statement. There is no scriptural authority cited, no discernible metaphor, no argument designed to out-argue rival schools. He is undeniably clearer than his predecessors, and employs an unusually operationalized terminology that is startling in a mystic. He dispenses with the notion of retrograde incarnation into animal forms from the human state, and adds much more in a coherent and logically refined explanation of the ascent through diverse evolutionary forms, or rather species.

The methodical sequence in this exposition is painstaking, and traces the evolutionary momentum to the first point of manifestation of the latent *lahar*, a point referred to as the Om-point, which is described as being of unlimited scope for the projection of the expanding *lahar*. The "most gross first impression (*sanskara*)" is specified as resulting from the reverberations of this first urge, which objectifies a particle of the infinite existence as "the most absolute opposite and most finite gross counterpart of the Infinite." In other words, the individual soul arises through ignorance of the underlying infinitude. Impressions limit consciousness to forms, and the most rudimentary of these are described in terms of "diverse innumerable species of forms, of which there are seven major different kinds of most, most-finite and most, most-gross gaseous forms."[104]

Through a process of mechanically explicable and mathematically logical momentum, the soul successively identifies with and dissociates from these and other rudimentary forms, passing through the newly arising stone-forms, mineral forms, and plant-forms. The key to this process of infinitesimally increasing consciousness is in the balance of impressions. For instance, it is only when the impressions of the last species of stone-form are exhausted that the consciousness of the soul dissociates itself from the "most-first species of metal-form." Yet although the consciousness has thus freed itself from stone-forms, it is now trapped in the impressions accumulated of the most-first species of metal-forms, which compels it to identify with the "most-next species of metal-form." This explanation is unique insofar as I know; it is also incredibly explicable as a working rationale of regular momentum through species-forms if it is taken into sufficient account that consciousness is extremely rudimentary in these lower species, and not consciousness in terms of human associations. Yet consciousness in plant forms is not a strange concept to some horticulturalists, and hence the thesis gains a much greater weight in its methodical evolutionist sweep from this point onwards.

The sequence continues in this way into insects, worms and reptiles, fish, birds, and animals, in a successive manner, and with no reversions from a more advanced species to a lesser one. This principle continues into human forms, though with a much more complex consciousness that requires an elucidation of an important extension of Meher Baba's thesis. This relates to the subtle and mental bodies of the soul, which are respectively connected with the subtle and mental spheres abovementioned. These finer-than-physical bodies are already present in the very lowest species, but in a correspondingly undeveloped form to that of the human counterparts. The association of the soul with these two higher bodies is unconscious, but from the subtle body it derives energy necessary for evolutionary momentum in the sequence of forms, while the mental body serves to accommodate and reflect the increasingly varied impressions acquired in consciousness. In the lower species, the mental form is developed only in respect of instinct, but in the human it has the quality of intellect. In the lower species, these higher bodies participate in the "survival of the fittest,"[105] but this concept is not applicable to the human species. For one thing, the subtle and mental bodies achieve their full development once the soul acquires a human incarnation. The human form entails a full experience of the physical (gross) world, and hence there is no further need for any further evolution of forms. But there is a need for the further development of consciousness, since the inchoate human awareness is trapped in the network of purely physical impressions, which prevent any consciousness of the subtle and mental bodies, and hence the subtle and mental spheres. Hence consciousness is drastically incomplete, though the process of "mechanical" evolution is fulfilled.

The lengthy phase of human reincarnations does not involve any reversion to animal forms. This latter idea is solely one of popular superstition and/or symbolic reference.

Each human incarnation of the evolving soul is motivated by the momentum of impressions lodged in the mental body (and also mediated via the subtle body), impressions which are a legacy from the directly preceding incarnation. The most primitive human types are much nearer the animal level of incarnation, therefore. But primitive characteristics can continue for a very lengthy period in the span of human incarnations. Meanwhile, the soul unconsciously (and instinctively) utilizes the mind (*manas*) "through various gross aspects of mind such as desires, emotions and thoughts." Desires are specifically stated to be the predominant aspect of the mind.[106] Note that emotion is here an aspect of mind, not of the subtle body. This has important implications for the attempted control of mind, which is very much more difficult than generally assumed.

Meher Baba's version of the "higher bodies" of the evolving entity compares very favourably with the modern Western occultist explanations, some of which can politely be described as inferior rehashes of Neoplatonist originals sparsely extant. Such concepts are often mistakenly regarded as exclusively oriental. In actual fact, these concepts have a lengthy history in European thought also, and were taught in variants by parties as diverse as the Cambridge Platonists of the seventeenth century and Porphyry and Iamblichus, two contrasting Neoplatonists of the late classical era. A much earlier origin in Greek philosophy is also inferable, if more obscure. It is probable that such concepts go back to remote antiquity. These concepts have been a recurring theme through the centuries in the works of mystical philosophers, though expressed in variants, and greatly surpass the more limited repertory of the Christian mystics and other groupings. In fact, it can be said that they are part of the intrinsic philosophy which has been marred by orthodox theology, rationalism, and scientific materialism alike.

The erudite Cambridge Platonist Ralph Cudworth defended at length the subject of the "astral body" in his *Intellectual System*, though his writings do also exhibit strong features of Christian bias. Several centuries earlier, Michael Psellus aired the subject during the Byzantine Renaissance, while some centuries before him in turn, the

Neoplatonist Olympiodorus of Alexandria stated that the "astral body" was egg-shaped. Non-Christian Neoplatonism was less diluted in its conceptual data, though Iamblichus was not the most perceptive of "pagans" to judge from his *De Mysteriis*, which exalted theurgy and divination, and gave a lop-sided context for the "astral body." This astral sheath was not always well defined, and there are apparently conflicting accounts of it in the sources, which have not always been interpreted very well by modern scholars. Plotinus and Porphyry were amongst those who said that it was acquired during the descent of the soul from the upper regions and discarded in the reascent. But Iamblichus, Origen, and others expressed the view that the "astral body" is permanently attached to the soul. The version of Proclus, who lived at a later date, has been considered to combine these apparently conflicting versions, but it is perhaps more accurate to deduce that he was merely giving a fuller version of a phenomenon more partially reported in other sources. Proclus specifies two ethereal "vehicles of the soul" – a higher one which is "original" and imperishable, and a lower one which is temporary in componency.[107] These might be compared to what Meher Baba calls the mental body and subtle body respectively, though the Iranian mystic is much more precise as to the phases of evolutionary development, and gives many more permutations regarding eventualities.

Comparatively few investigators have yet caught up with the fact that there were earlier Iranian versions of the higher "vehicles of the soul," which persisted in a variant until the nineteenth century, when the Shi'ite movement known as Shaikhism adapted earlier gnostic perspectives to Quranic eschatology. But though there is a definite recognition of finer-than-physical bodies in Shaikhism, there is no evolutionary sequence to round out this subject in the necessary cosmological terms of reference.[108] This evolutionary sequence had been blotted out in philosophies of the Shi'ite milieu during the Safavid era, when the influential Mulla Sadra Shirazi (d. 1640) had excised the more advanced themes in both sufi and ishraqi (illuminist) repertories by opting for Quranic literalism as interpreted by the official Shi'ism of the new Safavid clergy.[109]

The role of the subtle and mental bodies in evolution is the primary explanation for the phenomenon of after-death existence, variously denied by materialists and literally interpreted by religionists. Meher Baba admits temporary states of "heaven" and "hell" during this regular interval of the reincarnation process, but his explanation of these states is quite different from the hellfire preaching idiom.

Although the consciousness of the soul dissociates from the physical body at death, it cannot dissociate from the subtle and mental bodies. At death, what happens is that the discarnate individual now experiences through these finer bodies the impressions which are retained of existence in the last physical body. These impressions are necessarily comprised of the opposites (e.g. joy and suffering, virtue and vice), but one or other trend of experience predominates in relation to polarities, and this causes states of "relived" experience which may be compared to a comparative "heaven" or "hell." These words accurately refer to states of consciousness in myriadal variants, and not to places in the hereafter as crudely conceptualized elsewhere. What requires to be taken into account here is the extreme subjectivity of the after-death state of awareness, which is thrown back upon the impressions lodged in the mental body with a vastly magnified degree of vividness owing to the lack of physical ballast (which generally reduces the intensity of consciousness). The experiences of pain and pleasure, in all their manifold degrees and variations, become substantially more intense, and it is these that respectively comprise "hell" and "heaven." This is largely owing to the factor of desire-nature, which is accordingly magnified. The finer types of desire are not limited to gratification by sense-impression, and hence these confer a comparative heaven of fulfilment via thought and/or feeling. Whereas the coarser types of desire are dependant upon physical gratification, which is absent in the after-death state. This leads to a preponderant balance of suffering over pleasure, and hence the state of "hell" is experienced. Such states of mind are determined in their duration by the quantity and intensity of the accumulated impressions from physical existence. As with physical life, they are transitory, but it is possible to suffer far more in the after-death condition than in physical life owing to crude impressions.

The rationale for this whole process is that an extensive series of human reincarnations is sustained by residual impressions which never quite balance out in terms of annulment through experience of the opposites, e.g. poverty and riches, male and female, failure and success, illness and health. A see-sawing between either polarity is in continual occurrence, in human life and in the after-death states, first one and then the other aggregate of "predominant opposite impressions" being in ascendancy. The complexity of this aggregate would inevitably belie simplistic categorizations of binary associations. Fresh impressions of opposites are continually accumulated even while others are annulled by appropriate experiences. Each physical form expires at a point when it is just about to exhaust the impressions which brought it into existence; the residual opposite impressions determine the nature of the after-death state (or states). But complete equipoise between the opposites can only be achieved in the physical world, and hence there is continually a residue of impressions in discarnate existence which cause the individual consciousness to identify with a new physical body. There is no escape from having to experience and exhaust the impressions, which become very thickly concentrated in the mental body.[110] This process is too mathematically realistic for some who like short-cuts or who prefer to believe in oblivion; a vast number of births and deaths are indicated for the individual soul,[111] involving male and female incarnations and different ethnic identities.

At this point some readers may feel that the evolutionist framework presented by Meher Baba is too "mechanistic," too inexorable in its specifications of life-events determined by arrangements of impressions requiring an elusive equipoise. For some minds, there might seem too much of a similarity with the human condition of mechanicality emphasized by Gurdjieff,[112] or even the proposition of David Hume that the human entity amounts to no more than a mere bundle of perceptions or impressions.[113] Hume's sceptical realism has still not been resolved in Western philosophy and psychology, which still carry the burden of eighteenth century concepts deriving from a severe reaction to conventional religion. There is indeed ample indication in Meher Baba that the average human is substantially "mechanical" in his or her ordered flux of sanskaric patterns, but the explicit undertones and overtones of this evolutionist view are radically different from the realism of Hume. Nor does the Iranian admit the extreme mechanicality evinced in the more (than Hume) esoteric psychology of Gurdjieff, whose cosmological system lacks evolutionist criteria, a system which was mediated by the Russian philosopher P.D.Ouspensky.

There are pronounced extensions to Meher Baba's basic theme of alternating experiences moving between opposite polarities. In *God Speaks* he was primarily concerned with charting the sanskaric theme in a methodical evolutionist framework, lending to the term *sanskara* an operationalized value not found elsewhere. But in his *Discourses* he elaborates closely related aspects of the same phenomenon, and here gives to the term *karma* a much more precise and complex range of significations than is generally made. In fact, the Sanskrit word *karma* has become so devalued in current Western usage that it is worthwhile to point out some of the systematic experiential implications of the customary phrase: "as a man sows, so shall he reap."

The successive human reincarnations of the soul are "unfailingly determined by a rational law" which provides the opportunity of moulding the future of the individual through intelligent action. What Meher Baba calls the "ego-mind" is stated to be centred in the mental body, and it is this sanskaric projection of the soul which is the principle motivating the reincarnation process. The impressions comprising this ego-mind will determine the length of incarnation, the physical characteristics of body, the acuity or otherwise of intellect, and other details of personality. The disconnected nature of successive reincarnations is only apparent, since if a person develops special tendencies or capacities in one incarnation, he or she will continue these in subsequent lives. The law of cause and effect (= *karma*) works through impressions lodged in the mental body, which the ego-mind cannot erase at will. Karmic links arise between individuals, whether on a basis of affinity or repulsion, and these links recur in permutations over a span of lives. Any exchange between individuals is liable to create bindings when motivated by the ego-mind, which is subject to the polarities existent in the flux of impressions. "The law of *karma* is the law exhibiting itself through continuously changing mutual adjustments" is an indication of the interpersonal complexities involved. The rhythm existent in relationships tends to perpetuate itself unless this rhythm is changed "through fresh intelligent *karma*," which improves the nature of relationships. Once commenced, a particular karmic pattern "has a certain inertia of its own," i.e. it falls into a habitual pattern. Before any such pattern is created or fixed, "the individual has a sort of freedom to choose what it (the *karma*) shall be." There is thus a definite, if bounded, element of freewill in the selectivities of individual life pattern. Meher Baba emphasizes that karmic determinism is not an oppressive principle (unless of course it is made such) but represents the experiential train set into motion by the individual. Though past *karma* shapes the present of every individual, this past *karma* can "be modified, remoulded, and even undone through *karma* in the present life." The *karma* in physical life can be creative, and effective in "reshaping the impressions in the ego-mind," thus providing a fresh momentum for the future of the individual. It is through such creative *karma* that emancipation from the otherwise inexorable round of karmic determinism can potentially occur, though this is a very complex matter of long-term commitment.

Karma is of two basic kinds: "good" *karma* and "bad" *karma*. Even the former can bind, owing to motivations from the ego-mind which derives a sense of separateness from everything it does. Creative *karma* requires an advanced understanding in order to be maximally effective. Intelligent action is of varying kinds. *Karma* "persists until it bears its own fruit or is undone through counter-*karma*." If any individual harms another in any way, this will eventually rebound upon the former, and appears to be much more complex than the well known adage of "a tooth for a tooth and an eye for an eye." One gets the impression that if A kills B, he will end up being the slave of B rather than a mere victim of murder.

Meher Baba likens *karma* to a web of myriadal "debts to pay and dues to recover," an arrangement of exchange with other humans which it is impossible to avoid for any entity subject to sanskaras. Reincarnation occurs because of the need to "clear up the account," but even when the best tendencies in the individual incline to this, in practice it is very often not possible to do so in the short-term. Conscious capacity would need to be very high to meet such requirements. All the many persons involved in the individual web of *karma* may not be in incarnation at the same time, constituting a substantial hindrance. Further, in the very act of making "good" *karma* in relation to past human links, the individual cannot help "creating fresh claims and counterclaims" in this insidious web of exchange.[114]

This sociology of karmic patterns gains a further twist in an overarching consideration relating to impressions. A crucial change in the concentrated skein of sanskaras lodged in the mental body occurs at a point in the reincarnation process when consciousness commences upon the climactic phase termed *involution* by Meher Baba. This happens when gross (i.e. physical) impressions of the opposites gradually become fainter and less concentrated, since the gross impressions reach a surfeit point which causes consciousness to turn in upon itself to a much greater degree than before. These gross impressions merge into subtle impressions, enabling a direct link with awareness of the subtle world, which remains a closed book in experience prior to this phase of involution.

The ego-mind is now confronted by the levels of experience which Baba refers to in terms of the "subtle planes," meaning zones of consciousness extending from the subtle world. Owing to the accessibility of subtle energy existent in the subtle sphere, the individual who traverses these planes can gain "subtle powers" (*siddhis*) of the type which are crudely reflected in much hagiology. But the subtle planes represent a danger zone, since they comprise only reflections in a subtle form of ultimate reality. But persons gaining subtle consciousness (or degrees of it) usually confuse these diluted reflections with the ultimate; many so-called gurus and "masters" have not reached beyond this danger-sector, and represent a network of delusion for the unwary (particularly since their emanation is often hypnotic). Subtle characteristics tend to be sensational, and not infrequently sensate. Egoism can become uncontrollable in this sector.

The climax of subtle experiences are operative on the "fourth plane" of cosmic consciousness, i.e. the dividing line between the subtle and mental spheres. At this stage of involution the ego-mind can take a dangerous turn for the worse. This is because such a mind gains control of the vast energy of the subtle world, but is simultaneously exposed to the intense influences of the mental sphere which are not as yet under control. These mental sphere impulses come in the form of intense desires and emotions, aspects of mind which are outside the limited range of subtle control (which can only control and manipulate subtle energy, not mind). These unrestrained impulses can overpower the ego-mind which has flaws, with the consequence that a misuse of subtle power occurs. According to Meher Baba, this misuse of abilities can be so serious that a violent disintegration of consciousness occurs in such cases, causing the soul to revert to primitive identification with the stone-form. The process of evolution through species-forms then has to begin all over again. This is the *only* reverse to a lower species in the entire sequence of evolution as specified by Meher Baba, and significantly, it is *not* animal consciousness that is reverted to. This striking detail serves to clearly underline the gravity of potential shortcomings in "mysticism" (or rather occultism, to be more precise), and also to distinguish this version of transmigration from the popular Indian and ancient Greek counterparts. It is apparent that the ego-mind possesses a pronounced degree of freewill at this critical juncture of experience, an amplitude of choice which it can either use to benefit others or to wreak havoc in the world for selfish purposes.

Even while the "fourth plane" is a danger-point of such magnitude, it is also a possible springboard for further advancement. If the ego-mind does not allow itself to be overpowered by desires and does not misuse its resources but employs them wisely, then its intact consciousness can actually jump the next plane (the fifth) and establish itself in a much finer state of consciousness that has very different attributes to any lesser level of the path of involution.[115]

The impressions constricting consciousness undergo a further refinement in the transition from subtle to mental planes. Subtle impressions are metamorphosed into mental impressions, though the physical body can be maintained. Here there is the factor stipulated of different types of orientation in the involution process, which involve different combinations of the advanced subtle and mental consciousness with physical function.[116] But this is liable to misunderstanding in a summary, though it requires to be said here that in addition to the *masts* (discussed briefly in Part One), there is the category of the "God-communed" whose introspective concentration is not a perpetual state like that of *masts*, but whose consciousness is "constantly diverted by irrelevant attractions,"[117] i.e., the residue of physicalized impressions which acts as a weight upon the focus of inner attention.

The mental sphere has two planes of expanded consciousness, here the fifth and sixth planes in due order of ascent from the subtle counterparts. The soul is now identified directly with mind, which on the fifth plane exists only as thoughts. The adept of the fifth plane cannot slide downwards as happens occasionally on the fourth plane, and is capable of the mastery of thought but not of the mastery of feeling. He loses all ability in *siddhis* (occult powers), with which he is not concerned, knowing these to be the most serious pitfall imaginable. Since he is no longer oriented to the subtle world, he cannot manipulate subtle energy, but he is capable of controlling the thoughts of gross-conscious and subtle-conscious individuals. He can thus effectively act as a regulator in respect of proclivities in the subtle world, though it is not (ordinarily) possible to revoke karmic laws. The fifth plane is a very rare state, and lacks sensational attributes.

The characteristics of the sixth plane are also non-sensational, though they are very different to fifth plane attributes. In the sixth plane, the ego-mind exists only in a very refined form – almost egoless – and is identified with the aspect of mind that functions as feelings. Here thoughts are transcended, since the mastery of thought has occurred in the fifth plane. The sixth plane adept has the continual experience of "seeing God" via the process of "divine love," something not reducible to verbal formats. But the factor of duality persists, and the sixth plane soul yearns for the ultimate reality as something separate from himself or herself. Ironically, to the ordinary observer, the sixth plane adept might appear to be less advanced than the fifth, since the intensity of feeling might appear distraught by comparison with the more detached attributes of the fifth plane adept; appearances are never any adequate gauge, since both types can easily be simulated.

Some people interested in mysticism tend very easily to imagine that they are on the fifth or sixth planes by virtue of the most generalized criteria. It is worthwhile to point out the prodigious error here, since there is no reason to think that the game of convenient imagination will stop in the foreseeable future. Persons of a vaguely "intellectual" disposition tend to be elevated to fifth plane status, while persons of an emotive temperament mysteriously become sixth plane saints. This sort of selection by random associations neglects the rather obvious factor of there being very numerous types of both "intellectual" and "emotive" at the preliminary stages of the path of inner development – preliminary stages occurring well before the first subtle plane is encountered. Meher Baba defined two of these preliminary stages as *hawa* and seekership. The Arabic word *hawa* means passion, and is used in some Sufi texts to designate desire of certain kinds. Meher Baba's usage is different; he employed this word to describe a specific "condition of permanent relationship to the spiritual path." The man or woman in *hawa* is not yet on the path however, and is further from it than the category of "seeker," compared to a person searching for the commencement of a footpath,[118] and being more determined to find it than those behind him.

When the reader understands that Baba further analyzed the seven cosmic planes of consciousness in terms of forty-nine stages, it will (or should) become evident that there is a great deal more to the experiential contours of "development" than the rather lazy associations of binary polarities. One suspects that even *hawa* is an advanced condition by comparison with the infatuation for occult kicks amongst many rather gross-conscious (?) dabblers in fads and fashions. It should be added that the higher subtle planes (i.e. the third and fourth) might transpire to be bewilderingly "intellectual" in not a few cases for those accustomed to condense wide-ranging categories into thimble-portmanteaux of slipshod reference.

In referring to forty-nine stages on the path, Meher Baba added that these are not evenly distributed within the seven planes, and warned against the tendency to create undue symmetry in such concepts.[119] He notably did not elaborate very much on this more complex theme, perhaps because he knew that seven gradations would be more digestible than a much larger number, in the absence of actual experience.

The sixth plane condition experiences the last trace of dual impressions of the opposites. According to Baba, it is not possible for the soul to finally dissociate from the consciousness of mind without the assistance of a person who has already made this leap, which involves the total annihilation of impressions. Only then is consciousness free to reflect the ultimate reality, as distinct from mind. This achievement is designated as *fana* (annihilation), a Sufi term which Baba uses quite distinctively, and much more clearly than is done in Islamic Sufism. In this connection he also makes one of his rare references to a term of Buddhist derivation, proffering a clarification of one of the most debated words in the Buddhist vocabulary.

He divides *fana* into two stages: *fana* and *fana-fillah*. A synonym of *fana* is here *nirvana*, a Sanskrit word employed much in the Pali texts in the linguistic variant of *nibbana*. The state of consciousness signified by Meher Baba under the rubric of *nirvana* is the original absolute vacuum-state of the Beyond-Beyond God. This is only of fleeting duration in experience, understandably enough, since consciousness wiped clean of *sanskaras* now merely reflects the absolute vacuum state which prevailed before the train of impressions commenced. This does logically follow, though it is a unique explanation in extant texts insofar as I am aware. According to Meher Baba, this state was what the Buddha was actually referring to in his use of the word *nirvana*, a significance which was later misinterpreted by Theravada Buddhism in terms of the "no god, no soul" doctrine commonly extrapolated from the Pali Canon. Different scholars have entertained different views of meanings afforded by the Pali scriptures, and Meher Baba's interpretation is not incompatible with the more extensively analytical of these investigations. Gautama Buddha definitely appears to have couched his teachings in a different idiom to that of Upanishadic doctrines, but nuances allowable in textual readings indicate that later doctrinal interpretation was too inflexible in its semantic categories.[120]

Our Iranian metaphysicist is similarly quite specific concerning the meaning of the term *fana-fillah* (literally meaning, "passing away into Allah"). The conscious experience of absolute vacuum changes immediately into conscious experience of the real and unlimited "I" and its attributes of infinite power-knowledge-bliss. Once gained, this is a permanent experience. There is nothing of the attempt at orthodox qualification that can be found in numerous Sufi works in Arabic and Persian. Meher Baba's version does not concede any diminution of impact, since the soul here achieves apotheosis and is quite literally super-conscious on this "seventh plane." The equivalent term in Vedantic parlance is *nirvikalpa samadhi*, the "inconceptual realization," though Meher Baba does verbalize it to an unusually satisfying extent.[121]

This constitutes the end of the "First Journey," as Baba calls it. There are three further "Journeys," though not all souls undertake these. The Second Journey consists of the transition to *baqa-billah*, which is a state of consciousness inadequately defined in "popular Sufism" owing to confusing theological premises. Meher Baba's definition is very precise, and the more difficult for pedestrian conceptions. This ultimate *baqa* or stabilization involves the *full* consciousness of the phenomenal universe in addition to consciousness of the seventh plane.

The Third Journey involves the transition to the very

rare condition of *qutubiyat*, which only five entities achieve at any one time. This condition involves the same consciousness as in *baqa-billah*, but with a crucial addition in range of function that enables the carrying out of special duties for the benefit of those trapped in illusion. The Fourth Journey is hardly mentioned, and it is obvious that Meher Baba deemed this ultimate refinement to be elusive of description.[122]

What Meher Baba calls the "spiritual hierarchy" or "functioning hierarchy" has strong similarities to the Sufi concept of the hierarchy of saints believed to exert an influence upon mundane events. This concept is traceable to Hakim Tirmizi (d.*c.* 900), a Central Asian writer on Sufism whose thesis on saintship (*wilaya*)[123] was subsequently taken up by Ibn al-Arabi and others. Meher Baba is more specific about the degree of spiritual advancement applying to the members of this hierarchy. These seven thousand members are almost exclusively drawn from those traversing the six planes, with the addition of only eight persons on the seventh plane. This theme does not constitute any major part of *God Speaks*, and does not in fact appear in the text but gains a few pages only in the supplement. Many of the members are not highly advanced, being only on the subtle planes,[124] and hence it is apparent that this contingent are able to perform services coordinated by those higher in rank, services which feasibly contribute to their involution.

Psychology

It will already be evident that much of Meher Baba's psychological teaching revolves upon the crucial theme of impressions, or *sanskaras*. This concept has the advantage of explaining a great deal with regard to mental contents, and avoids the awkward angles of conventional mysticism which invoke states of mind without giving these any logical context of operation.

It has been remarked that *sanskara* (*samskara*) is an important concept in the *Yoga Sutra* of Patanjali, but that the meaning afforded to it by many scholars does not seem to be appropriate. Though the term has aptly been translated as "impression," there is a scholarly tendency to use this word in a static manner. It is more accurate to regard these impressions as dynamic urges or tendencies of the mind, which include unconscious (or subconscious) motives.[125]

Since there is no close parallel to *sanskaras* in Western psychology, the Humean associations of "impression" are to be avoided. But Yoga philosophy has also been subject to crippling conventionalities of interpretation. It has been said that the sole purpose of Patanjali's philosophy is to inform how *sanskaras* "can be controlled volitionally by generating such *samskaras* which will destroy all those *samskaras* which bind the self."[126] But the problem with Patanjali's text is its aphoristic nature, complicated by obscure idioms some two thousand years old. It was admired by a medieval savant of the calibre of Al-Biruni, who in the eleventh century translated it into Arabic for the benefit of interested Muslims. A version of this has survived,[127] which includes a very brief comparison of Hindu philosophy with that of Greek philosophy, Christianity, and Sufi mysticism. Meher Baba might be considered an updated sequel to this intercultural venture, though he never focusses upon the *Yoga-Sutra*. Indeed, he was at pains to point out that the preoccupation with *siddhis* (occult powers) is a serious defect, and can not only mislead, but can also prove dangerous to the wellbeing of any practitioner. *Siddhis* are mentioned in the Patanjali text, though the references have been given different interpretations.

Patanjali does not give any evolutionist context for his psychological reflections. Indeed, the extant teaching of the ancient Indian Yoga school can be regarded as fragmentary, and currently the sport of the simplistic yoga fads which have abounded in the West since the hippy boom.

Nor does Patanjali pick out the complexities of the sanskaric process in any great detail. The author of the *Yoga Sutra* asserts that *sanskaras* are "to be conquered by resolving them into their causal state," but does not chart exactly how this is to be done. In his commentary, Swami Vivekananda observed that meditation cannot destroy the *sanskaras*; meditation can only exercise an influence upon the gross outworking of the "mind-waves" (*chitta-vrittis*). The *chitta* or mind-stuff contains the *sanskaras*, the subconscious layer of experience which is at the core of the reincarnatory momentum.[128] Even Vivekananda (d. 1902) did not work out a detailed version of the *sanskara* theme, though he did exposit Vedantic and Yoga philosophy in an unusually scientific variant. What makes Meher Baba's version so distinctive is its systematic nature, and which is intimately related to his evolutionism and cosmology.

According to Meher Baba, the release from *sanskaras* can be variously, and in varying degrees, accomplished by (a) the cessation of new *sanskaras* (b) the wearing out of old *sanskaras* (c) the unwinding of past *sanskaras* (d) the dispersion and exhaustion of some *sanskaras* (e) the complete annihilation of *sanskaras*. The first four (a-d) represent overlapping principles of a process which culminates in (e).

One recourse for both (a) and (b) is that of renunciation (*vairagya*), which is ideally an inward attitude, but which can be greatly aided by external renunciation in some cases. Solitude and fasting are both recommended as features of external renunciation. The adoption of a conscientious attitude of "repentance" can contribute to (c), in the sense of mentally reversing the process leading to the formation of obstructing *sanskaras*. The momentum of "unwinding" *sanskaras* can also be furthered by the mental attitude here described in terms of the application of "*Neti, neti*" (Not-this, not-this), associated with the discipline of Advaita Vedanta. This is the attitude of detachment from all external *and* inward stimuli, whether agreeable or non-agreeable. This is of course a commonly presumed achievement; less common are Meher Baba's warnings against perversions, subtle egoism expressing itself through aloofness, and sheer inability to cope with the stress of worldly life. It is "a healthy form of asceticism" that is required, not anything unhealthy, which can easily occur in flawed individuals.

The orientation implied by "*neti, neti*," if sufficiently powerful, can loosen the hold of physical, subtle, and mental *sanskaras*. But it can also condition as well as decondition the mind, creating a new problem in identification with a "negative" disposition. Hence, this orientation must itself eventually be renounced. (The habit of self-reliance, for instance, may require correction in the light of instruction from a suitable teacher).

This method of negation is contrasted with the "method of sublimation," which has the effect of replacing lower values with higher ones via meditation, the selfless service of humanity, and devotion. Many sanskaric patterns constitute false values, and the search for true values occurs with varying degrees of clarity according to the density of the veil of *sanskaras*. Though ultimate illumination is prevented by this veil, it is still possible to clarify the consciousness to an advanced extent by "diverting the psychic energy locked up in the old *sanskaras* towards creative and spiritual ends." This has the effect of dispersing and exhausting some sanskaric patterns. This is particularly true with respect to the refinement of devotion (*bhakti*) which becomes *parabhakti* or "divine love" (literally: supreme *bhakti*). This comes into operation on the sixth plane, but even this does not achieve the complete annihilation of *sanskaras*, which only becomes possible through the intervention of a seventh plane adept.[129]

The master-disciple relationship is uncompromisingly stressed by Baba as the ultimate means of freedom from karmic bindings. The problem is that real masters are very rare, there being only five of them at any one time in the world. This diminutive number would appear to match the rare capacity to become a disciple in the true sense of the word.

The disintegration of the false ego is a necessary condition for the realization of truth. The mind of every person continually passes through a series of conflicts, and the ego attempts to establish a balance between these conflicts. But it does so by false valuation and wrong choice. Meher Baba characterizes the ego as treating "all that is unimportant as important and all that is important as unimportant." Power, fame, wealth, and other attributes of worldly success are taken as guiding criteria for the separative life of the ego, which rejects as unimportant the criteria of "true spirituality." This situation is complicated by the fact that persons interested in the so-called spiritual life are motivated by the false ego. It is nowadays very common to hear talk about, e.g. "the ego versus the essence," by the most crass individuals with a personal record of gross (and sometimes criminal ?) indulgence, and until more people can discern the difference between motivations, there is little point in doing more than repeating such observations as that of Meher Baba: "the elimination of conflict (in the mind) is possible only through conscious control over the psychic forces in the subconscious."[130]

The thick layer of accumulated *sanskaras* that prevents greater perception in the individual consciousness is often accomodated to external codes of religious injunction. This is explained by Baba as the easiest way for such people to placate their conscience, though externalist codes tend to promote mechanical attitudes and foster an insidious egotism. But in the opposite camp, sensationalists opt for the unconventional merely for reasons of novelty, deriving an egoistic sense of "being different" from the hidebound. It is a mere reaction to other habit-patterns, whatever significances are given to the novelties. In brief, this addiction to novelty represents an uncritical reaction to customs. In contrast, true freedom from convention is accomplished through the exercise of critical thought, involving a constant discrimination between false and true values, irrespective of whether these seem to be conventional or unconventional.[131]

This critical spirit has to be carried into the sphere of occultism,[132] where it is important to recognize that there are supra-physical forces relaying both beneficial and harmful influences. The conditioned attitude of disbelief in all paranormal events is about as scientific as the gullible acceptance of all the commercial fads currently purveyed to the victims of occultmania by various types of delinquent. The attitude of critical inquiry will quickly grasp that exploiters of four-letter word occultism and other social maladies have nothing to do with the truth, but only with the illusion in its worst forms.

At the time of dictating his *Discourses*, Meher Baba emphasized the value of meditation much more than he did in his last years. But he was also careful to point out that even the higher flights of meditation, which impart a sense of expansion and freedom, are not permanent in their effects, since in most cases the aspirant reverts to his ordinary mental state shackled by sanskaric limitations.[133]

He distinguished meditation from *concentration*, the latter being the higher aspect of mind. Persons who lack the capacity of intense concentration have to begin with meditation. In concentration, "there is practically no movement of the mind," whereas in meditation the mind can move from one relevant idea to another.[134] Nowadays, the excess of "meditation masters" will doubtless ensure that concentration is never achieved in those prone to believe that meditation requires formal credentials.

The traditional Hindu lore concerning *kundalini* is one of the most commercially abused topics in the occultist repertoire. Meher Baba never taught it, and for good reasons. He explained that *kundalini* is a latent energy in the higher bodies, but that the "awakened" *kundalini* cannot by itself confer seventh plane consciousness. This energy can be awakened by a competent yogi, but the resulting experiences have both advantages *and* disadvantages. Further, indiscriminate or premature awakening of this energy "is fraught with dangers of self-deception as well as misuse of powers." [135] Poison exists in many forms, and most especially in egoistic yogis and occultists of all nationalities. The awakened *kundalini* does not ensure any progress; rather, it may well prove retrograde under the wrong influences.

Of a more urgent psychological value than *kundalini* symbolism is the *fana-baqa* of the seven planes, a basic alternation operative at every major level of development, but one very seldom dwelt upon owing to common ignorance of it. The seventh plane represents the ultimate *fana* (i.e. *fana-fillah*) and the ultimate *baqa* (i.e. *baqa-billah*), but lesser degrees of *fana* and *baqa* exist on every one of the six lower planes.[136] Though Meher Baba does not greatly elaborate upon this theme, it amounts to a clarification of that earlier expressed by Ibn al-Arabi, who taught that *fana* is a gradual process consisting of seven stages, to every one of which corresponds a stage of *baqa*. In every one of these stages, a "veil" is removed.[137] This is a complement to the schema of the "seven selves," phases of the *nafs* (secondary self) which feature in Sufi terminology.[138] These seven selves are not be equated with the seven planes. The *nafs*, or ego, undergoes successive transmutations, its common manifestation as *nafsi-i-ammara* (commanding self) being crudely gross, i.e., the gross-conscious personality. The problem for many investigators lies in grasping the continued limitations of the *nafs* on the inner planes, and the way in which polarities of consciousness temper the evolving (or rather involving) entity subject to a field of impressions that may or may not speedily unwind into a more causal state.

Sociology

Since Meher Baba specifically disowned being a teacher in such statements as: "I have come not to teach but to awaken," it is the more surprising that so much cosmology and psychology is to be found in the products of his dictation. He did not express any regular sociology, and definitely not in a text-book idiom, but nevertheless, various messages and discourses do exhibit ingredients of a sociological perspective.

A universalist in outlook, and specifically catering for an inter-religious following, he disdained all religious ritual and formalism. This might be considered the hallmark of a genuine universalist, since parochial frameworks tend to persist via the repetition of formal observances dogmatically adhered to.

"I am, therefore, not interested in founding a new religion." This statement of Baba's comes from a message given in India in 1944, though his emphasis in this direction was consistent through the years. This is a corollary of his teaching that both partisans and critics have often missed; the attempt to glorify him as an *avatar* figurehead is in contradiction to his own observations on the superfluity of dogmas and beliefs present in the world. “I have not come to give another cage for man,” he insists in the same message. He did state that “the new Enlightened Humanity has to be born” from the travail and suffering of the contemporary era, but this is far removed from prescribing a religion.

He was never keen upon people changing one religion for another, and compared this to swapping cages. The organized religions, he said, often failed to express the vision of those entities considered to have been their founders. “Dogmas and beliefs, rituals and ceremonies” are in general not only ineffective, but also harmful – “they not only feed the ego of the priest-class, but also serve as an instrument for the exploitation of the credulous.” [139]

In another message, he stated that when rituals and ceremonies are mechanically followed, they can be said to be even more dangerous than other forms of unintelligent action, since they are undertaken in the belief that they are spiritually beneficial. Through sheer force of habit, men become so attached to these externals that disillusionment with them is only incurred by intense suffering. [140]

At the time of the Second World War, he gave a number of messages which related to current affairs. He was requested to explain the issue of violence and non-violence, and notably would not endorse the Gandhian ideal of literal non-violence in the face of an aggressor. It was impractical, he said, to insist upon such non-violence in relation to the masses; it is possible only for advanced souls who have undergone rigorous discipline. He maintained that if such an ideal was implemented amongst the masses, there would be a tendency to use it as an excuse for the “servile acceptance of ignoble conditions and contemptible desertion of a clear duty.” It was the clear duty of the ordinary man to resist aggression in self-defence or in the defence of weaker parties. [141]

The above statements came from his message entitled “The Need for Creative Leadership in India,” released in March 1942. In another message given at that time, he reiterated his emphasis upon this theme, stating that to defend the weak is an important form of selfless service and a part of Karma-yoga. But any fighting involved in such a justifiable cause requires to be undertaken without any selfish motives or hatred. He likened this situation to that of defending a woman from a rapist and correcting the attacking man by punishing him and making him repent. He warned against the danger of facile acceptance of slogans like "non-violence," and advised careful analysis of all such catchwords in order to ensure intelligent action. He gave the example of a mad dog running amok amongst schoolchildren; it would be the duty of the teachers to destroy this dog in order to protect the children, though this act of violence would have no hatred as motivation.[142]

This realistic form of idealism is apparent in other memoranda. In rather different circumstances to those of the war years in India, at a general reception awarded him at a hotel in Hollywood in May 1932, he remarked that he had been asked many times in America what solution he had brought for the social problems confronting the country. He gave a square answer as to the root of both individual and social difficulties: these are caused by self-interest. This was what caused corrupt politicians to accept bribes, caused bootleggers to break the law in the pursuit of profit, caused "the exploitation of great masses of humanity by individuals or groups of individuals seeking personal gain," caused the shelving of inventions that could contribute to human welfare, caused the wanton destruction of large quantities of food in order to maintain market prices even while people were starving. This was also what caused the hoarding of large quantities of gold when world welfare required its circulation.[143] Insistence upon some of these points would have made him a very unwelcome visitor on American shores, and if pressed to a logical conclusion, might have resulted in deportment. He went on to give the more "fantastic" part of his message, centering upon the power of his silence, but he had not evaded the issue of what was wrong in practical affairs. There would seem to be some justification for his references to the "unevolved souls" who maintain a low level of thought and action.

Nearly a decade later, in 1940, he dictated his message entitled "The New Humanity," which makes several unusual statements with the minimum of verbosity. The problem facing humanity , he asserted, was not merely war; the world war was the external symptom of something more grave. Mere propaganda against wars is of limited utility, he stressed, and insufficient to avoid them. Even when military wars were not being waged, human groupings were constantly engaged in "economic or some other subtle form of warfare." Military wars "arise only when these underground causes are aggravated." The root-cause of the collective chaos was that "most persons are in the grip of egoism and selfish considerations."

Wars, he stressed, do not arise merely in order to secure material adjustments. "They are often the product of uncritical identification with the narrow interests" of a local social arrangement. One has only to think of the fanatical indoctrination then at work amongst both the Germans and the Japanese to realize that neither Westerners or Easterners use their critical faculties as often as they ought.

"To understand the problem of humanity as merely the problem of bread is to reduce humanity to the level of animality," he continued. Yet the level of animality is still preferred by certain of the major ideologies in the world. According to Meher Baba, economic adjustment is impossible while self-interest continues, even with the best of equipment and numerical efficiency. There will still be mutual conflict in the absence of true cooperative action. An understanding of the spiritual dimensions of the human situation is essential, but this is still ignored at reckless cost.

The "new humanity" would have to emerge from the travail of struggle and suffering. It would not be able to ignore science. "It is a mistake to look upon science as anti-spiritual," he affirmed, which makes a refreshing change from some credos. Science can be a help or a hindrance according to the use to which it is put. Scientific truths concerning the physical body and the gross world "can become a medium for the soul to know itself," but in order for this purpose to be served, scientific data must be adequately integrated into a larger perspective of spiritual understanding which is capable of an unfluctuating perception of true and viable values. In the absence of such understanding, scientific findings would be used for mutual destruction.

Another relevant point is clarified here. Though spiritual experience cannot arise from the unaided intellect, the intellect can be of help in the communication of such experience. Baba repudiated the conventional notion that mysticism is something anti-intellectual, impractical, and unrelated to experience. "There is nothing irrational in true mysticism," which can instead be described as "the final understanding of all experience." Genuine spiritual experience involves an effective attitude to worldly duties and everyday life, not a neurotic reaction. Here he warned against the escapist tendency to seek shelter in a false sense of self-completeness; the New Humanity would need to avoid this cul-de-sac, and Meher Baba himself probably deemed the hippy boom an example of this neurotic reaction nearly a generation later.

On the other hand, conservatives are here viewed as liable to seek to preserve their separative ego-experience through an "uncritical identification with forms, ceremonies and rituals, or with traditions and conventions." He predicted that the New Humanity would "break the attachment to external forms." He warned against "identification with some narrow class, creed, sect or religion, or with the divisions based upon sex." The separative self finds fuel in such incomplete mergings with a larger whole, and takes delight in the feeling of being separate from other nationalities, creeds, and so forth. Since the mass of humanity is enmeshed in such separative and assertive tendencies, those who look only at the surface of events will inevitably feel despair as to the human fate. But Meher Baba asserted that the New Humanity "will learn the art of cooperative and harmonious life; it will free itself from the tyranny of dead forms and release the creative life of spiritual wisdom." This would originate "through the spiritual awakening brought about by the masters (i.e. *qutubs*, *sadgurus*)," despite the apparent hopelessness of mass insanity and mechanical patterns of response.[144]

If this sounds visionary to some critics, then it is no more an unrealistic prospect than other sociological reflections made by such academics as Marx and Weber. The current attempts at a "new age" amongst the Western bourgeoisie have not yet, for the most part, caught up with the standards set by Meher Baba, whose critical attitude to both elites and majorities left ample scope for freewill in the right direction on the part of those not neglecting the critical and intuitive faculties of the human psyche.

PART THREE

A SEQUEL TO THE KAIVANI PHENOMENON

The question of Meher Baba's background context has to date been neglected. The devotional movement associated with his name has never shown any interest in antecedents. Former biographers have exhibited an ignorance of philosophical links pertaining to the subject's ethnic and ideational heritage. These omissions require correction, not least because of the instructive nature of the links discernible.

The tradition which calls for attention in this respect is that associated with Azar Kaivan (d. 1618), the Iranian ishraqi philosopher who was a Zoroastrian by birth. Meher Baba himself did not explicitly claim any identity with this tradition, and the indications in this direction are of an implicit nature therefore. But owing to the intercultural nature of this tradition, which I have chosen to call Kaivani,[145] it is not at all inapplicable to dwell upon similarities in approach or orientation which can be attested. Meher Baba may be viewed as a sequel to the Kaivani tradition of Mughal India, with due latitude given to inevitable changes in environment and language media.

One of the most obvious points of comparison is the ethnic link. Azar Kaivan and his core group of emigrant disciples were Irani Zoroastrians who settled in North India from their original home in Safavid Iran. Meher Baba was an Irani Zoroastrian by blood, and a Parsi only by virtue of his environment, since both his parents were emigrants from Iran. His father Sheriar Mundegar (d. 1932) was an unusual self-taught individual who knew both Arabic and Persian, and the key to his studies was, as I have shown elsewhere, the affinity with Kaivan's disposition as this survived in exceptional entities like himself. Sheriar was an ex-dervish who had settled in Poona, an unusually literate man who found it difficult to communicate his knowledge to his less expansive Zoroastrian milieu.[146] His son Merwan did not learn Arabic, but was fluent in Persian, and probably imbibed much more from his father than was readily apparent to his less intelligent relatives.

An important point to grasp is that the Kaivanis were never a sect in the usual sense of the word. They are most accurately described as circles of disciples grouped around certain teachers during the late sixteenth century and the seventeenth century. They did not crystallize into an organization, and appear to have died out as a distinct trend during the mid-seventeenth century. This is in contrast to the pattern of popular movements, e.g. the dervish orders, which rarely maintained the original dynamic. The Kaivanis were primarily philosophers and mystics, not religionists, though they were misinterpreted in some features by nineteenth century religionists. Memory of them persisted strongly amongst the Zoroastrian literati, and they continued to provide inspiration owing to the literature deriving from Kaivani circles, mainly the works known as the *Dabistan i-Mazahib* and the *Desatir*. Kaivani teaching was eclectic in a very sophisticated sense; they eschewed orthodox Zoroastrianism, and taught in terms of *ishraqi* philosophy as adapted to an Indian milieu of mystico-philosophical thought. Sufism, Vedanta, Yoga, and Greek philosophy were all facets of this distinctive approach, and Kaivani circles included members drawn from a surprising number of different religious traditions – including Irani and Parsi Zoroastrians, Muslims, Hindus, Jews, and at least one (Portuguese) Christian.

The intercultural and non-dogmatic attitude of the Kaivani groups tends very much to be independent of labels, including "Kaivani," which is a convenient categorization. Their own literature refers to them by several different terms, none of which are particularly well known. One is left with the impression that if they did somehow survive, then they would no longer have been known by the same words. Meher Baba himself disliked labels, and is known to have specifically dissociated himself from categorization in terms of any ism.[147] This might be called a Kaivani trait, bearing in mind that "Kaivani" is itself merely a convenient classification for an outstandingly liberal philosophical and mystical trend.

It is apt enough that both of Meher Baba's masters, Hazrat Babajan and Upasni Maharaj, were of an intercultural complexion in the context of their training. Babajan had a Hindu mentor prior to her Muslim teacher at Multan, while Upasni (a Hindu) trained under the bizarre Sai Baba of Shirdi, a Muslim who was mistakenly identified as a Hindu by a large sector of his subsequent following. As one of the sufi *majazib* (illuminati) of the Deccan,[148] Sai Baba of Shirdi connects with the *qalandar* lifestyle demonstrated by such outstanding entities of the Mughal era as Sarmad (d. 1660/1), the "Jewish sufi" who is implicated in Kaivani activity.

Intercultural affinities in this highly specialized context do not merely grant the ability to synthesize apparently disparate elements, but also the ability to criticize the more pedestrian aspects of different traditions. Meher Baba demonstrated this critical spleen on an occasion when he referred to Azar Kaivan as "the last true *dastur*," a reference to the mystical capacities of the latter as distinct from the priestly etiquette associated with the term *dastur*.

Though it was believed by nineteenth century Zoroastrian priests that Azar Kaivan was a *dastur* (high priest), there is no evidence that he ever had any such sacerdotal role. This status rests upon assumption, and can be explained in terms of a priestly milieu wishing to assimilate a mystical entity to their own canons. However, Meher Baba's use of the term *dastur* was, in this instance, made in the Kaivani spirit of essential significances of canonical terms, and was combined with an unusually caustic assessment of traditional lapses from significance.

It was on February 7th, 1928, that two Zoroastrian dasturs visited Meher Baba at Meherabad ashram. In the course of conversation, he said to the visitors (via the alphabet board) that the "prayer books of all the religions . . . have nothing to do with the truth." He indicated that all the recognized scriptures were inadequate records of ancient teachings, and now taken out of context by bombastic sacerdotalists and clergy of all types. He specified the Zend-Avesta, the Bible of the Christians, the Vedas, the Quran, and "all the other religious books." But the brunt of his disapproval fell upon his native Zoroastrian tradition. Giving an example of the orthodox alterations to teachings, he said that Zarathushtra had taught that the "heart" should burn in love for God, but that the Zoroastrian priests had subsequently interpreted this emphasis to mean "burning" in the ritualistic sense. This was an attack upon a fundamental priestly code relating to sacred fires. Other doctrines and prayers found in the Avesta had all been altered at various times, he added.

Baba went on to affirm that Zarathushtra had fourteen disciples whom he made God-realized, but that afterwards there was only one God-realized entity in the Zoroastrian community, from whom derived a knowledge which "enlightened the community for seven hundred years." It is not clear whether Baba here meant a succession of such teachers, i.e. one at a time, or literally only one. But this knowledge became regarded as a hereditary accomplishment, passed down orally from father to son amongst the priests. "The last true *dastur* was Azar Kaivan," he added, after whom "there has been no realized perfect saint amongst the Zoroastrians." The report clearly indicates that Meher Baba regarded Kaivan as a God-realized entity, i.e. a seventh plane adept. The "true *dastur*" Azar Kaivan is here contrasted with the many "false priests among the Zoroastrians who have been giving their own versions of the Avesta." He makes it quite clear that all the religious books of the Zoroastrians (i.e. the Avesta and the Pahlavi works) were the creation of the priests and not Zarathushtra. Western scholars had discovered during the nineteenth century that only the Gathas could be attributed to Zarathushtra, contrary to priestly ideas on this subject, but Meher Baba appears to have meant that even the Gathas are similarly the product of priestly arrangement. This seems reinforced by his affirmation that Zarathushtra "taught a few gems of truth, but these are not known to the people today." Zarathushtra's essential knowledge and experience was transmitted to his inner circle of fourteen disciples, though "to the world he gave a way of life."

Zarathushtra has posed problems for modern scholars. His date is uncertain, and also his place of origin. There have been numerous arguments over what the Gathas mean, the Gathas being archaic "hymns" in the ancient Avestan language which may represent a redaction of teachings surviving from the time of Zarathushtra.[149]

In a further vein of critique, Meher Baba urged that there had been similar alterations made in the Bible and the Quran, though "sometimes these changes came about without the intention of doing so." An original explanation for some of these alterations is that followers of the *avatar*, i.e. Zarathushtra, Christ, and Muhammad, would address large crowds of people, and their words were subsequently confused with those of the prophet.[150] Some scholars of religion might concede such a possibility more readily in the cases of Zarathushtra and Jesus, as the Quran is generally considered unusually authentic owing to its early date of copying down. But it is perhaps incumbent here to point out the known facts of Quranic transcription. When Muhammad died, the Quran did not exist as a codified book. He had not written it down, and nor is he known to have given instructions for it to be written down. Scholars think that some of his revelations had probably been recorded on palm leaves, lambskins, shoulder bones, and stones – typical media of those times in Arabia – but most of his communcations were preserved orally. But when the first Quran-reciters began to die in the wars of Islamic expansion, there was consternation at the prospect of Muhammad's communications passing into oblivion. The first Caliph Abu Bakr (rgd. 632-4) commissioned a collection of all the revelations of Muhammad that were available. But by the time of the third Caliph Uthman (rgd. 644-56), different versions of the Quran were in circulation. The Caliph accordingly gave instructions for an editorial committee to establish an official recension. All other versions were destroyed by royal decree.[151] These developments seem likely to have given scope for omissions and variants, however unintentional;

official preference is not always the best guide to authenticity.

Though Meher Baba is known to have referred eulogistcally to Azar Kaivan, I have not been able to find any reference of his to Shaikh Sohravardi Maqtul (d. 1191), the Iranian Muslim who is generally credited with the initial formulation of ishraqi philosophy. Kaivan taught a variant of ishraqi philosophy, and his disciples have been dubbed "Zoroastrian ishraqis," appropriately enough. The Kaivanis used ishraqi elements outside the Islamic framework of reference employed by Muslim ishraqis, an understandable feature of cross-cultural adaptation. The Zoroastrian version of *ishraq* (illuminism) has rarely been understood in due focus, but then it is arguable that the Muslim equivalent has also been misrepresented by theologically conditioned parties. The philosophy of *ishraq* (illumination) gained an exposure amongst the Shi'ite literati of the Safavid era at a time when Imami Shi'ism gained a newly codified interpretation that was endorsed by monarchical interests and furthered by the new clerical establishment of the *mujtahids*. This exposure meant that ishraqi thought frequently became "orthodox," but this definitely does not apply to the Zoroastrian ishraqis, who avoided conversion to Shia Islam and retained an underdog status in Iranian society. This did not prevent assiduous learning on their part, though they did have to take precautions against oppressive social discrimination. This was one of the reasons why Azar Kaivan and his disciples emigrated to North India during the reign of the liberal monarch Akbar, an exceptional Muslim ruler who extended an unprecedented toleration to Hindus.

The philosophy of *ishraq* had strong affinities with Greek philosophy as mediated by the medieval Muslim literati. Shaikh Sohravardi Maqtul emphasized the antecedents of his philosophy in Neoplatonism and in the pre-Islamic thought of Iran. This latter should not be confused with orthodox Zoroastrianism; he specifically referred to unorthodox mystics of pre-Islamic Iran who were not magian priests. There is some reason to link these precursors with the dissenters of Sassanian Iran who have recently emerged into a clearer (though still very sparse) focus.[152] These dissenters were ascetics and mystics who probably contributed to the intercultural tradition associated with the accommodation of Greek learning in Sassanian circles. There were different groupings amongst these dissenters, and one radical extreme became known as the Mazdakites, some of whom were social revolutionaries.

Sohravardi Maqtul's philosophy is highly symbolic in content, with references to Zoroastrian angelology, amongst other features. This allusiveness was carried over into the Kaivani literature, which frequently employed a "Pahlavi style" context of reference that is not easy for a casual reader to unravel. Greek philosophy rarely emerges in Kaivani treatises, since the aim was not to repeat formal aspects of a philosophical repertory, which had largely been stereotyped by the Muslim Peripatetics – though there were exceptional men amongst the latter who participated in Kaivan's activity, notably Mir Abu'l Qasim Findiriski (d. 1641), a mystical Aristotelian, though he can also be described as a sufi.

Maqtul, who forfeited his life in the friction with Islamic orthodoxy,[153] may have had some contact with the diverse Zurvanite attitudes preserved by the Zoroastrians of twelfth century Iran. Certainly, his acknowledgment of the best in pre-Islamic Iranian thought is a notable feature of the liberal disposition of "high Sufism," a term which can appropriately be used for the *ishraqi* tradition. The associations of popular Sufism accordingly require to be suspended. Maqtul included amongst his precursors three of the major Iranian sufis, all distinctive for their unorthodox attitude: namely Bayazid Bistami (d.*c.* 874), Hallaj (d. 922), and Abu'l Hasan Kharaqani (d. 1033). In all of these, the bold pantheistic spirit of Iranian Sufism makes itself apparent. The Iranian *hululi* sufis retained much of the esoteric dispositon of the Iranian *ghulat* ("extremists"), early and radical Shi'ites (of diverse background and tendencies) who have been linked with the survival of older Mazdakite teachings. If this series is viewed as a whole – which is a perspective of anthropography – then there is much to be said for an underlying continuum of Iranian mystical traits which refused to compromise with orthodox pressures of conformism. In Meher Baba, the investigator has the opportunity to view at close range the Iranian spirit divested of Zoroastrian and Islamic dogma and ritualism. He is as much "Mazdakite" and Zurvanite as he is sufi; he is both *ishraqi* and *irfani* (gnostic) in affiliated perspective, and yet at the same time elusive of ready-made labels which require a deeper understanding than customarily awarded them.

I have observed above that Meher Baba (insofar as I have been able to discover) never referred to Sohravardi Maqtul by name. This cannot be said to mean that there was no intrinsic affinity, since it was foreign to Meher Baba's method to cite authority figures. It is useless to look in his dictations for "Maqtul says" or "Kaivan says." Neither of them were poets, and it is only poets whom Baba would cite. The old *qalandar* spirit of independence from authority was very strong in him; qalandars were known in Iran during the medieval era,[154] though one can conclude that the *qalandar* disposition represents but one more aspect of the Mazdakite and *dris-den* gnostic trends of pre-Islamic Iran, which quite conceivably date back to the time of Zarathushtra (even if this was as early as the second millenium B.C.)

For those who are pedantic about classifications, it is perhaps best to describe Meher Baba as a neo-Kaivani, just as the Kaivanis can be termed neo-ishraqi in their departure from Islamic idioms. The gnostic dynamic does not stand still in its intercultural avenues of expression, and indeed, if it does so in a mono-cultural guise, it is likely to be no longer a dynamic but merely petrified conditioning. The easiest thing for anybody to do is to repeat secondhand material; the consequence is generally unenlightened dogmatism, not to mention distortion.

Since Meher Baba made reference to Hallaj in his youthful poetry written in a mystical vein,[155] I see no reason why he cannot also be described as a Hallajian, hence adding to the list of those Hallajians charted by Louis Massignon.[156] In fact, Meher Baba deserves the classification more than some other names recorded in this context, since he did not compromise *hululi* principles as so many did in Islamic milieux. Hallaj paid for his refusal to do so with his life, and his teachings are still obscure for the most part.

One graphic feature of Baba's reference to Hallaj is his classification of the latter as one of those who gained the consciousness of a *qutub*, and who experienced the bliss of the "I am God" state even while physically undergoing acute sufferings at his execution.[157]

In an early discourse, Baba emphasized the importance of the stance taken by Hallaj in declaring "the fact that he had realized (God) fully and completely," and thereby contesting conventional ideas of *baqa*. Baba adds that there were many contemporary sufi saints "who knew through personal experience that Mansur (i.e. Hallaj) was speaking the truth." But nevertheless, some of these latter "thought it proper to maintain silence and some gave their tacit consent very reluctantly to the tragedy" of his death. Baba goes on to concede the validity of the Junaydi viewpoint in being reticent before the masses on sufi subjects, but stressed that there was "no lack of explicit confirmation of Mansur's claim by many eminent *qutubs*" of later centuries, including the recent Ghaous Ali Shah Qalandar of Panipat, a nineteenth century adept.[158]

The term of Hallajian should properly be distinguished from Hallaji, which was a sectarian label by the eleventh century. In his *Kashf al-Mahjub*, Hujwiri referred to the contemporary sect of Hallajis in Iraq, who vilified the earlier (Hallajian) exponent Faris Dinwari, who had championed the *hululi* teachings of Hallaj. These teachings were diluted to suit orthodox consumption, and Hujwiri himself, an "orthodox sufi," was one of those who censured *hulul* and the related teaching of the *tanasukhiyan*, those who believe in transmigration.[159]

The philosopher Abu Bakr Razi (d.c. 925), a true Hallajian by textual implication, would have had cause to wrangle with the dogmatists who denied reincarnation because it was not mentioned in the Quran. *Tanasukh* has recently emerged as a vintage Iranian teaching, going back at least to the Sassanian milieux of the dissenting gnostics –

though not merely to the Manichaeans, who were only one of the gnostic groupings of that era in Iranian territory. This teaching was retained in early ishraqi circles (doubtless clandestinely for the most part), but was eschewed by later Muslim ishraqis. The major case in point was Mulla Sadra Shirazi (d. 1640), who accommodated ishraqi philosophy and *irfan* (gnosis, associated with Ibn al-Arabi) to the newly established Shi'ite doctrines of Safavid Iran. Mulla Sadra, as his name implies, was a religious scholar in an official capacity, quite different to the position of the Zoroastrian ishraqis. Sadra supported the anti-transmigrationist arguments of the Aristotelian philosopher Ibn Sina (Avicenna), and in this contrasts with the example of the earlier ishraqi Qutubuddin Shirazi (d. 1311), who was inclined to support *tanasukh*.[160] Qutubuddin was a distinguished scientist, one of those associated with the Maraghah observatory in north-west Iran. He lived in the more tolerant era of the Ilkhanid rulers, deriving from the Mongol invasions, and was a discerning commentator on the Arabic writings of Maqtul, who has in general received much gloss.

Meher Baba's teaching compares very well with that of Mulla Sadra's anti-evolutionist *kalam* (scholastic theology). Sadra incorporated Peripatetic philosophy in his writings, but his use of the sciences allows for no evolutionism, and is accordingly at a disadvantage. Though there are some unusual and innovative features in Sadra's expositions, his dogmatic tendencies do not permit much rein to either science or gnosis, and the modern physicist, biologist, and psychologist is likely to feel much more at home in the pages of *God Speaks* than in *Al-Hiqmat al-mutaaliyah* and other works of Sadra.

Tanasukh was retained by the Kaivanis, though Meher Baba's version far surpasses the extant expression of this perspective in Kaivani treatises.[161] Nevertheless, the Kaivani literature is notable for its stress upon *ahimsa* (nonviolence), and is particularly concerned to protect "harmless animals" from human molestation. This emphasis has been viewed by some scholars as a consequence of Akbar's policy of conciliation with Hindu customs, but this interpretation can be viewed as only partially correct, since *tanasukh* was part of the ancient Iranian heritage as well as the Indian. Meher Baba himself was an advocate of *ahimsa*, being a vegetarian and permitting no creatures to be killed at his ashram other than the poisonous varieties (e.g. snakes, scorpions, mosquitoes). But as I have indicated in Part Two, his non-violence allowed for practical considerations; he was quite specific about the problem of mad dogs, for instance, and differed from extremists on this issue.[162]

During the reign of the Mughal emperors Akbar and Jehangir, Azar Kaivan lived a retiring existence at Patna in North India. His lifestyle was ascetic, and he enjoined a prudent reticence upon his disciples concerning his teaching. The idea sometimes encountered that he had a son who succeeded him is based upon a misextrapolation from the sources. He was anything but a professional high priest, and likewise avoided the role of a professional philosopher. His attitude was one of a very liberal tolerance towards all religions, reflected in the cosmopolitan membership of the Kaivani groups. This latitude is also demonstrated in the treatise entitled *Dabistan i-Mazahib*, written in Persian in the mid-seventeenth century by a writer who was reared in Kaivani circles. The name of this writer has been the subject of confusion, but there are strong grounds for the conclusion that he was a Zoroastrian by birth, though participating in the non-insular Kaivani approach which gives a bewildering impression of eclectic tendencies to those unaccustomed to such thought. One of the names adhering to him in manuscripts is Mobad Shah, *mobad* being a Zoroastrian title for a priest of a fire temple, though here its usage is poetic, typical of Kaivani nomenclature.

The *Dabistan* has often been cited in its ponderous (and frequently inaccurate) English translation, but has rarely been assessed adequately. It gives a coverage of numerous religions and sects, including Hinduism, Islam, Sufism, Jainism, Sikhism, Tibetan Buddhism, Christianity, and Judaism. It has a chapter on the philosophers and a biography of Ibn Sina, and a lengthy section on "Zoroastrian" sects, which includes a review of Kaivani (=Sipasi) history and lore. The author was clearly striving to demonstrate liberality, and succeeded; he was not concerned with critique of disparate elements (though this does occur in an adroitly low profile), since there was a desperate need in his time for liberal attitudes in religion. The format of the book has puzzled some analysts unnecessarily. For instance, the author writes in the "Zoroastrian" chapter as if he were a Kaivani partisan, but also writes in the section on Sufism as if he was similarly a partisan. There is no contradiction save for insular attitudes of the kind which affirm that sufis are distinct from Zoroastrians and Hindus, and vice versa. The Kaivanis themselves seem to have felt strongly that all insularists were mad, and required to be duly humoured on appropriate occasions. The esoteric measures of Azar Kaivan can be explained in this light.

Though the *Dabistan* was clearly intended for a general audience, and despite certain deficiencies in close reporting, it is a monument to broad-mindedness. It is, by its own hints, a diluted reflection of the universalist impact occurring in Akbarian India. It is possible, as I have indicated elsewhere, that Azar Kaivan and his Shiraz-Patna circle contributed to the Akbarian policy of *sulh-i-kul* ("peace with all"), a policy known to have been stimulated by Abu'l Fazl Allami,[163] a prominent minister at Akbar's court, whose ishraqi father Shaikh Mubarak Nagauri[164] would have been highly sensitive to whatever currents of philosophical expertise were operative in his time. It is a tangible fact that Azar Kaivan's universalist perspective attracted two of the leading scientists in Safavid Iran, namely Mir Abu'l Qasim Findiriski and Bahauddin Amili.

The chapter on Sufism in the *Dabistan* focusses, in the biographical section, on the contemporary "Qadiri" phenomenon[165] associated with Dara Shikoh and his *pir* Mulla Shah Badakhshi, who in turn derived inspiration from the sufi exponent Miyan Mir. Dara Shikoh (d. 1659) was a liberal Mughal prince who championed understanding and toleration between Hindus and Muslims. He not only presided over a translation of the Upanishads into Persian, but wrote a distinctive treatise of his own entitled *Majma al-Bahrain* (Confluence of the Two Seas), which outlined the convergence between the monistic traditions of Sufism and Hinduism (more specifically, Vedanta).[166] This treatise can be regarded as a precursor to the similar latitude displayed in Meher Baba's *God Speaks*, though the latter work is much more detailed and considerably more integrative.

Shikoh's eventual teacher was Sarmad, the heretical Jewish sufi, a man who defies insular labels in significant ways. He was erudite in the Arabic tradition of Peripatetic philosophy, and also in Jewish literature, and judging from Mobad Shah's description, was a distinctive Qabbalist of the intrinsic variety. He had adopted the lifestyle of a *qalandar*, going naked like Hindu sadhus and yogis, with whom he was on the best of terms. He was a friend of Mobad Shah, and was also linked with the Peripatetic Kaivani Abu'l Qasim Findiriski. Sarmad opposed the narrowness of the Islamic *ulama* (doctors of the law) at the Mughal court, and was detested by that faction. He was executed shortly after his patron and pupil Dara Shikoh lost his own life in the struggle with Aurangzeb, the new Mughal emperor. The doctrinaire fanaticism of Aurangzeb subsequently sent liberal philosophy and mystical influences underground, though these survived outside the political arena, in milieux like those created by the *majazib* (illuminati) of the Deccan.

Illustrating the Kaivani attitude in the spirit of "high Sufism" is a comment of Mobad Shah in his chapter on Vedanta. A Hindu known as Binavali was a Vedantic *jnani*, but gained the poetic name of Wali (a Sufi stylism) owing to his poetry; he became a disciple of Mulla Shah Badakhshi, the liberal Qadiri, whom he stayed with in Kashmir, subsequently acquiring the knowledge (*jnana*) that he sought. The author of the *Dabistan* comments: "The Sufi is by no necessity bound to a creed; no faith nor religion fetters his choice; he befriends the idol and the temple of the idol, and is no stranger to the mosque; by the power of ecstasy, not by any external knowledge, he utters sublime speeches."[167] (Mobad Shah became a friend of Binavali in 1640).

The nineteenth century was not lacking in Zoroastrian admirers of the Kaivani phenomenon, though various extrapolations and theories of these enthusiasts require to be met with reserve, owing to the theological glosses applied. This applies to such individuals as Mobad Fardunji Marzban, who during the early nineteenth century gained the reputation of being a "sadhu" of Kaivani type. But the problem with nominal sequels is always one of a superficial rendering of the original, very marked in sectarian activities of all kinds. Much more impressive is the low profile sequel apparent in the life of Sheriar Mundegar Irani (1853-1932), who scrupulously refrained from advertising his affiliations. Though he lived for a decade as a dervish in India, his earlier background was actually that of *dervishi* in Qajar Iran, where he had the opportunity to contact the various forms of oral lore that included ishraqi and irfani ingredients. Some of these oral ingredients were doubtless much distorted, though there were current some emphases which skilfully denied the resurrection of the body, a theological concept which had taken deep root in popular thinking. The nineteenth century traveller Edward Glanville Browne recorded some relevant data, mostly of a negative nature,[168] but did not himself come to grips with the underlying experiential heritage of Iranian *qalandar* types. The difference between "popular Sufism" and "high Sufism" is such that the majority-minority ratio is very pronounced; the Kaivani version of *qalandari* disposition was a minority achievement, and rather more complex than the popular versions.

One feature in which Sheriar differed from his more famous son Merwan, alias Meher Baba, is the totally reticent attitude of the former in respect of gnosis, combined with a mercantile lifestyle in the former's mature years. This gives him a "Junaydi" semblance by comparison with the more overtly "Hallajian" tangent of his son. But both of these polarities of approach were evident in the Kaivani phenomenon of the Mughal era. The disciples of Azar Kaivan included *qalandar* types who were to a considerable extent compatible with Hindu ascetics, and also men of a mercantile career. Meher Baba demonstrates the *qalandar* polarity, and was never mercantile – save during the phase in his early years when he took charge of a shop while training under Upasni Maharaj.

The old Iranian theme of *malamat* (an Arabic word

meaning "blame") can apply to both of the abovementioned polarities, but in general is a misunderstood word, like so many in the sufi vocabulary. Its misuse during the medieval era by hedonistic opportunists has served to distort its original significance. There was nothing hedonistic about Meher Baba or his father, and it is possible to see in them much of the old Iranian *malamati* depth. The *malamati* tradition is chiefly associated with Khorasan, though this represents a geographical contraction, and was exemplified by such classical sufi exponents as Abu Hafs Haddad (d. 883) and Abu Said ibn Abu'l Khair (d. 1049).[169] The genuine *malamati* may either totally conceal his attainments, or else use these to shock conditioned social strata and hence invoke blame or censure. Meher Baba fits the latter category, as he demonstrated in his friction with conservative Parsi priests who maligned him. This form of shock tactic should be carefully distinguished from "gnostic hedonism," which is very common nowadays and of a totally reprobate nature designed to appeal to vulgar audiences desiring sensation.

Azar Kaivan appears to have opted for concealment tactics in his ascetic vocation. The Kaivanis had a fear of divulging esoteric fundamentals even to their relatives, a reflection of the traditional philosophical (in the real sense) attitude to those unprepared for deeper truths, i.e. insights which must be guarded from hedonists and others who would misuse them, or suppress them. This seems to have been Sheriar Mundegar's view, though in his case he found one relative from whom there was no need to conceal, since his second son met with his own experience of how time-place conditioning constrained human thinking. Fortunately enough, Meher Baba was not a carbon copy of Azar Kaivan or his father, and as a consequence he did not hesitate to round out a coherent non-symbolical philosophy that allows insight into many matters only hinted at in Kaivani lore. In addition to necessary precautions against transgressors of unseen laws, there is also the necessity to educate a reading public in favourable climates who might in this way learn basic distinctions in preparation for a more advanced range of experience.

A feature in which Meher Baba did closely follow the Kaivani precedent was his liberal and non-sectarian spirit. In making a complete break with conventional Zoroastrianism, he demonstrated a universal range that simultaneously allowed for others to retain their native religion even while participating in his own worldview. This tactic may be described in terms of: allowing crutches for those who need them, since to break their crutches while they are still invalids (i.e. non-completed) may be a criminal act equivalent to breaking their limbs. He would not, however, tolerate insularity between the members of different religions, which is a serious social and psychological disease. He early broke down the barriers between his Hindu and Muslim pupils, barriers which included separate eating arrangements.

In India, Meher Baba had strong links with the Parsi, Hindu, and Muslim populations, though the Muslims had practically died out at his ashrams by the time of his "Humiliation" during the post-New Life phase. The absence of the Muslim element seems to underline the exoteric tendencies of the predominantly Parsi settlement at Meherazad. The "Humiliation" of Meher Baba as an exoterically advertised figure even while he lived in almost total seclusion is unlikely to be comprehended by those with simplistic religious ideas that can easily attach to a "saviour" figure. Such ideas are what gave rise to religions, and Meher Baba specifically stated on numerous occasions that he did not wish to establish any new religion.

His contact with Parsis and Hindus encompassed a substantial number of members of the Theosophical Society, particularly in the 1920's and 1930's. His attitude towards Theosophy was one of amiable tolerance, though he was known to express an amused criticism of several Theosophical concepts, particularly that relating to the "masters" of the Himalayas, which he stated to be an error. Theosophy had acquired (via Colonel Olcott) an erroneous perspective of some Kaivani literature, but this Baba does not seem to have referred to explicitly.

His following in the West was predominantly of a Christian background, though by no means exclusively. Various conditioned religious concepts are detectable in the accounts of him written by Westerners (as also by Easterners of different persuasions). His own assessment of Christianity was very much a mystical one. He pointedly remarked upon the comparative absence of seventh plane adepts in medieval and later Christianity in contrast to Muslim and Hindu religious sectors. He awarded to Francis of Assisi the high status of a "Perfect Master" (*qutub*), but expressly indicated the extreme rarity of this status in the West during the Christian era. He referred to other Christian mystics, but only in the context of sainthood, not masterhood. He is also known to have referred very favourably to Hugh of St. Victor (d. 1141),[170] who is frequently ignored by annalists of mysticism as a "scholastic philosopher," in much the same manner as Roger Bacon is ignored. A modern Christian theologian has described Hugh disapprovingly in terms of "the most Buddhistic" of all the Christian mystics, "in that he thirsts for the unmoving peace of nirvana," a comment of typically pious insularity, as is the accusation: "His (Hugh's) God is the God of the pantheists."[171]

Meher Baba's teaching was definitely pantheistic in tone, but not for that reason to be dismissed by bigots. He quite frequently used mystical poetry to supplement his emphases, and this gives his communications a refreshingly non-dogmatic complexion. The three poets whom he quoted most often were Hafiz of Shiraz, Kabir, and Tukaram. Of these, Hafiz gained the lion's share of citation, and affords a further instance of Baba's affinities with Iranian sufi tradition. Hafiz was a fourteenth century figure whose life is obscure, though his *Diwan* became one of the most oft-quoted collections of poetry in the Persian language. He is often associated with a (very) mild erotic idiom, and has been misunderstood by some Western commentators; his terminology is startling and highly allusive, fitting the more enlightened sufi attempts to speak in a language unhampered by dogmatic considerations.[172] Meher Baba's quotations and renditions into English are of good quality and consistently mystical in their interpretative appendages. Though some Western scholars have described Hafiz as a "court poet," Meher Baba was quite definitive in describing this poet as a *qutub*.

Kabir was probably the second most oft-quoted poet in Baba's repertory, and applicably enough, was one of those sufi exponents who spoke in a language encompassing the lore of Yoga to a marked extent. Born a Muslim weaver in North India, there is little that is concretely known of this fifteenth century teacher and poet, and much of the poetry attributed to him is now known to be in his "style" and not actually written by him. He is a significant figure in the obscure history of intercultural Sufism in medieval India;[173] Sai Baba of Shirdi described himself as a Kabiri in religion,[174] indicative of his intercultural stance between Hindus and Muslims. Kabir was one of the small number of historical entities whom Meher Baba described as a *qutub*.

Tukaram (1608-49) was one of the major mystical poets of Maharashtra, born into a low caste family of *shudras*. This peasant farmer made himself literate in the Vaishnava tradition of Hinduism, which is notable for its poetical expression of *bhakti* and *para-bhakti*. His verses (*abhangas*) in the Marathi dialect were well known in the Deccan, and it is quite clear that Meher Baba preferred these to the Vedas.

The "enlightened theism" of Tukaram is not by any means worlds apart from the counterpart expressed in an Islamic guise in the sufi tradition of *wahdat al-wujud* (Unity of Being) associated chiefly with Ibn al-Arabi. This tradition became popular amongst Indian Muslims, though its textual dimensions are currently known only to a small number of scholars. In Iran it was known as *irfan* (gnosis), and was often studied in conjunction with ishraqi philosophy by connoisseurs of esoteric literature. But *wujudi* philosophy also has strong Arab and Turkish affiliations, not least owing to the example of Arabi and his Turkish disciple Sadruddin Qonawi (d. 1273).[175] Dr. Abdul Ghani Munsiff was quite extensively familiar with *wujudi* philosophy, and his relationship with Meher Baba followed in a long tradition of teacher-pupil links in *wujudi* milieux.

A continuation of the *wujudi* tradition in realistic social terms was the *majazib* activity in the Deccan, which bridged the gap in time between the Mughal era and the phase of British Empire, two periods of colonial domination.

The *majazib* were not persecuted by the new empire urbanity, as they had been under Islamic rule, but the "natives" were all considered backward by the British, who found this condescension convenient for economic exploitation. Their talents remained a closed book in official circles therefore. Liberal wujudis were often designated by the term *majzub* (plural: *majazib*), which was a stigma in orthodox Islamic eyes; the Muslim ruling elite had found it convenient to stipulate the inferiority of Hindu religion, but the *majazib* had frequently lived like Hindu sadhus, part of the defiant *qalandar* methodology. Sai Baba of Shirdi emerges as a "majzub" purist, undefiled by orthodox insularity and operating outside the limitations of the dervish order mentality. Meher Baba can also be considered a "majzub" in this sociological sense, though he proffered a technical definition of the word *majzub* which equates it exclusively with *fana-fillah*. It is a useful operationalized application of the word, and should not be confused with the general associations of the word *majzub* in earlier centuries.

Meher Baba's disposition was markedly more amiable than that of either Sai Baba or Upasni Maharaj. At the end of his life in particular, it is rather easy to criticize him for his open-handed policy of letting all devotees have their way in the manner in which they represented him, which was often atrocious. Yet ironically, even his phase of "Humiliation" has Kaivani undertones, since it was a characteristic of Azar Kaivan and his circle to allow free rein to the personal expression of spiritually immature persons – persons who were humoured and not chastised for their ignorance. The comparison breaks down in that Meher Baba had no esoteric circle at Meherazad, only an exoteric one, but there was thus all the more opportunity for him to exercise an enduring *batini* characteristic.

PART FOUR

CRITICS AND ADMIRERS

It seems necessary for the historian to extend treatment to both the critics and the admirers of any famous figure. As an entity well known for statements of a gnostic character, Meher Baba has had both detractors seeking to defame him and admirers who have supported what they considered to be his merits. The former have varied in their motivations for criticism; the latter have also fitted a varying spectrum, including at its worst a gushing sentiment which, ironically, misrepresents the subject as much as certain well known opponents have done. I believe that this chapter will be of interest to persons not requiring to define themselves as either critics or partisans, since what matters most in anthropographic terms is whether the subject is being represented accurately.

The Secrets of Paul Brunton

The most celebrated critic of Meher Baba was a London journalist whose (later) name was Paul Brunton (1898-1981). His account of Baba appeared in a book that rapidly became a bestseller. This book fits a definite genre: travel in the exotic East in search of esoteric knowledge. It was entitled *A Search in Secret India*, being first published in 1934. Unfortunately, it contained only a selected version of the facts insofar as Meher Baba was concerned, as other extant documentation reveals. The motivation behind the late Paul Brunton's account of Baba requires due analysis if it is history that is in demand.

Brunton gave his readers the impression that he was a very impartial critic who was quite foreign to the milieu of

Meherabad ashram. He could not be duped by the sham "messiah," and passed on to greater things. His reputation as an impartial, detached observer was long afterwards sustained via Sir Francis Younghusband, who assumed that Brunton passed amongst the inhabitants of the Indian bush with a flair typical of Sir Richard Burton. Historically, this reputation is somewhat dampened by the more relevant consideration that Brunton's tour of India lasted only for a few weeks. This reputation is even more suspect when the nature of his visit to India becomes evident from the unpublicized facts. One hopes that the more complete data will serve to warn the readers of many semi-fictitious travelogues of the type which it is very easy to write.

H. Raphael Hirsch, alias Paul Brunton, was born in London in 1898. He became a journalist, with strong personal interests in mysticism and the occult. He came to hear of Meher Baba's existence by 1929, probably as a consequence of the activities of Meredith Starr, one of the earliest Western pupils of Baba. Hirsch entered into a correspondence with one of Baba's followers (either Starr or K.J. Dastur, it is not clear which), and made it evident that he regarded Baba as a guru of rare authority. He was intrigued by the issue of "messiahship" which some followers spoke of (an issue which was not at all clear). Hirsch wrote a poem entitled "Born Again" which he sent to Khaikhushru J. Dastur in the new year of 1930 for use in the latter's magazine *The Meher Message*. The poem was duly published by Dastur, whose periodical fortunately enables the investigator to trace some of the complexities which Hirsch subsequently omitted from his bestseller.

In the autumn of 1930, Hirsch embarked upon a voyage to India, intending primarily to see Baba, and also to undertake a brief tour of the country in an attempt to penetrate the "secrets" of the holy men. It is evident that he was seeking "signs and wonders," to use Charles Purdom's phrase.[176] Hirsch arrived in India in late November 1930, docking at Bombay, where two of Baba's Parsi *mandali* came to escort him to the Meherabad ashram. They reached their destination the next day, November 22nd, but since Hirsch later gave a misleading report of his first meeting with Baba, I will instead pass on here to events which he did not choose to record and which cast a very different light upon his narration.

After staying three days at Meherabad, Hirsch departed on his projected tour, having made an arrangement to spend a longer period with Baba after a couple of months had elapsed. He gives the impression that he departed alone and that he was merely intent upon seeking out yogis and faqirs. In actual fact he travelled with two men who were both followers of Meher Baba, one of whom was the latter's brother Jal. The other was an Englishman who had become known as Swami Prajnananda owing to his adoption of the Hindu monastic life; he was one of the first Westerners to have met Baba, and like Hirsch, regarded Baba as a spiritual master. The trio made a brief stop in Bombay, where Hirsch says that he encountered an elderly Parsi known as Khandalawalla, a former Judge who harboured a grudge against Upasni Maharaj but who was deferential towards Hazrat Babajan. The travellers were en route to Poona in order to meet Babajan, with Jal acting as the interpreter. Hirsch included the meeting in his subsequent book, but in a manner very favourable to his own talents, and the account may therefore be studiously incomplete. He certainly found it desirable to exclude all reference to the visit he made soon afterwards to the cave at Tiger Valley, Panchgani, where Meher Baba had retired into seclusion the previous year. This cave was specifically associated with Meher Baba, having been hollowed out of the rock solely for his use. Hirsch was also warmly received by various of Baba's devotees at Panchgani, Kolhapur, and Bijapur. At Hubli, Jal Irani parted company with his two English friends, being under instruction to rejoin Baba at Meherabad. Hirsch and Prajnananda continued on to Madras, where they had made arrangements to stay with more followers of Meher Baba, though in *Secret India* even Prajnananda is scrupulously deleted from the pages of "history."

Arriving in Madras on December 2nd 1930, the two travellers became the guests of the Saidapet ashram, which was well known for its affinities with Baba. Their hosts were C.V. Sampath Aiyengar and his daughter V.T. Lakshmi, both of them well-educated Hindus who accomplished humanitarian work under Baba's auspices in the local area. Aiyangar was a retired Judge of Kurnaul, and at that time one of the most eminent Hindu adherents of Baba. The travellers here received the same warm hospitality which other devotees had accorded them. In the contemporary pages of *The Meher Message*, Hirsch was considered a follower of Meher Baba, and as the earlier of the two extant reports, is to be regarded as the more accurate source. Aiyengar was able to advise his guests as to suitable holy men of talent in the local area, and they accordingly visited the Ramakrishna Math, Rajgopal Swami, and Ramana Maharshi. But the major event in the eyes of Hirsch at that time was a function held at the Saidapet ashram on December 7th. I will narrate this in some detail.

Hirsch was arranging to form an extension of the Meher League upon his return to England. This League had been created by the Saidapet ashram, and was dedicated to sponsoring concepts of universal brotherhood. On the afternoon of December 7th, the members of this League were "at home" to the two Englishmen, which involved a large meeting held under the chairmanship of Sampath Aiyengar and which was the occasion for some very revealing addresses. At four p.m. an address was given at the Saidapet ashram in honour of the two English guests, from which I reproduce relevant extracts here as given in *The Meher Message* of 1931. The name Hirsch is given as Hurst, which was the preferred literary name of the man under discussion[177] at that time:

To Raphael Hurst Esq.,
Bhikkhu Prajnananda.

Dear Brothers,

We, the members of Meher League, approach you with feelings of fellowship, and offer our heart-felt welcome to you in our midst. We look upon this, your first visit to this place, as a unique event in the history of this *asramam* which was opened by our master . . .

We welcome you, brother Raphael Hurst, as the founder of the Meher League in England. Your sincere words, "Our hearts are with every one of you who are serving the master's cause (i.e. Baba's cause) in India. Brotherly greetings to every devotee," are ever ringing in our ears . . . We earnestly request you to convey our fraternal greetings to our comrades in the West. We pray that under the benign care and guidance of the master and with your co-operation, that influences for good may unceasingly flow from this *asramam* . . . May the master give you long life to accomplish his work.

Meher Asramam, We remain,
Saidapet, Yours fraternally,
Madras: India. Members of Meher League (India).
7th December 1930.

Nor was this all. Swami (Bhikkhu) Prajnananda then delivered a lecture on "Shri Meher Baba and his work." This ex-Major of the British army possessed something of an oratorical eloquence, and spoke of the depth of Baba's inner activity which the latter was silently engaged upon. Prajnananda said that his personal contact with Baba had convinced him that the world would eventually be bettered by Baba's influence, and that his present followers were fortunate to be connected with him. Prajnananda appealed to the audience to accomplish their part of the "work" with one-pointedness.

Not to be outdone, Raphael Hirsch, alias Paul Brunton, then lectured on the meaning of life. The *Meher Message* specifically states that he related a few of his "personal telepathic experiences" in connection with Baba. These were emphasized as contacts transcendent of normal communication. Further, Hirsch said that Baba was immersed in the highest state of God-consciousness every moment, and that he functioned in all the invisible worlds. Yet in his subsequent book, Hirsch gave a diametrically opposite impression of his views at this period.

The chairman Sampath Aiyengar then related some of his own experiences pertaining to Baba, and exhorted the audience to cleanse India of accretionary customs adopted in the name of the *sanatana dharma* (eternal religion).[178] This latter was in conformity with Baba's own emphases, to which Hirsch was very partial. The English journalist must have found it gratifying that this meeting was thought to be one of the best ever held at the Saidapet ashram. His "telepathic experiences" gave him an aura of secret knowledge.

About a week later Hirsch and Prajnananda left Madras for Calcutta. At some point he made a brief excursion from Madras to nearby Tiruvannamalai, a small town near to which was the ashram of Ramana Maharshi (d. 1950), who proved aloof from the journalistic questioning of the Londoner. Hirsch later wrote up this episode in his typically verbose style, calculated to give the maximal credit to his own receipt of blessings. It is obvious to the factual investigator that Ramana Maharshi did not loom large upon the visitor's horizons at that date.

Brunton's travel story is undated throughout. Many uninformed readers were under the impression that he spent a lengthy period investigating "secret India." In actual fact, his tour took only some six weeks to complete after leaving Madras. He wrote about the Madras phase as though it too were lengthy, but the reality was a fortnight at most.

At Calcutta he made a sensible visit to the aged Mahendranath Gupta (alias Mahasaya), who was one of the few surviving pupils of Ramakrishna (d. 1886). Otherwise, our tourist moved to places on the beaten track like Benares and Agra, meeting an assortment of sadhus and faqirs such as every traveller in the Hind was likely to see. These contacts were written up with the journalistic stylisms that made the name of Paul Brunton famous to many armchair readers in the West.

When the representative of the Meher League arrived at Nasik on February 1st 1931, he became an inmate of Baba's ashram at this place for five weeks. This sojourn was practically as long as the "tour" from Madras to Agra, and yet was allotted a brief chapter of only ten pages in *Secret India*. One can legitimately draw the conclusion that something was being concealed, as the facts of documentation attest. The real "secret" of Brunton's sojourn in India was locked up in the Nasik ashram, and left padlocked by journalistic preferences of retrospect.

Impartial historians will readily concede that the acute differences between Brunton's version of his trip to India and the earlier version written by Indians constitutes a reversal of the more calculating data. The generally assumed accuracy of Brunton's report is invalidated by the earlier extant evidence. Brunton's version of himself as a consistent critic of Meher Baba from the very start is not only manifestly untrue, but affords a graphic insight into the distortions caused by a thwarting of personal ambitions.

Brunton's explanation of why he spent such a lengthy period with Meher Baba at the Nasik ashram is not convincing. "It is with no keen desire that I return to him," says the author of *Secret India* in retrospect. "I do not believe that the Parsee messiah can keep the extraordinary promises of wonderful experiences which he has made me."[179] The facts indicate very much to the contrary of what Brunton later chose to believe, though whether Baba had actually made any such "promises" is very much in doubt. A man like Brunton did not spend over a month in an ashram for nothing; his journalistic time was evidently precious to him, and he was under an injunction not to take down any notes of Baba's words. Typically, Brunton ascribes to his actions the highest possible motive: he had made a "pledge" to spend a month with Baba, and this was not to be lightly broken. Further, adds our journalist with a flourish, he went to Nasik so "that he (Baba) may not accuse me of never having given him the chance to prove his alleged powers."[180] This is very misleading. Baba was not in the habit of extracting pledges to stay with him; rather, it was considered a privilege for anyone to stay at the ashram, permission for which was usually refused. Even more to the point, Baba consistently zero-rated stunts involving occult powers. This factual aspect of Meher Baba's life, as proven over a span of several decades, tends very much to throw Brunton's version into sharp relief.

There is little doubt from the overall body of facts on Brunton at this stage of his career that he was very preoccupied with "telepathic experiences" of Meher Baba and other extradimensional occurrences. His contacts with yogis and faqirs attest Brunton's fascination with paranormal phenomena, and he clearly believed that it was possible to gain "powers," known in India as *siddhis*, a customary yogic preoccupation. Brunton was quite ready to talk about his telepathic experiences in a way that caused devotees of Meher Baba to exalt him accordingly. It is worth observing here that Baba is known to have frequently expressed a low rating of persons disposed to seek "wonders" amongst the sadhu population of India, since the attendant overload of superstition and cultivation of *siddhis* were deemed by him as harmful to serious aspirants.

The expectation of miracles was evidently high on Baba's blacklist. There is no doubt that he disliked exponents of *siddhis*. There is some evidence that he adopted special tactics with certain persons who had expectations of the miraculous. Brunton fitted a specific category of "follower" – he wanted to be esteemed as a great disciple possessing telepathic abilities, and also wanted to slot in this feted discipleship with whatever else was happening of paranormal appeal. Since Brunton consigned the real facts to oblivion, and these can only be partially reconstructed from other sources, the present author proffers the following reconstruction based upon the source materials for the biography of Meher Baba:

Baba would probably have expressed surprise that Brunton wished to join him at his ashram and yet first undertake a lengthy expedition into sadhu milieux. If Meher Baba was anything of a psychologist (as the evidence does strongly indicate), then he would have perceived typical traits in Brunton of the "siddhis" mentality, i.e., a desire for occult powers and attributes of greatness. Since such people are in general unfit for discipleship, he would have done the next best thing possible: teach the candidate for honours a necessary lesson. When he had fixed the date of February 1st for the journalist's stay at Nasik, Baba had quite possibly appended various hints and suggestions (but not definite clauses) as to what might happen. He is quite likely to have said (or rather dictated) something like: "You will gain deep inner experiences *if* you become my disciple," but the subtleties of this approach would have been lost upon a person who assumed that discipleship was equivalent to a desire for powers and status.

As it transpired, the Western journalist later did his best to caricature the man whom he felt had snubbed him. The main target in *Secret India* is Meher Baba, despite the comparatively small amount of space devoted to him. It was convenient for Brunton's itinerary to mix ostentatious discipleship with tourism; he was certainly not the only person to desire this sort of juxtaposition.[181] He arrived at Nasik in anticipation of more occult thrills, particularly perhaps, since he had then grasped that many of India's holy men were indeed as mediocre as persons like Meher Baba indicated. He would have regarded the Nasik ashram as the climax of his itinerary, not as the damp squib he later wished his readers to think. Memory can play strange tricks in the light of aggravated emotions.

Very revealing of Brunton's attitude is his careful interposition at the beginning of his chapter on his Nasik sojourn. During his travels, he says, he had investigated "the few so-called miracles of healing which he (Baba) is alleged to have performed," and found these to be exaggerated. This should be understood as a symptom of Brunton's interest in Meher Baba, an interest which focussed upon miraculous elements. Baba himself never claimed healing powers; he considered these as of no consequence. In fact, Baba's zero-rating of such powers is one of the most impressive features of his biography, and compares markedly well with not a few other biographies in the mystical field. Some of his Indian devotees did choose to emphasize "miracles" in both the earlier and later years of his career, but the haphazard nature of the devotee mentality is not at issue with the present author, and at any rate blends well in its less discerning modes with Bruntonian proclivities.

On the next page of his diluted memoir, Brunton's sour penchant for vengeance makes itself felt in relation to the *mandali* – all "forty" of them, who are described as a retinue who "wander aimlessly about the place,"[182] i.e. the Nasik ashram. That was very unfair reporting, since whatever deficiencies may have been discernible in some of the *mandali*, aimlessness was not one of these. Every resident of the ashram had a full programme, or rota, of duties and instructions which had to be meticulously fulfilled; lazy persons were liable to very sharp rebukes in those years. Brunton himself was possibly given menial tasks which he found too lowly for his elect tastes.

Brunton's reminiscences of his conversations with Baba appear to have undergone pronounced chronological distortion, which tends to be underlined by the fact that he was not allowed to take notes of these meetings. His very first meeting with Baba at Nasik is presented as being unfavourable to his host owing to the visitor's superior logic. "It is not possible to argue rationally in such an atmosphere, so I let the matter drop,"[183] adds the dubious narration. While this may well have been Brunton's mood at the end of his Nasik sojourn, it is most unlikely to be an accurate insight into his thinking at the commencement of that sojourn. The budding representative of Meher League, the recipient of awesome telepathic communications, had as yet no incentive to feel rationally piqued. He was much too intent upon acquiring the powers which he believed were in the offing from the man who functioned "in all the invisible worlds" as Brunton had declared at Saidapet ashram.

Brunton saw Baba for an unspecified length of time every day. Baba answered "many questions" of the visitor, but these solutions are not vouchsafed to the reader. Brunton's main refrain is that Baba made no reference to the "strange promises" given at Meherabad. There was evidently no mention of any inner experiences which the visitor might expect. There was nothing miraculous in Baba's answers, no talk of powers. One might conclude that Baba's unrecorded answers provided the solution to Brunton's obsession with the sensational, but not all solutions are directly acceptable to those requiring the answers to pet dilemmas.

Brunton says that he formulated a "constant rain of questions" which he put to both Baba and the *mandali*. Brunton was evidently not as meditative then as he later claimed to be. In order to quieten him down, Baba loaned him lengthy diaries written by two of the *mandali*, totalling "nearly two thousand pages of loosely written manuscript." The date he was given these diaries is not stated, as with all the other dates missing from *Secret India*. It may have been at the same juncture that Baba limited his daily meetings with the visitor to only a few minutes. "I wait for the wonderful experiences he has promised me, though I never expect them to arrive,"[184] writes Brunton in a vein of contradiction. Baba no longer seemed interested in him, was no longer amenable to his questions. This amounted to a rebuff in the mind of Brunton. The "cold" treatment invariably causes upheavals in individuals who like the limelight. The disciple of telepathic prowess was now dwarfed into a mere tiresome visitor who could not stop asking questions.

The deflation caused Brunton to turn against his mentor with a distinctive venom. This did not happen overtly all at once. In early March 1931 the journalist prepared to leave. He gives the impression that he himself set the date of departure, though this is questionable. But one may take it as factual that Brunton brought up the matter of the missing "experiences." According to Brunton, Baba then calmly postponed the date of the supposed marvels to a couple of months in the future, and then dismissed the matter. But another source supplies a detail that gives a more pronounced twist to Brunton's tactics. Charles Purdom met Brunton a few years later, and the latter affirmed that he had no doubt Baba was false, since he (Brunton) had asked Baba to perform a miracle but Baba could not do so.[185] The non-gratification of childish desires often results in a childish reaction.

Though Brunton does once refer to his "foolish attempt to take this man (Baba) at his word,"[186] the context of foolishness on the author's part is heavily glossed to the point of dishonesty. To psychologists, it is quite evident that Brunton had set much store on the possibility of miracles, and that he was acutely piqued when these were not forthcoming. Two major features of his psychology after that time were (a) to cover up the fact that he had been an admirer of Meher Baba to a pronounced degree (b) to give a much lower rating to miraculous elements and instead to assume a critical stance, though not invariably. In other words, it is possible to discern that Brunton learnt something he needed to know, and which he could not have learnt by mere words (which were freely available to him), but only by a process of shock that cut at his ego.

Brunton departed from the Nasik ashram on March 8th, 1931.[187] He went to Bombay, intending to return to England that same month. In the metropolis he felt depleted and ill, on the edge of a nervous breakdown as he informs his readers. His search after paranormal demonstrations had not brought him fulfilment. Though he does not give the due context, it is evident that the deflation he had experienced at Nasik had made its mark, and was not by any means as casual as the more superficial readers might have thought.

Just before his ship sailed, he received a letter from a follower of Ramana Maharshi, suggesting that he revisit the latter's ashram. Brunton did not want to return to England bereft of consolation, and so he made the journey across the peninsula to Tiruvannamalai. His harrowed frame of mind seems to have (initially at least) created in him a more appropriate attitude. His memory of Maharshi is reported in terms of: "He had seemed so aloof, so remote from a European mentality, and so indifferent whether I became his pupil or not."[188] Upon meeting Ramana Maharshi the second time, the visitor asked to become his disciple, but the sage evaded the question and told him to "find the master within you." Brunton adds, "I am slightly conscious of an initial rebuff,"[189] but this time was sufficiently sensitive to the requirements of the occasion not to leave with a display of wounded pride.

Brunton seems to have assumed that he became a disciple of Ramana Maharshi, though discipleship is a glib topic in general that is confused with other categories of admirer. Our journalist spent a few weeks at Maharshi's ashram at the foot of Arunachala Hill. He saw the sage every day, though in rather different circumstances to those pertaining to Meher Baba's ashram. The Maharshi spent his time in a hall where visitors and residents were able to come and go at most times of the day; in contrast, Meher Baba was inaccessible for much of the day. But a similar disposition was evoked in Brunton: an admiration for the teacher, and the desire to be in close communication with him. For instance, Brunton writes of one occasion spent in Ramana Maharshi's company: "I am perfectly aware that the sublime realization which has suddenly fallen upon me is nothing else than a spreading ripple of telepathic radiation."[190] Note the superlatives; there was nothing ordinary for Paul Brunton. The total evidence attests that this had also been his attitude with Meher Baba. What he did was to switch the same focus to Maharshi, and in the process, turn vindictively upon his earlier mentor who had discomforted him. The sequence of events is no reflection upon either of the teachers, neither of whom were backbiting gossipers, only upon the Western seeker of miracles, knowledge, and plaudits.

Brunton's new-found psychological stabilization unfortunately did not decrease his tendency to exalt his personal achievements. A rather glaring example of this tendency is afforded by the reported episode of a meditation of his which lasted for nearly two hours in the audience-hall of the Maharshi. Many other people have had similar meditations in which they feel uplifted, but Brunton's encounter with "starry (*sic*) truths" is transposed into several pages of prolix and pretentious revelation which are subsumed under the chapter-title of "Tablets of Forgotten Truth." Brunton did indeed forget some of his own sentiments. "He who has once seen his real self will never again hate another,"[191] he says in one revelation, and it is therefore the more incongruous that his vindictiveness is clearly discernible in his distorted account of Meher Baba.

When he returned to England in the spring of 1931, Paul Brunton had spent five months or less in India. He resumed his London activities as a journalist, but soon became a more renowned entity owing to his purported illuminations. The Cockney sage wrote an account of his Indian travels which quickly became a popular seller and enabled him to give talks and lectures before admiring audiences of the "esoteric" type. He was widely regarded as an authority on Yoga. The reading public believed every word he wrote. *A*

Search in Secret India and his subsequent books became bestsellers in a dozen languages. Typical of the publicity for *Secret India* was the review which stated: "He (Brunton) visits the Fakirs and Yogis and Sages, beholds their extraordinary feats, wins their confidence, learns many closely guarded secrets, writes down their uttered wisdom and lives in their secluded hermitages and jungle retreats." The vast majority of his readers had no idea how short a time this achievement took.

Some literary critics must have winced at Brunton's rhetorical flourishes even at the time of first publication. *Secret India* begins with a chapter entitled "Wherein I Bow to the Reader." Such humility doubtless enchanted those not intelligent enough to realize that the author's insistence upon his critical acumen was no guarantee of authenticity or insight. In that chapter Brunton criticizes the reports of Hindu writers as being unreliable, viewing these as inferior to his own. Typical of his self-congratulatory style is the attendant statement: "I thanked Heaven for such scientific training as the West has given me and for the commonsense attitude which journalistic experience had instilled in me."[192] It should now be added that journalists were not exempt from the patronizing attitude of the British Empire, and furthermore, lacked the accuracy of scholars and seasoned explorers which the Empire sometimes produced.

In *Secret India* were included two chapters on Meher Baba entitled "I Meet a Messiah" and "At the Parsee Messiah's Headquarters," treating of the author's sojourns at Meherabad and Nasik respectively. In some respects, the first of these two chapters is even more misleading than the second, and was written in a very lethal spirit of revenge. The characterization as a "Parsee Messiah" was an attempt to depict Baba as a self-laudatory fraud who was always wrong, and whose disposition differed strongly from that of Ramana Maharshi. There were actually some notable similarities between the latter two; like Baba, the Maharshi was taciturn, and he never sanctioned "hit back" tactics like those of Brunton. Though Ramana Maharshi was very much more accessible in his audience-hall than Meher Baba, to a certain extent he compensated for this by sometimes giving an impression of aloofness. He must have been able to see though a self-glorifying tourist like Raphael Hurst.

Brunton's effacement of his earlier name was not his only sense of security against little known facts committed to paper. He must have known of the details concerning him in a certain Indian periodical, but these he would doubtless have dismissed as inferior native accounts. This tactic would have been rendered easier in his mind by the fact that K.J Dastur, editor of *The Meher Message*, had himself defected from Baba only a few months after Brunton. Further, Meredith Starr, another English occultist, subsequently defected in 1932, which would have emboldened a defector of a similar type but with more public fame. As it transpired, Brunton escaped an attack from Meher Baba's following owing to Baba's typical attitude of indifference to criticism and the latter's uncommon assertion that even calumnies were serving the purposes of his work. Pens like those of Charles Purdom were accordingly restrained, though history suffered owing to this charity.[193]

The chapter entitled "I Meet a Messiah"[194] is Brunton's extremely calculated version of the three days he spent with Meher Baba in late November 1930 at Meherabad ashram. With the exception of a few paragraphs, none of the section relating to Baba can be taken as an accurate report. The most well known error is the author's description of Baba's facial features; Baba's forehead is stated to be "so low as to appear less than average height, and it is so receding as to make me wonder." Brunton adds suggestively: "Does a man's forehead indicate his powers of thought?" If so, then Meher Baba was a more sophisticated thinker than Paul Brunton. The copious photographic documentation on Meher Baba proves indisputably a high forehead and an unusually large cranium for his height and build. One might charitably conclude that Brunton's occular powers were deficient. This observation necessarily extends to the journalist's characterization of Baba's white robe as looking "ludicrously like an old-fashioned English nightshirt." This comparison of apparel is a much less serious reflection, but strangely indicative of the depreciation reserved even for small details relating to the stigmatized entity. (Ramana Maharshi wore a loincloth).

One point upon which Brunton was an honest reporter is the detail that Baba asked him not to take notes while in his presence, and hence all statements were recalled from memory. This at least explains some of the anomalies, though Brunton was much less honest in concealing the context of his visit to Meherabad. *Secret India* gives the impression that the critical questioner knew next to nothing about Baba, though he had arrived as a result of his expressed desires to be in rapport with Baba. Brunton wanted to give the impression that he was an outsider, and continually incredulous of all he was told. His version of the conversations, replete with the author's interposed comments and insinuations, was designed to portray Baba as a sort of imbecile or maniac. The reality of the situation was that Brunton believed himself to be in telepathic affinity with Baba and was ready to be a representative in England of the Meher League arranged by the Saidapet ashram at Madras. Baba's reference to such interests is worded by Brunton with typical truncation. Baba is represented as urging a reluctant and totally uncommitted critic to "Go to the West as my representative!"[195] Brunton preferred such deviousness because the truth would have caused complications in his account of the critical and rational journalist who was destined to become an illuminated disciple of Ramana Maharshi after negotiating false prophets. In order to explain his later stay at Nasik, Brunton had to write: "I decide to investigate the whole thing with an open mind,"[196] which was the most minimal statement possible of the actual situation.

It would look petty to pick out every error in Brunton's chapters on the "Messiah." Yet there are so many errors that at least a few of them require clarification. For instance, Brunton gives the impression that he could wander in and out of Baba's ashram just when he wanted to, a literary device emphasizing his (Brunton's) supposed aloofness. While it is true that Brunton wished to combine a tour of India with the benefits accruing from Meher Baba, the leisurely nature of arrangements ends on this point. Unlike the ashram of Ramana Maharshi, the ashram of Meher Baba was a "closed" ashram, i.e., visitors could not go there unless specifically invited. It was not easy to stay there even for a few days on these select terms, let alone weeks. Neither the Meherabad or Nasik ashrams were open to the public. A very different situation existed at Ramanashram, where the Maharshi allowed all-comers to visit him and left the administration of the place to an ashram management of brahmins. Despite the Maharshi's aloof *jnani* features of temperament, he was very easy-going with visitors. Despite Meher Baba's amiable temperament, he was extremely firm in his policies of ashram discipline; he himself was in charge of all the running arrangements, and there was no separate management. He was in general exacting to the last detail. The situation was quite unlike that prevailing in many ashrams throughout India, where management by a caste hierarchy was a traditional feature.

Brunton's description of Baba's method of dictating words on the alphabet board was in terms of "this dumb pantomime manner." Brunton was evidently a very vocal type, and may have assumed he was at liberty to lavishly reword the dumb statements. Not all of the sentence structure reported by the journalist fits the alphabet board idiom; though a number of the phrases used are probably approximately correct, others present characteristics of embellishment. Brunton dwells markedly on alleged statements of Baba concerning his mission as the messiah. While Meher Baba did indeed frequently make extravagent-sounding gnostic statements, these require to be accurately reported and in due context. If Baba really made statements to Brunton like: "If I play the role of a messiah it will be because world conditions require it,"[197] then it would be a very rare instance of his use of the word "messiah." Meher Baba was not in the habit of referring to himself as a "prophet" or "messiah," though these terms frequently occur in Brunton's report. He was known (though very rarely at this period) to employ the term *avatar*, but this term is not used by Brunton. Other terms and phrases (missing in *Secret India*) were used by Baba in reference to rare functions, but all such references were brief, and usually allusive and difficult to pin down in terms of definite meanings. Such references were not made in the systematized form appearing in *Secret India*. Such references were nearly always made in reply to questions. Devotees interpreted these references differently.

Other sources give a more accurate idea of Baba's "messiah" statements at that time. Diary notes and records of questions and answers (on-the-spot reports, that is) reveal a markedly sporadic and fragmentary emphasis in this type of statement. In 1932 (in England) he told another London reporter that: "Christ, Buddha, Krishna . . . these are names for states of consciousness."[198] Ramju Abdulla reported the question: "Does Shri Meher Baba claim to be the Avatar of the new dispensation?" The reply to this is given as: "Such a claim would have no value until it were substantiated, and once it were substantiated, there would be no need of claims."[199]

A more pointed statement of Baba that comes from this early period is: "I never wish to be called Redeemer, Saviour, Divine Majesty. The devotees, through their love, faith, and enthusiasm, give me such titles."[200] Another, and much more common, title awarded him was Sadguru, though the author of *Secret India* inaccurately affirms that Baba called himself by this Hindu title.

It is worth noting that Baba was very oblique in communicating with journalists. He carefully avoided giving newspaper representatives any definite statement as to his "spiritual identity." He would refer to the *avatar* concept impersonally, and not in relation to himself. These tactics were long-established, and as a consequence the majority of his following were uncertain of his precise definition of himself until as late as the mid-1950's. Even then, his more personal statements on the *avatar* theme require careful evaluation such as is not always given them. His predominant public audience was Hindu.

One has to view with due suspicion Brunton's version of Baba's words on the subject of "once I publicly announce myself as a messiah." Brunton has the words: "I shall openly work miracles in proof of my mission . . . restoring sight to the blind, healing the sick, maimed and crippled, yes, even raising the dead – these things will be child's play to me!"[201] Through a comparison with other contemporary reported statements of a more reliable nature, it is evident that the wrong sense has been given in *Secret India* to such ingredients of "dumb pantomime." Ramju Abdulla records that Baba stated at this time: "The ability to perform miracles does not necessarily imply high spirituality. Anyone who has attained perfection and enjoys the Christ-consciousness, can perform miracles. Healing the sick, giving sight to the blind, and even raising the dead is child's play to such a one." There was here the important corollary that persons on the subtle planes could perform these miracles.[202] Hence it was beneath the dignity of more advanced entities to dabble in such displays of subtle energy. This is clearly the sense of other statements also that were recorded at this period.[203]

Revealing enough is Brunton's admission of interest in the "marvellous things" attributed to Baba by one of the Hindu *mandali*. When the journalist pressed for details of these "reputed marvels" in Baba's presence, the latter parried by telling him to consult Vishnu Deorukhkar (the interpreter) on another occasion.[204] This rings true, since Baba allowed people to make what they liked of various events while himself shrugging them off as secondary phenomena non-relevant to discussion. Baba's own angle was "experiences," not miracles, though subtleties were apt to be lost upon those who desired powers and telepathic status.

Brunton's misinterpretation can in part be attributed to a lack of assimilation of basic emphases he gleaned from Baba. The latter did not deny the paranormal powers in which Brunton was so interested, but referred to them as "child's play" which was more suited to persons traversing the subtle planes of the inner path. Brunton may have assumed that this meant he himself could become a miracle-worker on the subtle planes, while yet being a follower of the "messiah," who could bestow upon him such powers. This would be quite consistent with other details, and perhaps more reliable than the journalistic report of the last interview at Meherabad, in which Brunton has it that Baba predicted that he (Brunton) would perform miracles in the West. "I will help you to obtain advanced powers," are the words attributed to Baba, though on the very next page Baba is reported to have communicated: "I will give you wonderful spiritual experiences." [205] This confusing matter is clearly at the root of Brunton's subsequent disgruntlement. The misunderstandings of would-be disciples are not an uncommon occurrence, though the literary venom surfacing from the depths of *Secret India* is much less frequent. Brunton affords an interesting example of an admirer turned critic of a virulent type. He ran into deep water with the "work" statements of Meher Baba, the most complex sector of the latter's repertory and one that was so variously interpreted. Baba seems to have used many of these statements as psychological probes; reactions to matters of this nature are often far more revealing than reactions to systematic teachings.

The reader will perhaps already have grasped that Brunton desired his "experiences" in the space of only a few weeks, with the least amount of effort and with as much personal attention and adulation as he could meanwhile acquire. His constant questions were somehow to be regarded as a priority. There are a surprisingly large number of people like him who are interested in "spiritual" matters. When thwarted, they can prove distinctly underhand, and numerous other descriptions would also fit them. This is not to say that they do not learn anything in the process, but such fruits are rarely attributed to their rightful source.

Brunton's desire to present Meher Baba in the worst possible light is also reflected in his brief account of the latter's life. There are some factual inaccuracies such as the statement that Baba's father Sheriar concluded that his son had been overstudying at the time of the "realization" triggered by Hazrat Babajan. It was actually Baba's mother Shirin who arrived at such conclusions; Meher Baba himself is on record as saying that his father understood his condition at that time. Brunton also depicts the Meherabad colony phase as being concurrent with the Prem Ashram, which is a chronological mistake, though he was more concerned to hoot at the report of an "enthusiastic devotee" that Baba had cured five lepers during the colony phase. While it is easy to understand criticisms of devotee stories, it is much less easy to understand why the Prem Ashram received such derogatory treatment. This is described as a "curious educational institution" which involved "religious hysteria." Yet in the same breath he affirms that there was nothing unusual about this institution, since "there are plenty of schools in England where pupils of different creeds foregather in a natural spontaneous manner." It is quite obvious that a pointed bias is at work here, in which the author was singularly determined not to credit any of Meher Baba's activities. Brunton's invocation of colonial standards compares poorly with the account of Ramju Abdulla, then available in published form, and which serves to give the lie to such supercilious coverage.[206]

These and other distortions are carried over into the description of events personally witnessed by Brunton at Meherabad. He was a spectator at a devotional *arati* ceremony in which Baba made himself available to the Hindu inhabitants of the nearby Arangaon village. The *arati* hymn was sung in Marathi, and was followed by *darshan*, in which devotees prostrated at Baba's feet. Brunton states that this ceremony was "repeated every evening wherever Meher may be at the time."[207] This is typically inaccurate. *Arati* and *darshan* were standard features of Hindu devotionalism; Baba drastically curtailed *darshan* procedures at his ashrams, though he made special concessions to the low-caste and outcaste Arangaon villagers. The Hindu *mandali* would enthusiastically join in these concessions, and often the Parsis, but Muslims were permitted to remain aloof. Baba did often permit the *arati* ceremony at Nasik from 1930, though it was non-operative while he was on tour, and he had not always allowed it even at Meherabad. In subsequent years, the *arati* ceremony became increasingly rare at all his ashrams, since he clearly evidenced that he only bore it on sufferance.

Brunton was trying to insinuate that in such features of his routine, Baba was permitting an unwarranted adulatory focus. He conveniently neglected to inform his readers that Ramana Maharshi also allowed *darshan* prostration, and to a much greater extent than the Parsi guru.[208]

Our journalist really ought to have presented a more accurate version of Baba's biography, since during his stay at the Nasik ashram, he was given the lengthy diaries of Ramju Abdulla and Behli J. Irani to peruse. Though these are characteristically described in *Secret India* as "secret diaries," nobody of consequence would have given secret documents to a man like Brunton. He did his best to denigrate the content of the "nearly two thousand" relevant pages in less than two pages of demeaning commentary. One of these diaries has since been published in a generally available form,[209] and readers are therefore better able to judge what was so hastily dismissed. Brunton retained some vestige of fair representation in a sentence which commenced in a condescending tone and ended with: "I candidly confess to myself that I have read lofty and soul-elevating discourses in them (the diaries), and that Meher Baba possesses religious genius."[210]

It is relevant to mention here the incident reported in these diaries that was singled out by Brunton as the most serious indictment of Baba that was contained in their pages. Since I have personally known Christian critics to make much of this incident, it seems particularly appropriate to dwell upon its extensions. We are told that Baba "struck one of his most intimate disciples a stinging blow on the ears during a train journey to Muttra, a blow so severe that the unfortunate follower had to seek medical attention."[211]Brunton carps at Baba's "gospel of divine love," and with typical brevity, distorts Baba's interpretation of the event in question. What readers ought to know, amongst other things, is that the victim of this blow on the ears was a sturdy fellow much bigger than Baba, who was slight in build and had slender hands. Most of the early *mandali* who accompanied Baba on his travels in the early 1920's (when this episode occurred) were stronger than average, and specially selected for their physical stamina. Several of the men concerned had known Upasni Maharaj, and were immune to possibilities of rough treatment, which insofar as Meher Baba was concerned, were very minimal. Baba never preached a "gospel of divine love," but a balanced teaching which stressed factors not always liked or preferred by religionists. There was a much stronger display of retribution on one occasion at the Manzil-e-Meem when Baba knocked one of his pupils down the stairs, but with no injuries in accompaniment. The man concerned was a heavyweight wrestler and as strong as an ox or very nearly so; he could have flattened Baba with a single blow if he had wished. Brunton may or may not have known (though he shows himself very ignorant of ethnographic details) that Indian Muslims in particular have often gone out of their way to invite the wrath of a saintly entity, believing this to be a sign of divine favour. The idea of saintly violence is not strange in India. As it transpired, Meher Baba gave a memorable display of "turning the other cheek" in relation to Paul Brunton's verbal scourge, which is more than one can say for third-rate journalism.

As a parting stab, the author of *Secret India* presents his explanation of what happened to Meher Baba when he met Hazrat Babajan during his college days. The accuracy of this explanation might best be illustrated by Brunton's reference to Baba's "small pointed chin" which he somehow discerned as being an eloquent testimony to irresoluteness. This further reflection upon bone structure is again totally invalidated by the extensive photographic evidence to the contrary. The chin of Meher Baba was amply proportioned and rounded, with no trace of pointedness; Brunton's reflection is the more suspicious owing to the fact that Baba had no beard at the time of the former's visits. Serious readers are likely to be amused at the attempt to interpret Baba's gentleness as a consequence of his frail physique, even though the subject has been castigated a few pages earlier for his violence. The only truth in these reflections would appear to be Brunton's attendant admission that at Meherabad "I was impressed by the peace and gentleness of his attitude." This had to be lived down in journalistic annals, and at some cost to history. The hapless Ramju Abdulla (there was only one Abdulla amongst the *mandali*) is quoted as saying he was a friend of Baba in the latter's youth, and never found him interested in religion or philosophy prior to his "sudden departure into spiritual matters." Since Ramju did not meet Baba until 1921, this testimony is impossible, though it may have been confused with a potted version of Dr. Ghani's reminiscences that was markedly incomplete in relation to the total data available. The point which Brunton awkwardly tries to make is that Babajan (to whom he conceded authenticity) imparted to Merwan Irani an experience for which he was totally unprepared, and which threw him "into a condition of semi-idiocy" and subsequent paranoia. This would of course make Babajan wildly inaccurate in her calculations, but Brunton chose not to dwell on this point. Brunton shows not the slightest awareness of the (often very abrupt) states encountered in Sufi lore, a lack entirely compatible with the drawing-room appetite for the Orient that was common amongst his readers. Brunton thought in terms of a stilted version of Yoga which involved very little Sanskrit, and compares Baba with those "men who want the exalted consciousness which Yoga promises its votaries, but are unwilling to pay the price in training and discipline which it demands." This is very ironic in view of the writer's unwillingness to stay in one place of discipline for more than a few weeks prior to becoming an assumed and presumed authority on Yoga.

Attention might instructively be drawn to the missing context of Brunton's allegation of "theatrical methods" used by Baba, methods which are stated to have contradicted "the spiritual etiquette of thousands of centuries." Brunton seems here to be laying claim to a long memory, though the accusation of theatre was based upon the publicity given to Baba's second visit to the West in 1932, which is referred to in terms of flashing "like a meteorite across the Western sky."[212] This publicity had been mounted by Baba's Western devotees, notably the Kimco women, without any instructions from him, and was accordingly never repeated, since he took the opportunity to drive home necessary lessons to the publicizers. If Brunton knew anything of the details, he did not disclose them, and instead chose to state: "Moreover, like a meteorite, he (Baba) will fall ingloriously to earth." The only justification for this insistence is the fact that press coverage ceased after the second visit to the

West, which is an unconvincing reflection upon the importance of the subject.

Brunton's own subsequent and rather well publicized career is relevant for a brief survey here. As might be expected, *Secret India* had a sequel. Two years later appeared *A Search in Secret Egypt*, which was similarly favoured by the reading public, though literary critics were more reserved. The publishing blurb appropriately described this sequel as "an account of sensational experiences and strange travels under the burning sun of the land of the Nile." In case the uninformed reader might imagine that this was some kind of research into contemporary dervishism as a complement to Yogic mysteries, it is incumbent to describe the contents in terms of the more popular "Western esoteric" field of interest. One press reviewer for *The Queen* wrote: "Important both to the layman and the expert (*sic*) are Mr. Brunton's researches into the meaning of the Sphinx and the numerous temples which abound in Egypt. His exposition, too, on the connecting link between the Atlantean and Egyptian civilizations is fascinating in the extreme, so that his pleasantly written and beautifully illustrated volume contains something for every taste." Yoga was apparently not sufficiently popular with Western audiences at that time.

Brunton's new recourse of hearing the saga of Atlantis from ethereal presences inside the Great Pyramid must have stretched the credulity of at least some of those readers otherwise addicted to old wive's tales of the occultist media. He describes how he spent a night inside the edifice at Gizeh which has become one of the major pitfalls for fabulators. "The great space of the King's Chamber," writes Brunton with a due superlative, "became for me – who had investigated deeply into the psychic, into the mysteries of the occult, into the sorceries and wizardries of the Orient – peopled with unseen beings, with spirits who guarded this age-old building." Nay more, he "tuned-in" by a "method of interiorized attention" which he had learnt long before, and became aware that hostile forces had invaded the chamber, etc. A nameless dread, as he describes it, flickered into his heart; malevolent countenances suddenly appeared quite close to his face. A dark apparition advanced, gazing at him with a fixed and sinister stare. Age-old spirits crept out of the neighbouring necropolis. A circle of antagonistic spirits surrounded our intrepid investigator. Monstrous elemental creations gathered around, afflicting him with unimaginable repulsion. "In a few minutes I lived through something which will leave a remembered record behind for all (*sic*) time." Brunton can only with difficulty be described as a modest reporter. Our critical enquirer into Indian secrets now found himself face to face with the High Priests of an ancient Egyptian cult; these were tall figures in white robes, and with sandalled feet and wise aspect. Light glimmered all around these High Priests in a most uncanny manner. They spoke to him quite dramatically, and in a rather quaint form of English, e.g., "Why dost thou come to this place?" The author writes that he then saw, as in a far-off vision, a great city with a maze of streets, etc.[213] Anyone who really thinks that Brunton was a rationalist reporter, impartial and non-gullible, is welcome to the rest of this flight of fancy. It doubtless had his fans on the edge of their armchairs. If Meher Baba was theatrical, then he was less talented in this respect than Paul Brunton. Meher Baba did not always give his audience what they wanted; Brunton did, with due reward.

Very soon afterwards appeared *A Hermit in the Himalayas*, which Brunton described in the dedication as being the "Journal of a Lonely Exile." This might have evoked pangs of sympathetic anguish from his more devoted readers. The mysterious mountains of the main title have elsewhere been credited as harbouring immortal yogis and miraculous Babajis who jump ravines and valleys with the greatest of ease, and one imagines that Brunton must have been in good company, wherever he was. A foreword stated to have been written by Prince Mussooree Shum Shere Jung Bahadur Rana, says: "This new book, being but a journal, is to me more interesting than a studiously composed work." It could also have been very easy to compose. The same writer of the foreword reports that the author of the journal had found his pages to read in a "horribly egotistical" vein, to the extent that he "felt inclined to consign them to burial under the mountains where they were written." This dramatic Bruntonian flourish was evidently intended as a guard against the increasing accusations from more critical readers. The writer of the foreword adds: "I assured him (Brunton) that egotism is an essential part of every memoir."[214] One might at least deem this an apt postscript to *Secret India* and *Secret Egypt*. Even more to the point perhaps, the foreword to the Himalayan revelations lamented reactions to *Secret Egypt*, since some critics had deemed the Great Pyramid "spirit experience" to be a mere journalistic stunt.

Books flowed rapidly from Brunton's pen and achieved an astonishing number of reprints. By the 1950's, one of his early books had gained its twenty-fifth impression. This was *The Secret Path*, the most popular seller of all in the trio of Secrets published in the mid-1930's. It can perhaps best be described as one of the dubious works in the overtly clandestine tradition of spinning a few yarns out of last year's old socks. The problem is not so much that Brunton divulged too much of the mysteries, but rather that he divulged too little. There is the typical esoteric patter incorporating *Gnothi Seauton* and the enigmatic statues on Easter Island. This manual opens with the promise that a high-powered Yogic technique will be revealed that will prove virtually indispensable for enlightenment. After ambling through numerous cliches, he discloses towards the end an elementary breathing exercise that any passenger might have heard about at Bombay docks.[215] Yet the carrot of secretiveness did not fail to gain such praise as that expressed by a reviewer of *Secret Egypt* in the *Daily Sketch*: "Paul Brunton, who knows more about Yoga than any living Englishman . . ." Is it that Great Britain had simply not bothered to learn anything about its colonial properties?

It is evident that some reactions to the propagation of secrets led Brunton to seek a more respectable niche amongst British writers. Subsequent books of his appeared with his new credentials as a Ph.D. in glowing prominence. The journalist now became Dr. Paul Brunton, though some of the critics were inclined to a conclusion equivalent to the proverb: "leopards do not change their spots." To do Brunton credit, it was an unusual tactic for an occultist author to employ, and indicates a very strong desire to affirm his equality amongst the literati. But a new problem was that his admirers now considered him to be beyond criticism, since there was (and still is) a naive belief that such credentials somehow confer an impeccability of expression.

Brunton's new-found transcendence seems reflected in the title of an opus which appeared in 1941, carrying the alluring title of *The Hidden Teaching Beyond Yoga*. True, he was making no secret of it, but one feels that Western esotericism was perhaps a shade too eager to keep ahead of rivals. The divulging of this innovative theme reached suitably dizzy heights at its end with a meditation "amid the vast deserted ruins" of ancient Angkor, which included the reflection that was it not wonderful that the immemorial wisdom had been extricated from the "burial-urn of the Past," and "moulded in an ultra-modern form to suit both our time and need." Rather pointedly perhaps, Brunton adds in relation to this wisdom that "its authenticity or truth may not be plainly recognizable to its present day Indian inheritors." Was even the Maharshi getting left behind ? Be that as it may, Dr. Brunton finished this eulogy to his own genius by bending in homage before the Himalayan intelligence of those sages who had kept truth alive since untraceable antiquity.[216] But some think that if Brunton had really bent in homage, it would have broken his back.

Two years later appeared a declared sequel, *The Wisdom of the Overself*, described on the dustjacket of reprints as: "The Magnum Opus of this Great Writer on Esoteric Wisdom." It was set in a small print unusual for popular books, and the prefatory chapter evidences Dr. Brunton's acknowledgment of "hasty criticisms" of the companion volume. Critics had clearly thought that the hidden teaching was in rather a low profile, but Brunton counters by saying that he had hidden it particularly deeply in the book in question. The sequel would now make it more clear. The precedent had "cleared a path for the still subtler revelations of the present volume," he added with due modesty. Dr. Brunton did not lag behind in the sequel, since the two volumes under discussion were described as the presentation of a teaching "which, in such explicit fullness, is for the first time written down in a Western language." This claim appears to be based upon Dr. Brunton's textual research. "I went to great pains," he says, "to explore the most recondite sources in quest of the material which has partly gone into the making of this book." He refers only very broadly to Sanskrit texts and their translations into Tokhari, Chinese, and Tibetan, and adds: "It would have been more self-flattering to parade the breadth of my learning by peppering both volumes with a thousand Sanskrit, Tibetan and Chinese quotations, names or words." The fact is that neither volume is so peppered; Brunton's magnum opus is unannotated, a characteristic of his works. Readers had to take on faith his assertion that: "Hundreds of texts were examined in the effort to trace and collate basic ideas." Dr. Brunton's obscure investigations into Buddhist philosophy and mysticism seem as transcendent as his conclusions concerning Yoga. It is evident from his style of discourse that he was impatient with the contradictions of textual traditions, and that he preferred the role "of disentangling myself from all authority whatsoever." This can of course have its advantages, but much will depend upon what the disentanglement involves.

Revealing is Dr. Brunton's statement in his magnum opus that "today I walk in utter independence of thought and, like Emerson, 'without school or master.'" No longer were the praises of Arunachala sung. Dr. Brunton did state in the same preface that "any higher rank than that of a student among students is hereby disclaimed," though it is quite obvious that he considered himself a student of singular importance. More dramatically, and in his earlier journalistic style, he interposes: "I know also unearthly visitations and heavenly communions and something that brooks no denial bids me leave a record before I pass from this earth."[217] As it transpired, Dr. Brunton had still plenty of time in which to express his "still subtler revelations," and he was certainly not denied a wide readership despite the smaller print and more philosophical stylisms of delivery. The two declaredly unique volumes gained nine and eight reprints respectively by the mid-1950's.

Readers might care to compare the two arcane rarities abovementioned with the *Discourses* of Meher Baba that achieved contemporary publication in the Deshmukh edition. There are more pages in Dr. Brunton's two books, though there is less metaphor and superlative in Meher Baba, even with Dr. Deshmukh's inflation of the text. In the *Discourses* there is a complete absence of personal references, though the subject matter is as broad-ranging as that of the English writer. The Iranian makes no claim of having read a single text, but is actually much broader in his philosophical and mystical terminology drawn from different Eastern traditions and employed in an original manner.

Dr. Brunton's later career continued to be successful. He had an apartment in New York and made frequent visits abroad, where he was also in much demand for his wisdom. It was even said that Rishikesh had come to New York, but if so, it should be remembered that the Indian sanctuary for holy men had changed drastically after the Second World War into a neon-light boulevard by comparison with earlier decades. Much of Brunton's subsequent eminence did not actually gain exposure in books, since he now relied upon reprints rather than newly written works. The "esoteric" grapevine was sufficient outlet for his talents. He claimed that during yogic trances he had entered the company of angelic figures who were concerned with the spiritual welfare of the mass of humanity, angelic beings who had come from another planet. It was about 1960 that Dr. Brunton became much more forward in respect of his achievements, announcing himself as an example of one who had finished the spiritual path. While his reprinted books continued to bear the name of Dr. Paul Brunton, he himself employed the new name of JR, which was an abbreviation for Jupiter Rex, an appellation which he said had been bestowed upon him by higher powers. This name had its historical precedent in the first of the Caesars, whose supporters conferred upon him this laudatory identity.

As Dr. Brunton's secretary later described, the Western adept would stipulate his requirements for (very brief) seclusion, the purpose of which was to attend to "his personal assignment which, he would say, involved the fate of millions."[218] Paul Brunton, alias Jupiter Rex, had achieved a deification whereby he could intervene in mass karma.

The concept of a "seclusion" for purposes of world amelioration has been copied by the more recent Western breed of guru associated with California. The origin of this concept is quite clearly certain statements and activities of Meher Baba. There are some very pronounced differences in the application of such concepts which are worthy of study. For instance, Meher Baba never attributed his new name to any otherworldly source, but only to one of his early followers, which is a historical fact.

The egocentrism of Paul Brunton is discernible in embryo in the pages of *Secret India.* His attack upon Meher Baba can be interpreted as a strangely accurate self-portrait, in consonance with psychological tendencies that are still being variously interpreted by professional psychologists. As Brunton himself wrote in his loaded reflections upon Meher Baba: "The deification of self, the belief that they are messiahs destined to save all mankind, is the final step taken by the audacious few."[219]

The Questions of Rom Landau

The most well known critic after Brunton was the writer of a book which was written in a different vein to that of *Secret India.* Rom Landau, in his earlier career, wrote *God is My Adventure*, which was published in 1935 and became a bestseller. Landau here recounted his various contacts with leading figures and unusual persons of mystical fame. One chapter related his brief contact with Meher Baba in 1932.[220] To the best of my knowledge, it is an honest report, quite lacking in the motivations of Brunton, and its style is much less objectionable. I propose to review the contents of the relevant chapter and to make some applicable comments in extension.

Landau begins by quoting a favourable report which appeared on the front page of the *Sunday Express*, April

10th, 1932. This report on Baba came from the pen of the popular British journalist James Douglas, who had arranged an interview with Baba and prepared a questionnaire with the help of Sir Denison Ross, the distinguished orientalist scholar. Sir Denison had collaborated in the hope of foiling the Iranian visitor, never having met him and judging him by hearsay. Douglas admitted that this questionnaire "was designed to trap the teacher, but he smilingly threaded his way through it without stumbling. His mastery of dialectic is consummate. It was quite Socratic in its ease. He frequently put questions to me which startled me by their penetration. But he never evaded a direct question."[221]

Landau appears to have envisaged a similar session of quick-witted questions and answers when he himself decided to visit Baba a few weeks later in London. It was mid-May 1932 when Landau sought Baba out in his lodgings at Lancaster Gate. Baba was staying at a hotel that was run by the Fellowship Club, which had transpired to be the only possible venue of stay, since elsewhere in London colour prejudice was too much in evidence. This Club accomodated Indians, and the rooms were inexpensive. Baba's room was on the top landing and was reached by five flights of stairs, which frequently constituted an impediment for visitors, particularly since there was no telephone extension. Baba spent five days in this hotel, and there were a fair number of visitors.[222]

Landau had managed to contact one of Baba's English followers named Quentin Tod, who duly arranged an interview for him. Upon arrival at the hotel one morning, he was confronted by a native domestic who said that she would call "one of them Arabs" for him in reply to his enquiry. After a few minutes one of the "Kimco" women appeared and said that she did not know of the interview arrangement but would ask on his behalf straightaway. A few more minutes elapsed and then one of the *mandali* appeared, dressed in European clothes. Landau reports his words: "Oh yes, Shri Meher Baba will be delighted to see you; he knows all about you, and it won't be a moment." The visitor was then left at the front door, and it was twenty minutes or so before another woman appeared and asked him to follow her upstairs. They climbed the laborious five flights of stairs, and then Landau was received on the top landing by another of the *mandali*, who said to him: "Baba has been expecting you."

The door of Baba's room was opened to reveal unostentatious furnishings typical of the small hotels in the district. The bed had not yet been made. Baba sat in an easy chair in the middle of the room. He was wearing a dressing-gown, bedroom slippers, and a woollen scarf around his neck (it was a chilly morning). He held his alphabet board, but did not seem inclined to make much use of it. Instead he took hold of Landau's hand when the latter sat next to him, caressed his arm in a characteristic manner, and laid his own hand upon the visitor's. This was a frequent feature of interviews and gave a very personal flavour to the interchanges. But Landau was one of those less receptive, and instead wished for a verbal encounter. He had prepared a series of questions, and lost little time in launching into these. Baba did not reply at any length. Two of the *mandali* stood near and interpreted aloud the quick movements of his fingers on the alphabet board. Landau writes that the response from Baba was almost invariably to the effect of: "This question requires a more elaborate answer and a longer discussion; I shall have a written answer sent to you in a day or two." Landau seems to have left of his own accord. He writes: "After this had been going on for about three quarters of an hour, I decided that it would be unfair to trespass any longer on my host's time." He said goodbye and turned towards the door. Baba suddenly began to flick his fingers again across the alphabet board, and one of the interpreters voiced aloud: "Baba says that he is going to help you in the future." The visitor expressed his thanks, and then left.

A week later, Landau received a lengthy letter, covered with the handwritten answers to his questions. He appears to have been under the misapprehension that Baba had written this epistle, though it was actually written by one of the *mandali* (doubtless F.H. Dadachanji) at Baba's instructions. Baba had then started on a voyage to America. This epistle seems to have largely consisted of extracts from messages which Baba had previously dictated, but also included were a few statements made by Baba at the time the letter was written. Landau reproduces one page of this letter, which included gnostic statements and references to Baba's "work." Landau found it hard to digest the gnostic statements, e.g.: "Nothing is beyond my knowledge. I am in everything. There is no time and space for me . . . I see the past and the future as clearly and vividly as you see material things about you." In retrospect, Landau cited Brunton's critique with evident approval (though unaware, like so many other readers, of the real facts). But at the time, Landau was not nearly so certain in his rebuttal; he himself writes that he continued to investigate Baba because there had been several sound statements in the letter received. This sanction refers to the more general and impersonal themes, which included:

"No general rule or process can be laid down for the attainment of the ultimate reality. Every individual has to work out his own salvation."

"Renunciation should be mental. One should live in the world, perform all legitimate duties, and yet feel mentally detached from everything. One should be in the world, but not of the world."

The last-quoted sentence closely reflected a choice Persian axiom of sufi lore; this particular emphasis was well known in sufi channels, but was obscured in the Western field of interest by a preoccupation with the conventional trappings of "spirituality." Rom Landau himself was to develop an increasing interest in Sufism over the years (mainly in its Arabic form), but he chose to reap stagnation in his efforts to understand Meher Baba by the deceptive expedient of judging him according to the standards imposed by a person considered to be his disciple. This was Princess Norina Matchabelli, who evidences not the slightest comprehension of antique Persian mysticism and very little of its modern variant as represented by her "master."

Though Landau did not again meet Meher Baba, he did encounter Princess Matchabelli in New York, and records a talk he had with her, though without referring to her by name. He described her as "one of his (Baba's) most experienced and most intelligent pupils," which doubtless reflected Matchabelli's view of herself, though it can be strongly repudiated here. She had known Baba for about a couple of years, and had formerly been an actress. Landau did not neglect to comment that the passion of the great actress had not left her. "It might have been the centre of a stage with thousands of spectators watching her, and not an apartment off Fifth Avenue." Matchabelli was doubtless a talented actress, though her exaggerated mannerisms were not the best guide to history. Even informal group photographs in which she appears alongside Baba reveal a "madonna" pose reminiscent of her theatrical performances in *The Miracle.* She regaled Landau with reminiscences depictive of Baba's own star role; her attitude to his "work" tended to be one of dramatic embellishment, in which she was by no means alone, though she was probably singular in her mode of expression. It is not surprising that Landau was offput by her version of the "master," though he made the mistake of assuming that she accurately represented Baba. His reaction, upon returning home, was to read Brunton's newly published critique, which evidently influenced him at the critical juncture. He approvingly quotes Brunton's verdict: "One is compelled to condemn the theatrical methods which he (Baba) has used." Landau was here confusing Baba with Princess Matchabelli, whatever Brunton's extrapolations from the publicity coverage by Western press men in 1932.

This confusion over theatrical auspices was equivalent to the historical error more recently appearing in a much-read work by the political satirist Bernard Levin, who misleadingly stated that when taken to see a performance of *White Horse Inn* at the Coliseum Theatre in 1931, Meher Baba "had apparently been so struck by what he saw that he determined to remain silent for the rest of his life."[223]

In a more political vein, Landau's decisive literary verdict against Baba incorporated his talk with Mahatma Gandhi's pupil Madeleine Slade, whom he represents as toning down the rumour of Baba's influence upon Gandhi. Miss Slade was concerned to state that it was Meher Baba who saw

Gandhi, and not vice versa, though it seems more historically decisive that it was originally the Lord Mayor of Karachi who advised Gandhi by wire to meet Baba on the steamship *Rajputana* in 1931.[224] But the argument here is inconsequential by comparison with Landau's deprecatory conclusion that: "In a world in which there is a Steiner there must also be room for a Shri Meher Baba."

From Landau's account of Baba, we learn primarily that (a) Landau did not expect to be kept waiting nearly half an hour for his interview (b) that he wanted his questions given a reply within three-quarters of an hour. Neither of these considerations proves that Baba was in error; he was under no obligation to play host to interrogations. Landau was probably not the only Western visitor to conceive of a sequel to the James Douglas interview, but the Iranian was perhaps tired of being baited by curious enquirers. If it was mysticism they really wanted, then it seems unreasonable by such standards to expect instant divulgence of profundities.

One wonders what curious enquirers would have thought of a meeting with Ibn al-Arabi (d. 1240), who was castigated by many of the theological scholars of his time, and afterwards by orthodox posterity for referring to himself as the *qutub*, a position of mystical eminence to say the least. It is much easier to make an armchair study of a dead sufi's remnant teaching than to become a working disciple (in the real sense) of the flesh and blood reality.

Subsequently a Professor of Islamic and North African Studies, one of Landau's later books was devoted to Ibn al-Arabi. It is a sympathetic study, though not a long one, and deals with the subject's life in only two pages before proceeding with a disquisition on Arabi's philosophy. It is evident that Ibn Arabi himself is comparatively obscure, though he is very likely to have made gnostic statements in private that would have been even more upsetting to religious scholars than his allusive writings. As Landau writes, it was inevitable that countless orthodox theologians were opposed to what appeared to be heterodox, and even scandalous, methods of Quranic exegesis employed by Ibn al-Arabi. The latter's views on the incarnation of God in man (*hulul*) or the identity of man with God (*ittihad*) were anathema to conventional thought.[225]

Meher Baba may well have judged Landau as an intellectual enquirer who wanted system at the expense of plus factors of impact. At the time of Landau's interview, there was no published teaching of Baba's generally available other than in newspaper reports. A few collections were published the following year, though Landau does not mention any of them, and may not have been able to obtain the most systematic of these (Ramju Abdulla's *Shri Meher Baba: his philosophy and teachings*) prior to his unfortunate contact with Matchabelli. It is worth noting that during this period he also met Gurdjieff, who was similarly non-compliant with Landau's demands. Gurdjieff told him that it was no good asking premature questions, and that he did not know what to ask. Despite the dubious moral background of this Armenian, who is implicated in having adopted some sufi methods, there may have been truth in some or many of his assessments.[226]

Other assessments of Meher Baba at that time were more favourable. One of the most distinctive came from the Buddhist fold, and contrasts markedly with that of Landau. Christmas Humphreys met Baba in London in 1932; he had founded the Buddhist Society of London in 1924, and was a lawyer by profession. It is notable that his high estimation of Baba was unaffected by the books of Brunton and Landau. Writing in 1941 in a little known article for a Buddhist readership, Humphreys reminisced on his meeting with the Iranian visitor: "It must be ten years since I was taken to a room in London to visit Meher Baba, and the recent receipt of literature about his life and work, has reminded me of one of the three most remarkable men I have ever met. I sat beside him cross-legged on a sofa while we talked – by means of an alphabet board, for he observed silence – of love, and the use of love and, if I remember rightly, of the doctrine of transmitted merit, whereby, it is said, the Bodhisattva hands over for the benefit of all mankind the karmic benefit of all his noble deeds. For the first time in my life, and I have not met another like him, I found myself in the aura of a man who literally radiated love. Like all great mystics, he combined the profundity of mystical experience with the guileless candour of a child, and his smile was as infectious as the words he used were immaterial. For I found, as I found with the Abbot Tai Hsu and Nicholas Roerich, that after a while there is no need of words, and one can speak from mind to mind in silence. And all the while he radiated such a pure affection that one wondered why, when all religions praise the value of pure love, it should be a memorable experience to meet one man who practised it."[227]

Humphreys went on to liken Baba's unpredictability to the techniques associated with Zen Buddhism, i.e., "using any method which will break the bonds of intellectual habit which enthral the higher mind." Humphreys himself wrote some books on Zen (Ch'an) Buddhism that were superior to most of those since in vogue in the West, though he was not sectarian in his approach to Buddhism. He was clearly impressed by certain other perspectives of Baba, including that expressed in the words of Charles Purdom: "He (Baba) is content that people should be brought into contact with him even by enemies . . . Indeed, I think he prefers attacks to praise because they arouse more feeling."

Humphreys' sense of Buddhist ethics evidently found satisfaction in the Iranian gnostic. "If there were more Meher Babas in the world today, war would end for want of causes; this man of love sets all men an example." Yet the President of the Buddhist Society was careful to stress that "there is nothing emotional about the emanations of this holy man,"[228] which is the impression too often given (inadvertently) in devotional literature.

Unfortunately, few people read the above-quoted article, and another sixteen years elapsed before another sympathetic Buddhist writer, Dr. W.Y. Evans-Wentz, favourably compared messages given by Meher Baba to those of the Tibetan yogi Milarepa,[229] giving a "Kargyutpa" colouring to a later visit which Baba made to the West.

The Loquacious and the Silent

An admirer who was apt to make a great deal of noise was

Khaikhushru Jamshed Dastur, a Parsi who lived at Meherabad in 1928. He witnessed many of the events relating to the Prem Ashram, and became such an ardent devotee that he was known to roll in the dust and exclaim that he was ready to wash Baba's feet with the blood of his heart. It should be noted that as a consequence of such displays and metaphor, Dastur gained a prestige amongst the devotees, including the *mandali*. This prestige tended to be accentuated by his above average background of literacy, which made his displays seem the more impressive. Dastur was not content with the role of a schoolteacher in the ashram, and made plans for a magazine entitled *The Meher Message*, with himself as the editor. It was the first of the "Meher" periodicals, and of very mixed content. What is important to understand is that Dastur undertook this literary task on his own initiative, and not at Baba's instruction.

Dastur was now regarded by some devotees and other more disinterested readers as the literary mouthpiece of the person whom he so lavishly described as "His Divine Majesty," i.e. Meher Baba. Dastur basked in the light of proclaimed discipleship, not being one to understate matters. Baba himself made no interference with Dastur's literary policies, though some of the *mandali* did express objections. As Charles Purdom later discerned, this openhandedness was typical of Baba's method.

After a couple of years of effusive verbalism, Dastur's enthusiasm began to wane. It is evident that he did not obtain what he had thought he would get. The motive of doing something in the expectation of due rewards is well known, though it is not always exposed. In Dastur's case, it was exposed, and the details are quite sufficient to indicate that his conception of discipleship was infantile.

In March 1931 Dastur had an interview with Baba, in which he presented his new objections and requests. Like some other admirers, Dastur had interpreted Baba's statements on his "manifestation" in a drastically literal manner. This imagined event was accordingly viewed as a source of benefits and glories. Dastur had been confident that this would happen quite quickly, but the absence of dramatic happenings left him in a situation that was becoming embarrassing to him, and also irksome. He made it evident that he desired some tangible revelation of Baba's function if he was to continue as a follower. It amounted to a request for miracles.

Baba's simple answer to this demand was to tell his faltering admirer to wait until the last day of October. Dastur agreed to wait until this date before expressing any adverse opinion in public.

Dastur's report of this interview appeared several months later in his magazine, though he had already evidenced his discontentment well prior to the agreed deadline. One of the topics he raised during the interview was the Prem Ashram. Previously he had written an account extolling the merits of this institution, but from now on he decided to think of it as a failure. The reasons for this *volte-face* are inadequately described by Dastur, whose relevant editorials in *The Meher Message* were strongly biased against Baba, though still self-congratulatory. He gave his readers the impression that Baba agreed with him that the Prem Ashram was a failure. The basis for this conclusion was Dastur's reflection that the leading figure Aga Ali had been forced away by an outside agency. Baba is stated to have said: "I did it before the time," an ambiguous statement which Dastur employed as an admission of failure. Baba is more likely to have been reflecting that Dastur's heart was not so free with its vaunted blood in the face of thwarted expectations.

By August Dastur heard that Baba had spoken with C.V. Sampath Aiyengar about the future of *The Meher Message*. Dastur evidences that he took this consultation as a personal affront. This matter is rather more complex than Dastur was prepared to admit. Sampath Aiyangar was a rival editor to Dastur, being the leader of the Saidapet ashram in Madras and editor of its new periodical *The Meher Gazette*. It was quite obvious that *The Meher Message* was considered dispensable (bearing in mind that Baba had not asked for either of these periodicals to be commenced).

In the October issue of *The Meher Message*, Dastur openly declared Baba to be a charlatan. He reasoned that Baba's consultation with Sampath Aiyengar had released him

(Dastur) from his promise to wait until the end of October. Dastur's reliability is thus very much in question. Certainly he was no more "The Disciple of His Divine Majesty." He had since turned his flitting attention to Theosophy, and had become an admirer of the deceased Madame Blavatsky. His magazine would henceforward be known as the *Mystic Review*. Though the wellsprings of Dastur's heart had evidently dried up, he found time for another of his editorials entitled "My Heart-to-Heart Talk," which reflected some literary honesty (though this was very much in his interests in order to lessen the gravity of his former mistaken beliefs). Dastur here expressed his apologies to the critics of Meher Baba for having denounced them formerly, but appended the consideration that some of the statements these critics had made against Baba "were entirely groundless and false." As examples of such errors, Dastur cites the biased statements "that Meher Baba was in the habit of privately speaking by word of mouth with certain female disciples, that he extorted money from his disciples and made a wrong use of it, and that the boys of his (Meher) Ashram did not receive good secular training and were not well taken care of." Dastur said moreover that "I am bound to assert that every *pie* that was given to him (Baba) was given entirely voluntarily by his disciples."

In a more malicious vein, Dastur expressed his view that Baba had performed a "spiritual experiment" upon the Prem Ashram boys which had been unjustified. The reasoning behind this seems to have been that most of the boys concerned had been sent back to their homes well prior to the end of the period originally stipulated. A study of the facts will reveal that the Prem Ashram was closed owing to reasons quite other than those implied by Dastur. Also relevant here is the consideration that Dastur himself had been closely involved in Prem Ashram events, and had acquired at that period his sense of flushed enthusiasm that knew no bounds according to the sentiments he had then expressed. Dastur was recorded in print as having rolled in the dust, doubtless embarrassing to him in retrospect, and hence experiments that had misfired were now the order of the day with regard to blood of the heart which had evaporated.

The editor in error stated that in April 1931 he had concluded "that Meher Baba was not real, and all his talk of manifesting himself as an avatar was bunkum." In more evasive explanation of why he had continued to wait in the offchance of something dramatic happening, he wrote: "The problem was very delicate, and I had to make my assurance doubly sure." Expectancy had died hard, it seems, and was effectively killed off by a shock to the ego rather than by impartial observation.

"I still love Meher Baba," added Dastur a little unconvincingly, and he generously conceded that his ex-teacher certainly possessed occult knowledge and powers.[230]

Khaikhushru Dastur had done a great deal of talking during the past few years, and perhaps affords as good an example as any of the uselessness of effusive admirers.

Another Parsi presents a strong contrast, and refreshingly enough, never proclaimed himself as a disciple. Yet Gustadji Hansotia would seem to merit the vaunted tag of "disciple" much more than many of his comrades. He was one of the resident *mandali* during the Prem Ashram period, and was known to Dastur, though Gustadji never spoke to him. The reason for this was that Gustadji observed strict silence of mouth at Baba's instruction from 1927 onwards. This instruction was maintained on a permanent basis, so that Gustadji died still silent. That was in 1957, after a full thirty years of silence. He was the only male amongst the *mandali* who was given such an instruction.

It is a strange fact that very little reference to Gustadji was made on the "devotee media" of the post-New Life phase. Adi K. Irani and others of the *mandali* received the plaudits, while Gustadji was rarely even mentioned. Yet it was he whom Baba had once used to refer to as his "shadow." This was in reference to Gustadji's constant association with him during the earliest years of his work. In his later life, Baba even stipulated that one of his "favourite photographs" was one taken of himself and Gustadji in 1922.[231] The conclusion is inescapable that some exceptional individuals remained in low profile, while others less deserving of spotlight attracted general attention.

Gustadji was born at Hansota in Gujerat *circa* 1890. As a boy he had lived in Bombay, attending the Fort High School. He left this institution to become a wage-earner, but his heart was not in material pursuits. In 1910 he became a pupil of Hazrat Sai Baba of Shirdi, and over the next several years stayed regularly with him, living an ascetic existence under Sai Baba's instructions. Before the latter's death, Gustadji was transferred to Upasni Maharaj, one of the comparatively few persons to gain this privilege of transfer. Several years later, Upasni in turn transferred him to Meher Baba, with whom he had been intimate since 1917. He was the only pupil of Baba who had trained at Shirdi, which tends to further underline the distinctions in his case.

In subsequent decades Gustadji continued to be a close companion of Baba, and this often meant that there were two silent persons in the travelling parties. Gustadji was notably averse to the tours in the West, though he was a regular feature of the "*mast* tours" in India. Like Baba, Gustadji often communicated via his sense of humour, which was a pronounced feature of his disposition. Yet there is very little information available about him; the fact that he was overshadowed by more officious entities is perhaps an inevitable accompaniment to depth occurrences. He had lived much of his life in ascetic and simple environments, one of the reasons for his aversion to travels in the West. He was one of the four men who accompanied Baba during the *manonash* phase of 1951–2, and a photograph taken of him at that time with Baba reveals a bearded figure who has a *mast*-like appearance, accentuated by a very heavily-patched pair of trousers and a ragged shirt.[232]

The "Old School" in England

Two of the most literate individuals amongst the British followers were Charles Purdom (d.1965) and Will Backett (d. 1963). They were of divergent temperament, though each had their merits. Neither of them had anything in common with the new "hip" wave of the late 1960's which engulfed the Western branches of the devotional movement. Indeed, neither of these men were typical devotees, particularly Purdom. In attempting to assess them, readers should therefore clearly understand that they were amongst the best representatives of what can here conveniently be dubbed the "old school," as distinct from the less disciplined tendencies of "pop culture" which gained influence and publicity after their deaths.

Will Backett had early been an admirer of Tolstoy, and *c.* 1905 had lived at a Tolstoy colony near London, working there in his spare time while continuing his business at his city office. Tolstoy's English followers were then engaged in a study of the *Bhagavad-Gita*, and this contact with Hindu philosophy led Backett to study the works of Swami Vivekananda, which greatly broadened his outlook. But despite Vivekananda's critique of Theosophical beliefs, and doubtless in part owing to the absence of a Vedanta Centre in London at that time, Backett subsequently joined the Theosophical Society, which was then in its heyday under the leadership of Annie Besant. He transited from this affiliation to the version of Sufism taught by Inayat Khan (d. 1927), whom he met in London. Both Backett and his wife Mary regarded Khan as their teacher, though it was Mary who received tuition in music, a reflection of the Chishti Sufism of India. After Khan's death, the Backetts' were dissatisfied with the perpetuation of the movement he had founded. They came into contact with Meredith Starr, one of the first Western pupils of Meher Baba. This led to their meeting with Baba in London in 1932. Unlike Starr, the Backetts remained firm in their new allegiance, though possessing a very different perspective to that of the "Kimco" group of English women who received a greater share of Baba's attention. The Backetts did not accompany him on his tours in Europe, but achieved a unique role on their native soil as intermediaries. Many of their friends believed that their intuitive affinity with Baba was much stronger than that of persons in his physical proximity. This does of course fit a sufi fact of experience in respect of the differences between pupils, but the devotional movement at large had little comprehension of such matters.

For some years Will Backett retained his office premises at Charing Cross, where he worked as an insurance broker. He was not a wealthy man, and lived in comparative simplicity at a country cottage near Sevenoaks, where his wife spun her own yarn in an atmosphere that would have done credit to a Gandhian ashram or a Tolstoy colony. Baba visited this cottage in 1933, and used Backett's office premises for private interviews in London, publicity being strictly discouraged. Backett was given the special privilege of sending weekly letters to Baba during the 1930's, and messages to other individuals were often relayed in the replies he received. This role as an intermediary continued until the New Life. But unlike some other persons, Backett did not vaunt his privileged role, and remained in surprisingly low profile until the end of his life.

Will Backett had disagreements with Charles Purdom. In Backett's eyes, Purdom was too "intellectual" and retained too much Christianity. Backett himself came of strong Puritan stock, but his Protestantism had been shattered by a confrontation with Robert Ingersoll and other agnostic writers. Purdom retained a Christian orientation, and accordingly found it difficult to adjust to certain features of Baba's evolutionist teaching. However, to Purdom's credit, his literary style was more incisive than Backett's, and he was indisputably correct in his affirmations that the *Discourses* frequently did not represent Baba's verbatim dictation (which Backett believed for a long time).

Purdom had a multi-faceted career. Distinctively self-taught, he had started off as an accountant in his industrious role as a pioneer in the Garden City Movement. As an architect he played a strong part in founding Welwyn Garden City, where he chose to live. He was also a journalist of calibre, and became noted for a new approach to Shakespeare criticism. He wrote books on politics, social economics, town-planning, and drama. His varied career gained further colour in providing the first published biography of Meher Baba. It is unfortunate that his book *The Perfect Master*, which appeared in 1937, was completely overshadowed by the earlier works of Brunton and Landau insofar as the reading public were concerned. Purdom was an exceptionally impartial biographer, to the extent that it is very difficult to describe his work as sectarian.

It was 1931 when Purdom first met Baba, but it was not until 1948 that he began to associate closely with the "London group" of Baba's followers. For seventeen years he had remained aloof from the movement (if such it could be called at that time), and it is a striking fact that he was a virtual stranger to the devotees despite his having written the only readily available biography of Baba. Even then, he only cooperated with the London group because Baba had specifically asked him to do so, nominating him as the first chairman of the "Universal Spiritual League" in England. Delia De Leon wrote: "We were all then enabled to know him better, and were stimulated by his many talks and writings."[233]

I was able to attend one of Purdom's talks shortly before he died in July 1965. He had prepared a paper on Ramakrishna of Dakshineswar, which was read out before a small gathering in a hired room in London. There was not the slightest bias against another "movement" in this paper, and I did not always find the same catholicity elsewhere.[234] The contrast with later sectarian developments occurring after the deaths of both Purdom and Baba was very pronounced, I may add, and I am led to think that a number of Purdom's talks went over the heads of certain of his audience. More educational to me than the "Family Newsletters" of Mani were the much more brief news-sheets of the London group which contained Purdom's reviews of new books. Whether it was Teilhard De Chardin's writings or the Discourses of Rumi (translated by Professor Arberry), Purdom was interested in everything else of philosophical value, and seemed intent upon enlarging the rather limited horizons of devotees with whom he was in contact.

As a personality, Charles Purdom closely fitted the typical image of the British literati: he spoke excellent English, was courteous and restrained in his deportment, and could easily give the impression of being aloof to people who did not know him well. Yet he was a true democrat, not a conservative. After his death, the tone of the London group meetings deteriorated.

When Purdom had first met Baba in 1931 at East Challacombe, Devon, he was then in his late forties and editor of the London *Everyman* magazine.

This editorial career he had taken up in 1928, when the publisher J. M. Dent had invited him to manage their newly revived literary weekly. Purdom had also been asked to become managing director of an important industrial firm, but he chose the less financially favourable alternative owing to his literary interests. As he wrote in his autobiography, he and the publishers did not compete in the field of other weeklies like *Tit-Bits* or *John o' London*, but aimed at a more serious-minded public interested in literature, the arts, and current ideas. As a consequence, it was difficult to sell enough copies of *Everyman* even at the competitive price of twopence. Purdom asked Bernard Shaw for a contribution, but this celebrity observed that they could not pay the four hundred guineas he would require, though he more generously agreed to sit for a portrait which appeared on the cover. This magazine was considered to be of exceptional quality, but the publishers steadily lost money owing to the slow increase in circulation. Purdom was determined to maintain high standards, evidenced in his notable statement: "To combine journalism and authorship is not possible . . . Many writers have found that to write books they must give up journalism, which is what I discovered."[235]

Purdom discovered other things also. In the summer of 1931 he felt the need of a holiday, though he had decided that his editorial work left no time for such luxury. But late in the season, a friend urged him to stay at a retreat in Devon, having just returned from this place with a glowing account of it. Purdom was able to make a quick booking for early September, and departed with the intention of staying a week only, or ten days at the most. His destination was the retreat at East Challacombe, near Combe Martin, an isolated farmhouse set in pleasant acres of rolling fields. It was run by Meredith Starr, who had earlier stayed with Baba in India. The regime was austere, with four hours daily being devoted to meditation (in solitude, not communally). There was work on the farmstead for those who wanted it. The atmosphere was distinctly contemplative; there was no contact with the outside world save for the visits of tradesmen. "It was the simplest and least pretentious life I had encountered," wrote Purdom, "and after a week I felt restored, a new man."

Starr was not dogmatic in his allegiance to Meher Baba, though he made it clear that the latter was the inspiration behind the retreat. He invited Purdom to stay a little longer, in order to meet Baba who was journeying to the West for the first time. Purdom agreed, feeling an interest in the visitor. In his autobiography, he compressed the details, since few of his readers were sufficiently interested. He described Baba in terms of a "dark-haired, bright-eyed Persian . . . he was without self-assertion, but had a princely bearing, and aroused amazing fervour of devotion among all the other persons present." With typical detachment, Purdom added: "I disliked this fervour and wished he had checked it, but he did not; I felt nothing of the kind, though I recognized an exceptional person." This was primarily a reference to the displays of weeping that were particularly noticeable in women. Purdom added with honesty: "It was impossible not to feel a sense of devotion," though he did not mean this in any extroverted sense. Despite Baba's silence, Purdom found that verbal communication was surprisingly fluent; in using the alphabet board, Baba abbreviated many words, and hence "soon one could read them (Baba's words) as quickly as speech." In this way Purdom had "long talks" with Baba, who "showed comprehensive understanding."

All this prompted Purdom to write an article about Baba, which the latter approved. "He asked for nothing of the sort, but was pleased when I suggested it." Purdom left after a few days, unable to delay his return to London any longer; Baba was himself departing for London soon after. Purdom lived in Welwyn Garden City, from where he commuted; he found the change in environment an unpleasant shock. The noise and bustle of mundane life required a prodigious effort of adjustment. "I looked upon the world with new eyes," he wrote. There seemed to be no room for meditation in city life, but he resolved to attempt regular meditation at all costs. "I had met the extreme of worldly life, and the contraries had to be reconciled." It should be stressed that Purdom was one of the few who did pursue a disciplined introspective course of meditation,[236] unlike "Kimco" and other devotees, who were more extroverted in temperament. He did not require to be told to do so by Baba, who in general left such matters open to personal inclination and capacity. Some people were not of sufficient depth to be able to hold such focus, including some of the *mandali*, who in later years attempted to insinuate that Baba had never sponsored meditation, contrary to the facts. Devotionalism is frequently an exercise in simplification, but Charles Purdom was not a devotee.

On September 24th, 1931, the *Everyman* contained an editorial article entitled "A Perfect Master." It was the first publicity of any kind that was accorded to Baba in the West. The title employed Baba's technical English equivalent for *qutub* and *sadguru*. The writer found that there was resistance to the information he divulged. "Mysterious calls arrived by telephone from unknown people bidding me beware." More directly, the journalist Raphael Hurst, alias Paul Brunton, called upon Purdom in person, warning him to avoid Baba, since he (Hurst) had met Baba in India and knew him to be a fraud, or at the least deluded.[237] Purdom was not to be intimidated, and was an unlikely candidate for Bruntonian views after being acquainted with the empirical evidence. When he later had the chance to read Brunton's *Secret India*, he did not admire either the accuracy of reporting or its literary style.

Purdom's controversial article merits inspection. It is not at all sensational, and makes no reference to any messianic idea. Baba is described simply as "a master." It was not a lengthy article. Some extracts are reproduced here:

"He (Baba) arrived in England quietly twelve days ago and went to an isolated place in the country where only a few people know of his presence . . . he has not spoken a word for over six years, and does not propose to speak now. Meher Baba has not come to this country with a 'message' or to give lectures, or to found a new sect. There is too much talking, he says, and there are plenty of religions. He has come to impart his knowledge of God to those who wish to receive it. His method is simple. He says to the inquirer, 'What I am, you are.' This seems nothing at all; but coming from him with the unmistakeable spiritual certainty that he possesses, it comes as a shock. What he does is to make the seeker after truth look into his own heart to find it. And, what is more significant, he gives him the power to find it. For from Meher Baba there flows power. He has no startling things to say . . . He does not need to speak; he has the power of truth in him.

"He is thirty-seven years old. His eyes are large and beaming, lighting up his face, which irradiates happiness. He has a great sense of fun, and is said to be a first-rate cricketer. He combines the simplicity of a child with the wisdom of the ages.

"He is willing at present to receive anyone who comes to him with a sincere mind; but he does not care to exhibit himself. It is not to be thought that he is an impractical mystic, out of touch with everyday affairs. His knowledge includes the concerns of ordinary men and women. He is one who brings into the world of commonplace things, experience of the superconscious.

"I have had several 'conversations' with him. But as I have said, to talk with him is not the important matter. It is sufficient to be in the same place. He asked me if knew the poems of Kabir . . .

"He makes no demands on anyone, but those who come to him for help have to be prepared to do what he says, which may be severe . . . The rules that he gives, so far as he gives anything at all, are inner recollectedness, selfless service, and pure intention. He does not ask the Christian to cease being a Christian, but to be a true follower of Christ, that is, to do what Christ said. He does not ask the sceptical man or woman of today to accept any dogma, but in the spirit of humility to obey the God in his (or her) heart. What Meher Baba says the mystics of the Western world have said; but he is its fullest expression. What he says, the psychologists of the West have also said in part; but he interprets their theories in practical life. It may be strange to find a spiritual master from the East speaking in terms that belong to our scientific textbooks . . ."

Unlike Rom Landau, Purdom early grasped that speech was not one of Baba's priorities. However, his initial statement that Baba's method was simple was subsequently to be extensively corrected in his later writings. The subtleties underlying the alphabet board could prove deceptively simple even to the more perceptive.

This sophisticated form of publicity was soon to be overshadowed by crude press coverage when Baba came to London in late September. Purdom records that a number of reporters were brought along to see Baba "by an enthusiastic admirer."[238] Purdom early witnessed the differences amongst admirers, who ranged from sensitive types to the more extroverted personalities. Newspaper reporters were usually only interested in scoops, with due losses in accuracy. Baba did not at this stage refuse to see journalists, though he did do so on later visits to the West.

Owing to the reactions to his earlier article in *Everyman,* and in view of the sensational tendencies of press men, Purdom's sequel editorial feature entitled *The Need of a Teacher* omitted any specific reference to Baba. But he touched upon aspects of the master-pupil relationship which were not well understood in general (and still are not):

"In psychological terms a teacher is one who throws light upon the unconscious – he is a mediator between the conscious and unconscious mind. He is able to show how repressed energies may be released for creative purposes. He does this not by argument, but by mere association with himself."

The last part of this statement reflects the sufi concept of *suhbat* (companionship), according to which the pupil learns by the teacher's personal example and emanation. The concept was popularized in dervish circles, and more recently, the modern theme of "repressed energies" has been grossly abused in Reichian and neo-Reichian interpretations. This has contributed to an almost total ignorance of the (authentic) master-pupil situation, an ignorance which is nowadays worse on average than it was in 1931. Purdom's remark in the above quoted article is now more relevant than ever: "We can meet teachers in books, but it is better if we meet them in the flesh; the difficulty is that they do not often let themselves be seen."

When Baba returned to England in the spring of 1932, he did allow himself to be seen in London by newspaper reporters. But it is important to grasp the background to this coverage. Some of his new English followers, including the "Kimco" women, demonstrated little or no understanding of his background and lifestyle. They actually believed that he would want to be made known to the British nation, and accordingly booked reporters. Baba did not stop these arrangements when he arrived, particularly since he was the guest in a private home and not in a hotel. Instead he capitulated to the various demands and expectations, and casually mentioned that he would "speak" in America. This was the prelude to a demonstration which revealed to Purdom and others certain important dimensions of his method not formerly so obvious. Purdom did not need to be told that newspaper publicity was a very mixed blessing, and mentioned this in another article he wrote for *Everyman*. This was after he had seen Baba several times in April at Kitty Davy's parental home in Kensington:

"During the past few days, the newspapers have been publishing sensational accounts of an Indian 'Messiah' who has lately come to this country. The subject of those accounts is the master about whom I wrote in these pages a little more than six months ago. I promised then to write more about him, and many readers have reminded me of that promise. If in fulfilling it, I tell a rather different story from that which has appeared in the newspapers, the reader can be sure that I have verified facts . . . His reason for visiting America is, he says, that America being most deeply engrossed in material things, and suffering most in consequence, is the soil in which a new spiritual rebirth will first take place . . . It would be easy to write a sensational story about this remarkable being, though he is himself the least sensational of men. It would not be difficult to make the most exaggerated claims for him . . . He does not shrink from contact with others, though he seeks to withdraw himself as much as he can. In appearance he is under middle height, delicately built, with a light brown skin, gentle brown eyes, long brown hair, strong features, and a serene expression. Perception silently emanates from his presence. He wears Eastern dress in the house, but in the street usually wears ordinary European clothes . . .

"He has no doctrine; he is a living truth. Therefore it is not what he says that matters. That is why the fact that he does not speak seems of such small consequence. Always it is the power of the realized truth that convinces, not the mere utterance of the truth. I have never before met a man of whom I could say that with such certainty. In his presence I feel that I know the answers to the questions that have hitherto perplexed me. Indeed, since I first met him just over six months ago, I have realized that the difficulty is not to get questions answered, but to act upon what one knows . . . If it is dangerous to ascend a difficult mountain without a guide, it is even more dangerous to attempt to disintegrate and reintegrate our personality without the help of a skilled teacher. The many failures of psychoanalysis have made this abundantly clear. A Perfect Master helps to break down our personality, because he helps us to get rid of the ego; but he also enables us to build it up again. I find Meher Baba to be above all practical. He is concerned with everyday life. He does not invite people to leave the world, but to make use of it, to raise it to spiritual values. We should live in the world, he says, and yet be not of it, attend to all worldly duties and yet be completely detached from their results.

"He does not seek to convert men to anything; certainly he does not attempt to change their religion . . . He does not bring Eastern ideas for us to act upon, but intends to help us to act upon what we already know. He revivifies unused knowledge. He does more than that of course, for he shows us the necessity for a change of heart and enables us to gain real knowledge through experience. Above all, he unites the mind and heart, so that we need no longer be divided personalities, but can live as entire men."[239]

The lastmentioned emphasis was characteristic of Baba, but in general strangely neglected by devotees. Will Backett records Baba's statement: "The true life is lived when one feels both heart and head balanced: intellect and feeling linked – materialism and spirituality blended. Then only can one realize the Infinite in every phase of life and be in harmony with everyone and everything, living in the world of matter and yet feeling detached."[240]

This emphasis upon the head and heart in balance was by no means new, and yet is even now neglected by too many partisans of the mystical. Self-professed intuitives shriek against the "head," preferring this ploy to that of coming to terms with the qualities of discrimination relevant to the "head." Purdom found that many devotees of Meher Baba were likewise disdainful of the "head," though he did not live to see the pathetic aftermath of mawkish "heart" preferences that were tied to the jargon of pop culture and sectarian Meherazad.

Purdom must have felt very disconcerted when Kitty Davy and others invited Paramount Studios to come and film Baba at the Davy home in Kensington. Purdom found himself in the garden of that suburban home reading out a message which Baba had consented to dictate for the occasion. He must have felt slightly incredulous that the film crew had expected Baba to speak while being filmed. Baba had apologetically declined to comply with this expectation. The brief film clip was subsequently included on the national newsreel shown in the cinemas.[241]

Baba did not let this matter rest in ignorance. Since certain English devotees were awaiting something dramatic, he rid himself of them by conceding to their desires for the spectacular. In the past he had indicated that he would "speak" at a time of crisis in the world. This was interpreted with an incredible literalness by those disposed to do so, and like K.J. Dastur, some pressed him for an imminent deadline. As Purdom wrote in his autobiography, "persistent demands from American devotees caused him to fix a date in 1932 when he would do so (i.e. speak) in Hollywood." A fairly large number of people were involved, some of whose tendencies were shallow to say the least. As Purdom wrote: "To be importunate with him usually meant that he gave the answer desired, just as any devotee who greatly wished to take any action was, after warning, allowed to do it."[242] There were some devotees who never grasped this, including some of the *mandali*; overestimation of personal abilities is not the best tendency for gaining perception.

When Baba gave in to the demands of admirers, he went to the extent of stating that he would break his silence over the radio in the Hollywood Bowl, introduced by Mary Pickford, and that his close disciples would gain God-realization. It is on reliable record that several women "paid immense amounts for what were to be their God-realization dresses."[243] They purchased these dresses of their own accord, so convinced were they that perfection would be theirs. The vanity of glamour often knows no limit.

Baba never appeared in the Hollywood Bowl. He was expected to do so after returning from China, but he went on to India instead, and sent word that he would not break his silence at that time. He gave no explanation for the missing event. Not everyone could take this in a spirit of approval, and Meredith Starr sent him a cablegram demanding: "Break your silence. Give me God-realization or four hundred dollars."[244] Both Starr and his wife thereafter repudiated Baba. Others were less drastic in their behaviour, but were still very vague as to priorities. In later years, Baba remarked to some of those concerned: "Did you really believe that I would do such a thing as break my silence in the Hollywood Bowl?"[245] The reply was in the affirmative.

To some, this might appear a contradiction to his ethical philosophy in stating what he knew to be an untruth – or rather a joke. But it would have been far more unethical for a teacher not to teach some of his pupils an elementary lesson of which they were in desperate need. It was a more effective way of humiliating unfledged, insistent desires than eloquent discourses such as some had hoped to hear. Ethically also, he was justified in imparting a shock to Meredith Starr, who had complacently apportioned himself the role of a St. Peter who could do no wrong and who was but a step away from the ultimate realization.

Baba had given a timely exposure of the crass disposition (and worse) of a section of his Western following. It would be misleading to say that all the relevant lessons were assimilated by all concerned at that time, but on the subject of publicity at least, Baba rammed home his real requirements in no uncertain manner. Some enthusiasts of the sensational had loudly proclaimed the coming glories to their acquaintances, and were not a little deflated as a consequence. Baba thereafter prohibited all publicity measures on subsequent visits to the West in the 1930's.

The Hollywood Bowl episode was one of the symptoms of devoteemania which caused Charles Purdom to remain aloof from other admirers for another sixteen years. He must have felt relieved not to be included in the group of Westerners who were domiciled in the Nasik ashram in 1937, a very mixed grouping which met with various internal upheavals and frictions. It was mistakenly assumed by some that inclusion in this ashram was a sign of elect stature, but "close disciples" are usually the very worst of pupils and require more time spent on their defects proportionately. The Backetts notably did not preen themselves, but Princess Matchabelli and others did.

Some may wonder why Baba was not more severe in dealing with superficial types. But to "break down the personality" of lop-sided types can amount to an act of cruelty, and would be liable to cause irreparable psychological damage. Baba did not tax people beyond their limits, which were often slight. He had to spend a certain amount of time in "building them up"; the onus was upon them in matters of motivation and behaviour, not upon him. A frequent consequence was an ego trip, sometimes pronounced, though not all managed to fly as high in the vapours of delusion as they might have wished.

The subtlety of Baba's "concessions" to the wishes of those around him is not easily elucidated in terms of the strait-jacket conventions commonly reserved for "spiritual masters." Though Baba stressed obedience to his instructions, his method frequently involved the very opposite of what devotees expected in terms of clear instructions. He would instead bend with their own expressed wishes, which they would *interpret* as an instruction. In this way also, hints and suggestions became headlines of concrete affirmation. Sufficient proof is available that he knew of the disparities this technique was likely to engender. It is more reminiscent of the Chinese to the average Western mind, but then Eastern psychology has been very much in abeyance in popular literature of all kinds, not to mention the shortcomings of academic literature.

Purdom continued to see Baba on the latter's visits to England, though he did not accompany the "Kimco" women on the Continental sojourns. Instead he gave time to preparing his biography of Baba entitled *The Perfect Master*. This project had arisen in 1932 when Purdom had asked Baba if he could do anything for him, and Baba replied by suggesting the biography. Baba approved the manuscript without alteration (though this was a typical habit of his), and it gained publication in 1937. It is worth noting that this book appeared the same year that the author was conspicuously absent from the Nasik "ashram for Westerners," and that his allegiance to Baba was permanent, whereas Quentin Tod, an Englishman who had accompanied the "Kimco" group on Baba's Continental tours, had since lost interest in Baba. This is further proof that the notion of physical proximity to Meher Baba representing an elect status is entirely unfounded, though it has been in currency for over half a century. In contrast with Purdom, Tod was an extrovert and in affinity with the superficial behaviour of "Kimco."

The Perfect Master was "entirely ignored by the press, with the exception of an account in a London evening newspaper, which treated it as news."[246] This situation was in stark contrast to the praises lavished upon the works of Brunton and Landau. Yet it is Purdom's book that is the most objectively written, even at the cost of occasionally making dull reading. Purdom's book still reads in a current style, whereas Brunton's *Secret India* is obviously outdated even to its partisans.

There was a revealing episode occurring nearly a decade after publication. In 1945 Purdom received a letter from the wife of a well known man of letters in London; she had obtained a copy of *The Perfect Master* from a public library and had been startled by the contents. This was because she had formerly read the critiques of Brunton and Landau, which had given her and her husband an unfavourable impression of Baba. Unlike Brunton's reprints, *The Perfect Master* had become generally unobtainable, and so she typed out some thousands of words from the library book which she now considered valuable. As a consequence of this discovery, her husband was also prepared to reconsider his opinion of Baba. This woman even wrote to Baba, and received several letters dictated by him. After five years, she still retained the sense of contact with him very strongly.[247]

A few years later, Purdom had some cause to write in his version of Baba's *Discourses* that: "This is not a book for those who do not want to be disturbed and who propose to go on living as they have always done. Such readers will not like it. This is not a book for idle reading."[248] Many readers of Brunton would not have recognized the "Parsee Messiah" in these teachings, and Landau's invidious comparison of Iranian mysticism with the occultism of Rudolf Steiner might have seemed biased to impartial readers.

Despite the difficulties which Purdom experienced in coming to terms with Baba's evolutionist teaching, he had an unusually penetrating approach to Baba's more informal gnostic statements which were given such extravagant amplification by less discerning individuals. In a rare article which he wrote for *The Awakener* during the late 1950's, he attempted to convey to devotees some of the complexities involved in an appreciation of Baba. "The idea that Baba intends to perform some sensational act in the world is a great error," he urged. This idea hinged upon Baba's references to "speaking," references which are rather obviously non-literal. Purdom quotes Baba's statement in "The Final Declaration" message of 1954: "I shall speak only One Word, and this Word will penetrate the hearts of all men." Purdom's interpretation of this was well above average, and he understood that "productive silence" would be necessary for the "inner ear" to hear this Word. "Baba's sensational act is in our interior world, and unless it explodes into activity there, it will be for us as though the Word had never been spoken."[249] This largely fell on deaf ears, since the general devotional interpretation expounded a literal word of some kind, as readers of Mani's Newsletters and similar literature will find.

Purdom was not afraid to voice unorthodox views. "Baba always says that we must obey our consciences. 'Leave me if your conscience says so; attack me if your conscience says so' is what he tells everyone . . . Only those who use their minds hear the voice of conscience." He was well aware that some did not use their minds, but were instead content with shallow sentiment. He advocated a "questioning and examining" attitude of a sophisticated kind with regard to Baba's statements. "I do not of course mean that we should be carpingly critical and receive what Baba says sceptically . . . What I do mean is that we should listen with devotion, but with active minds, realizing that Baba speaks his own language, so that we cannot enter into his meaning without meditation."[250] Such ideas were already a form of blasphemy to the hierarchy at Meherazad, who disclaimed the validity of meditation and opted for literal belief, annulling conscience in the pursuit of a blind obedience as promoted by officious persons like Adi K. Irani, the self-proclaimed disciple.

Purdom's amplified biography *The God-Man* appeared the year before his death. The interpretative section included some further very relevant and discerning comments. In relation to Baba's references to "the Word," he cites some apparently contradictory statements and reflections, but arrived at the conclusion that "the Word will be an inner word, heard by the inner ear only by those able to hear it."[251] This interpretation is consistent with Baba's many (usually very brief) references to the phenomenon. Purdom also relates a useful incident that had been narrated to him by Ramju Abdulla: Baba told some of the *mandali* that he intended to speak, and took them to a distant place, a journey which involved days of laborious walking. Upon arrival he made elaborate preparations for the anticipated event; each of his companions had to stand in a circle about twenty yards distant from him, and with their backs to him – when he clapped his hands, they were to turn towards him and he would speak. But when they turned to him in this manner, they heard nothing. He smiled and called them together again. They asked why he had not spoken, and he answered: "Do you not know I am always speaking?"[252]

It would have been embarrassing for some of the more

officious *mandali* to think along these lines rather than adopt the literal associations of "speaking," for they would then have been confronted by the unwelcome situation of their being completely deaf to finer-than-physical wave-lengths.

Also unwelcome to some was Purdom's explicit reminder of the secondhand nature of the words purporting to be Baba's. "Every time the words 'Baba says' appear, inverted commas should be used, and in documents bearing Baba's name the signature should be in inverted commas too." As a literary critic of some experience, Purdom's reflections are fully justified here. He hastened to add that "there are many declarations and messages in which he dictated exactly what he wished said," but Purdom was also at pains to point out the very obvious fact of "how often in messages Baba is made to refer to himself in the second person, which clearly indicates that someone is speaking for him." Purdom was indicating that the different interpreters of Baba's words, whether via the alphabet board or via gestures, left their respective imprints upon the communications in many instances. Relevant also is his observation that reports by different people of what Baba communicated on the same occasion "have only too often shown discrepancies . . . listeners do not always hear the same thing, and omissions of what has been said, as well as words introduced that have not been spoken, are frequent."[253]

Also well above average were Purdom's remarks upon Baba's "method," though in some respects he can be improved upon considerably. For instance, he says that: "Baba's praises and flattery are for those who are not near . . . it is impossible to be close to him without suffering loss of self-complacency and self-esteem." Purdom here seems to be subscribing to the general belief that the *mandali* at the ashram were ground to the metaphorical "dust" of egolessness in their relationship with Baba. But in practice only some of them were; others were markedly ready to assert their status at every opportunity, and clearly had not reached the stage of egolessness. In practice Baba frequently praised certain members of the *mandali*, sometimes to an exaggerated extent as reports attest.

Physical proximity should never be confused with spiritual affinity. It is doubtless correct, as Purdom wrote, that "there is nothing that a master will not do to put a disciple to the severest test," but the distinction between a devotee and a disciple was never generally recognized.[254] A disciple requires to stand upon his or her own feet, not as part of a status group receiving the homage of a whole movement of people. Men like Charles Purdom and Dr. Ghani might have qualified (or begun to qualify) as disciples in the real sense, and also others less well known to public limelight.

Aptly enough, Purdom reiterated his earlier observation in *The Perfect Master*: "It is Baba's practice to allow anyone who wishes to say what they think about him or his work to do so . . . He will therefore permit people to make statements about him that they may strongly desire to make, without checking them."[255] The point to grasp is that devotees frequently accepted such statements as the gospel truth, particularly when these statements were voiced or written by one of the *mandali*.

Purdom observed that the most constant complaint against Baba was his continual changes of plan. He would appear to make promises but did not keep to them; he gave instructions that were contradicted by other instructions. The "promises" mainly relate to his declarations of "speaking," for which there were often important extensions in communal expectancy. Yet at the same time Baba was constantly reminding people that he promised nothing, that they should approach him with no expectation of receiving anything. Purdom saw in all this a distinct method whereby Baba was continually testing his followers. Purdom pointed out that the "promise-breaking" in these matters was quite contrary to Baba's standard practice in mundane affairs, which "is scrupulous in its attention to precise detail, and he never neglects to keep commitments."[256] It is relevant to add that after the New Life phase, Baba more than once gave his followers the option to leave him honourably if they felt the inclination to do so, appropriately emphasizing the difficulties which some encountered in their commitment. Why it should still seem strange to some that there were such tests is an anomaly for critics no doubt, though some partisans had a poor record at the time of Baba's decease, when certain longstanding expectations were finally shattered.

"No one knows exactly what that Work is,"[257] wrote the author of *The God-Man* in relation to a major topic of Baba's statements. Purdom's version of Baba's "work" was accordingly suitably restrained, in contrast to other interpretations which have appeared since Baba's death. Some of these interpretations are very colourful and cannot always be found to have an adequate basis in Baba's extant statements.

The "Shadow" Self

In 1955 Baba made a formal statement inviting any of his followers to leave him if they so wished, emphasizing that it would cause no offence to him if they did. One who took this opportunity was Jean Schloss, better known as Jean Adriel, an American woman who had some years earlier written a book entitled *Avatar* that described her contact with Baba since 1931. She now retreated from association with Baba's devotees and affiliated herself with Sant Kirpal Singh, a guru of Sikh background whom Baba himself acknowledged as being on the fifth plane of cosmic consciousness.[258]

This episode gained much comment from American devotees, who believed that Adriel had taken a major step backwards. This was accompanied by a degree of self-complacency amongst the faithful in some quarters. There were also some differences of opinion as to what course personal allegiances could legitimately take. Some of the American devotees wished to receive initiation from Kirpal Singh during a visit he made to America. Others felt that this would constitute a grave act of disloyalty to Baba. This situation invited a response from Baba's sister Mani (Manija) at Meherazad ashram, whose interpretation of the matter was considered official by the devotees. There is much sense in Mani's argument in that it repudiated the value of such an external practice as initiation, which Baba *never* gave and had indicated to be a misleading avenue of approach for earnest seekers. If Mani had limited herself to such considerations, it would be very easy to agree with her perspective, but she also took the matter much further. "We cannot follow two living Masters at once," she asserted, and here she was impugning even the value of contact with a *sadguru* or *qutub*, i.e., a master of the seventh plane. This was stated on Mani's authority, as the relevant circular of 1956 makes clear.[259] But such a perspective omits subtleties. Mani made no reference, for instance, to Gulmai Irani, who had remained in contact with Upasni Maharaj until the end of his life. Gulmai was a Parsi woman who had been amongst the earliest pupils of Meher Baba, and who had retained her close link with both he and Upasni. Gulmai did "follow two living masters at once," but the significance of this was lost upon the generality of devotees. Gulmai tended to keep very much in the background of events, and left the limelight to others like her son Adi K. Irani, who does not appear to have assimilated all he could have learnt within his family.

Whether or not Jean Adriel did make a backward move, there is some evidence that she had formerly learnt more than some of her complacent critics. In her book *Avatar*, she explains some of her experiences with Baba in the light of modern psychiatry, which "had given me profound insight into many of the more puzzling aspects of Baba's technique with his disciples."[260] This helps to give a certain realism to her account, which is otherwise often gushingly written. No such interpretation of Baba's ways is evident in the literature prior to Adriel, with the exception of some comments made by Charles Purdom. Yet the contours are implicit in various dairy notes of those who encountered traumatic experiences, but who never evolved a working evaluation of these in effective terms. Adriel dwells to some extent upon the "shadow" side of the individual psychology that frequently emerged in events, particularly (but not invariably) in Baba's proximity. This darker side of the psychology was seldom acknowledged by individuals, not even when they demonstrated it noticeably, but Baba created situations in which it was evoked. It was sometimes confronted, but not invariably, though Adriel does not cover this important negative extension. If an oral report is correct, then it may in fact be that Adriel herself was unable to face her own "shadow" at a crucial juncture after having written her book.[261] This connects with a more collective series of occurrences which have never been adequately detailed in the literature.

Adriel probably felt eclipsed by the prominence accruing to Princess Norina Matchabelli, an acquaintance of hers since Baba's first visit to America in 1931. Matchabelli had at first reacted against Baba, but subsequently acted as if the chief feminine role in relation to Baba was her own. Not a few people seem to have believed this, and Matchabelli's continued (though intermittent) presence at the ashram in India seemed to support this notion. On such points Baba could be extremely subtle, and it is worth taking into consideration here his diverse references to the "Circle" which were the focus of much speculation and assumption. For instance, he told the Kimco group of English women that "we were of his Circle," as one of them expressed it, while in America he conveyed that "Jeanco" were also of his "Circle." The group known as "Jeanco" was named after Jean Schloss (Adriel), and included herself, Norina Matchabelli, Elizabeth Patterson, Anita De Caro (Vieillard), and Nadine Tolstoy.[262] The problem is that such references have been facilely interpreted. Baba's references in this vein were very frequently unclarified: for instance, he used to refer in a very general sense to the *mandali* as his "Circle." He did on rare occasions distinguish between an inner and an outer circle, though without specifying the identities of individuals. The one exception here seems to have been Matchabelli, whom he gave to understand was the head of his "outer circle."[263] Matchabelli made as much of this privilege as she could, but was perhaps a little frustrated that it was not the inner circle that was specified. In later years Baba stated that he had many "outer circles."[264] Thus simple references to his "Circle" should never be confused with the "inner circle," the members of which he never specified.[265]

Advocates of "Circle" elitism have a further difficulty in the obvious discrepancy between ascriptions and events. In the general devotional interpretation, Jean Adriel was a renegade from the cause, but it was her name that was originally given to "Jeanco," who acquired an aura of elite prestige. Similarly, the woman whose name became incorporated in the group designation of "Kimco" likewise dropped away, though in different circumstances. Kim Tolhurst did not remain Baba's follower for very long after 1931. Delia De Leon told me that after a couple of years Tolhurst lost interest owing to Baba having "turned the cold tap on."[266] Another member of Kimco who lost interest during the 1930's was Aminta Barton, De Leon's sister, who had earlier purchased an elaborate dress for her debut as a God-realized disciple at the Hollywood Bowl.[267] Lack of sensational profile all too frequently leaves nominal disciples with no stimulus for discipleship. The varied talk of the "Circle" was, one could logically infer, very much in a vein of encouragement to superficial hangers-on.

Jean Adriel did not make much of the "Circle" in her autobiography, but did make a misleading statement which acutely generalized Baba's tactics with individuals. She observes that at the beginning of contact with anyone, he would be easygoing "until he knows the moment has come to turn on the reverse current." Then would commence the real work of uprooting egoistic tendencies. But Adriel evinces the tendency to assume that Baba maintained this operation "until all the cankerous ego-growth is eliminated."[268] To the contrary, the evidence attests that this process was very gradual and intermittent in many cases, and in some cases postponed altogether.

Sufism Reoriented

An unusual example of "a movement within a movement" was that known as Sufism Reoriented, an identity tag which has provoked a variety of reactions. The members were followers of Meher Baba who preferred to retain their beliefs and practices in sufi tradition as represented by the offshoot grouping from Inayat Khan's version of Sufism. This offshoot grouping was led by the late Ivy Oneita Duce, an American woman whose pupils were predominantly American.

The present author is amongst those who can see no reason why there should not be an "American Sufism" in addition to the ethnic varieties found in other countries. On the credit side, Sufism Reoriented attracted many young people in the late 1960's and early 1970's and promoted Meher Baba's anti-drug emphases which were sorely needed in the diffuse sector of mystical interests attendant upon the hippy boom.

From its inception in the early 1950's, Sufism Reoriented encountered friction with "non-sufi" components of Meher Baba's following in America. Some devotees seemed to think they were in rivalry with a movement of superfluous auspices, and that the "non-sufi" approach to Meher Baba was the best one. This perspective always seemed a shallow one to onlookers like myself; in my own view, the outlook of Ivy Duce converged too closely with that of the devotee movement at large, limiting the range involved in the issue of Sufism. I do not deny that the activities of Ivy Duce had value, but I do hold the view that her version of Meher Baba *and* Sufism was incomplete.

Baba's link with the sufi tradition as a whole has rarely been well understood. During his lifetime, it did not even become general knowledge that one of his activities in 1948 concerned the direct patronage of "the Sufi Circle for India." This was founded at his instigation on September 8th, 1948, and prominently included Dr. Abdul Ghani Munsiff. An office was created at Poona, and several of Baba's followers were delegated tasks such as translating certain texts. Only a few weeks elapsed before the dissolution of this project, since Baba was dissatisfied with the standard of commitment to the tasks allotted. He emphasized "that anyone who felt deeply interested in Sufism would be permitted to work as a free-lance Sufi."[269] Ivy Duce and her associates in America were duly informed of what had transpired.

Duce had met Baba for the first time in January 1948, when she spent several days at Meherazad.[270] She was the wife of an oil company official, and had studied under Ada (Rabia) Martin (d.1947), who was a long-established pupil of Inayat Khan (d. 1927), the Chishti shaikh of India. Martin was the leader of what was known as the Sufi Order, a title adhering to the Inayat Khan sect of Sufism. Duce was appointed by Murshida Martin as the latter's successor, and accordingly became head of the "Sufi Order" in America at Martin's death. Murshida Duce clearly felt that she needed guidance in this undertaking, and in this direction followed the incentive of Rabia Martin herself, who at the end of her life gained the conviction that Meher Baba was the *qutub* of the age. Martin did not get the opportunity to meet Baba, and Duce was determined to rectify this in her own case.

This episode appropriately underlines the fact that some leaders of mystical organizations are aware of their incomplete range. The question of ultimate authority, which may even invalidate minor or assumed authorities, is rarely probed by the partisans of numerous mystical sects. The "Sufi Order" of Inayat Khan had already posed certain problems both for participants and observers. At his death in Delhi in 1927, the "Sufi Order" founded by Inayat Khan split into two separate factions. Rabia Martin, who was an American, believed herself to be Khan's successor owing to statements he had made to her in person and in letters, supported by assurances from Shaikh Hasan Nizami, a prominent Chishti colleague of Khan who was with him at the end of his life. But when Martin went to France in 1927 to take charge of the "Sufi Summer School," she encountered opposition from within the movement, to the extent that she lost control over the European sector of the Order. She thereafter confined her activities to America, Brazil, and Australia, while Inayat Khan's brother (and later Khan's son Pir Vilayat) took over the remainder of the Order (though they claimed to represent this exclusively). There were notably a number of Inayat Khan's followers who effectively seceded from the Order at the time of this schism, which appalled them; these dissidents would not continue their training with either of the new leaders. Will and Mary Backett were amongst this contingent, gravitating into Meher Baba's orbit by 1932.

The "Sufi Order" represented an extension of the eclectic attitude of the Chishti dervish order of India, stressing the unity of religions and similar themes. These concepts are easily assimilable and have proved popular, though they do not guarantee knowledge of the finer mechanics of teaching situations and teaching capacities.

Ivy Duce quickly identified herself as a pupil of Meher Baba, of whom she writes in glowing terms, and with a tendency to emphasize his omniscience. Her autobiography is of interest, but offputs some readers owing to the devotional overtones. In identifying with the devotional movement, Duce freely subscribed to the prevalent thinking attitudes of devotees, which tends to render her version of Sufism less objective than it might have been.

Duce found that Baba himself, though possessing an evidently deep knowledge of Sufism, would not specifically identify himself with it. Indeed, he seemed more intent upon reorienting it than in being a declared representative. This is very understandable when one considers the predominantly cult nature of "popular Sufism" which prevails in the public eye and in general assumptions concerning the subject. Insofar as Ivy Duce was concerned, it was specifically the "Sufi Order" which was the candidate for reorientation, though Baba was extremely polite on the matter and did not unduly press the point he was sometimes prepared to make.

When Duce and her daughter stayed at Meherazad, Baba specially assigned Dr. Ghani to be present. The latter usually lived at Poona, where he was regarded as the leader of a non-sectarian group of persons with sufi interests. This leadership had gained him the title of "Munsiff." During the last few years of his life, Dr. Ghani was the intermediary in the correspondence between Duce and Baba. Duce learnt that Ghani had known Inayat Khan and thought highly of him, though Ghani did not have any connection with the "Sufi Order." Ghani even asked Duce to send him all of Inayat Khan's books, which he subsequently studied in some puzzlement. The erudite Ghani is reported to have remarked to Dr. Donkin: "For heaven's sake, is this all the knowledge that Inayat Khan gave to the West? He knew far more!"[271]

Upon returning to America, Murshida Duce found that many of her associates in the Sufi Order were averse to her new-found commitment to Meher Baba, who in their eyes was a rival to Inayat Khan, whom they regarded as the highest authority. Duce felt that a living teacher was of more use, and regarded it as her task to reestablish the Sufi Order in America.

It was four years before she met Baba again, this time in America in 1952. In her description of this episode, she opens the relevant chapter with what strikes some as an incongruous Biblical literalism of the type which often preoccupies religious mentalities. Baba's arrival by aeroplane is viewed by Duce as fulfilling a prediction in the Book of Revelation – despite the fact that Baba himself explained the same Biblical reference in a context of symbolism of planes of consciousness.[272] The Christian upbringing of Murshida Duce had evidently left its traces. This type of conditioning can frequently distort events and dilute psychological impacts inherent in teaching situations.

At Myrtle Beach in May 1952, Duce had a long talk with Baba about Sufism, in which he said: "I am very serious about the reoriented Sufism." He added that he wanted to have the result "appearing all over the world."[273] It is evident enough that he was referring to cult Sufism and the abuses perpetrated by self-appointed teachers clamouring for the attention of *murids* (disciples). He affirmed that only the achievement of (the ultimate) *fana* and the acquisition of (the ultimate) *baqa* gives the ability to lead others to perfection. Absence of this ability amounts to an insult to Sufism, and yet "all over the East and West it is being done." A very serious statement in relation to this situation of exploitation was reported as: "I intend to change the whole affair, overhaul the whole thing, because I love Sufism with all my heart."[274]

In deferring to Baba, Duce was disavowing any claim to ultimate achievements, though she retained prestige as the head of an organization. Baba asked her to relinquish the Australian sector of her activity to Francis Brabazon, an Australian who first met him at Myrtle Beach on that same occasion in May 1952. Brabazon had been studying Sufism for some years, and was enthusiastic over Baba.[275] This situation, in which Baba said that both Duce and Brabazon would have to become "murshids," can be regarded as a test for both of them. Both of these individuals came to be highly regarded in the devotional movement, and particularly by the sufi-committed contingent; Brabazon gained an adulation that some would have found embarassing when he published his poetic work entitled *Stay With God* in 1959, a book which was awarded lavish praise by Baba.

It is a long-established sufi technique to nominate deputies as part of their training, the main purpose being to test their integrity and their susceptibility to egotism.

Baba referred to a new charter that he would give to these two deputies and their associates. A more public statement about this new charter was dictated the following month at Myrtle Beach and duly circulated. This message stressed that he was equally connected with "Islam and its Sufism, Christianity and its Mysticism, the Orient and its Vedantism, broad Buddhism, practical Zoroastrianism, Jainism and many other such 'isms' which all speak the same divine Truth." This message also stated that he was detached from all these isms and had to awaken the followers of these isms to their real meaning by reorienting them; in this capacity he had reoriented Sufism in a charter which was to be "universally adapted."[276] The charter, as a document, was then only at an initial stage comprising notes taken down by the *mandali*. The reader will observe that Sufism was specified here in an Islamic context, which is the context of much "popular Sufism." He subsequently began to hint of a much wider context for Sufism, and in this sense converges with what has recently been dubbed "high Sufism," which is not organizational and which exists outside labels such as Sufism. Meher Baba himself can be brought under this classification; he can be regarded as the embodiment of the principles and teachings of *hulul* (in its essentials) applying to the vintage Iranian tradition of mysticism originating from the pre-Islamic era. "Islamic Sufism" clearly cannot cover him, any more than Hindu Vedantism can directly equate with him.

The significance of his statements on "reorientation" was not generally assimilated during his lifetime, the more understandable perhaps in that most of these statements were never published prior to his death. These statements deserve closer attention than they have received to date, and taking into full account the ambiguous nature of some of them.

On July 20th 1952, at New York, Duce and her colleague Don Stevens gained a two hour interview with Baba. Stevens was a former member of Rabia Martin's group in San Francisco; he had found it difficult to transfer his allegiance to Baba from the deceased Inayat Khan, and had initially rebelled at Martin's new sense of commitment. He had since become the chief assistant of Duce, and was favourably impressed by his recent first meeting with Baba, who now specified that he would send them the complete charter for "Sufism Reoriented" by November 15th. Duce was proposing to adopt this tag for her organization. Stevens asked to read out questions they had devised in relation to the new charter and the future of the organization. One question reflected their preoccupation with avoiding any schism such as had occurred after the death of Inayat Khan. This is an amusing feature, since the concept of a perpetual sufi organization with officially smooth transitions from one generation to the next is rather like desiring an orthodox church in addition to the esoteric fare.

Baba insisted that a *murshid* (teacher) has to be illumined, since otherwise the teacher could not guide the students. There was an evident contradiction here, since Ivy Duce was known as a *murshida* but did not claim to be illumined. The matter of her status was a rather vague one; her students tended to regard her as someone illumined. Baba himself never acknowledged her as illumined, but only as someone under his guidance, someone whom he allowed to fill a prominent role in an organization prepared to follow his lead. Stevens requested Baba to ensure that they (Sufism Reoriented) should gain an illumined *murshid* when Duce died. This desire for guarantees in an organizational situation strikes some readers as markedly incongruous. Baba's reply to this pressing question was in the "exaggerated" vein which he sometimes employed. It is reported that he said: "I promise you that you will have an illumined *murshid* for the next seven hundred years,"[277] a reference to the avataric cycle he had recently been referring to. He added, in a more sober vein, that at that time (1952), there were "only five Sufi *murshids* in the entire world." He gave a geographical clarification here: one was in Mashad (in Iran), one in Egypt, one in Algiers, and two were in India. There were no further details of identity. "He felt that the western world was now ready for Sufism and must have a real *Murshid*."[278] But again, there was no specific identity supplied for the "real *Murshid*."

While Stevens wanted guarantees of illumined murshids, Duce herself expressed concern about whether "the Board of Directors" would agree to implement the plans of the *murshid* (meaning herself). The context of these preoccupations was clearly a limiting one of a formal organization, similar perhaps to a dervish order. Baba's general response was good-humoured, but his main emphasis was arguably very much at a tangent to the formalities. "Sufism is to be universal," he stated, "to embrace all other 'isms,' and yet to remain Sufism."[279]

Sufism primarily connotes an attitude of mind, not an organization, though this is too often forgotten by formalists. Baba himself can be said to have lived up to his own universal ideal of Sufism, since he never aligned himself with any organization. What he did was to give part of the Inayat Khan movement a charter containing guidelines, a charter which materialized in November 1952.[280]

Baba's ethnic predecessors included ishraqis who were never explicitly institutional since the death of Sohravardi Maqtul, who was officially condemned for the "wisdom of illumination" transcending Islam. More specifically, Baba's method had Kaivani overtones, including the latitude of allowing everyone their predilection of metaphysical background, which sometimes involved agreeing with, and even praising, their aptitude and view – even while attempting to enhance their aptitude by suggesting a step ahead (since two steps is generally far too much and invites more resistance). Sectarians find it difficult to meet universal standards, while those who pay lip service to the latter are often worse than the former.

On one occasion at Myrtle Beach in 1956, Baba singled out for attention the disparate situation in which non-sufi devotees were criticizing those who had the auspices of an "ism." Baba confronted a prominent American devotee, John Bass, who was the leader of a group of devotees and who regarded Sufism as an inferior approach quite distinct from his own "direct" approach (to Meher Baba). Baba defended Sufism Reoriented, and boldly stated: "I am the greatest Sufi of the past, present and future."[281]

Baba was then freely permitting his followers to assemble in groups which had recognized leaders. But he stressed that these groups should not be competitive and try to win over members of a different group (which is what tended to happen). He was beginning to use the term "lovers" for his devotees, and hence such statements of his as: "There may be greater lovers of Baba than the group heads . . . Someone who does not belong to any group may be the greatest lover of all."[282] But such remarks were not, in general, the most popular.

The desire to be part of a group is marked amongst many "spiritual aspirants." It gives them a stronger sense of identity, and serves to maintain their enthusiasm, which tends to evaporate in many cases without such a prop. Such groups often degenerate into entertainment programmes.

Those devotees who prided themselves upon their "direct" approach to Meher Baba merely exhibited features of another "ism" to outsiders owing to the cliches, sentiments, and beliefs that were disseminated, frequently with no great degree of discernment.

Ivy Duce was certainly not the only devotee to press publicity ventures upon Meher Baba, though in her case, the disparity with wisdom appears more marked. At the time of Baba's visit to America in 1956, she was preoccupied with press coverage of events[283] in a way that is reminiscent of earlier Western devotional enthusiasm in 1932. She reports that she had an ego-harrowing time during this visit; this is hardly surprising in view of such activities of hers as arranging to have a hair-do in order for her "to look nice" at a press conference at which television cameramen would be present. This press conference was arranged by her assistant Carvalho, whom Baba afterwards indicated was "confused." It is obvious that Duce thought that Baba's remarks went over the heads of the newspaper reporters; one might well think that he said much more that went over the heads of gushing devotees.

At a critical juncture Baba made it quite clear what his real attitude was to the publicity arranged for him. "A fleeting horrified expression came over Baba's face," writes Duce, when she mentioned to him that she and Bernard Carvalho (her publicity assistant) had arranged for a motorcycle escort of two policemen to rush Baba and his party through the crowds upon arrival at Washington. He then stated that "he did not like these press conferences where reporters only looked for sensationalism and often distorted what was said – nor the publicity, nor TV, nor any part of it."[284] He then pointedly asked Duce if she really thought that Jesus would have travelled through Washington with a police escort. Surprisingly, Duce glossed this rebuke with the statement that "he (Baba) had freely wanted publicity for his own purposes."[285] This gloss might be very partially excused on the basis that he had delegated the task of publishing and distributing *God Speaks* to her, but it amounts, in context, to an inability to accept criticism and to remedy defects. Duce adds that Baba acted as if he would go through with the publicity since it had been arranged, and she gave no more thought to it.[286] Further thought given to these matters by Duce and others might usefully have cancelled all the arrangements imposed. As it transpired, the motorcycle escort was dispensed with, but photographers were still in evidence at Washington, while later in Los Angeles, Duce and Don Stevens presided over more press arrangements. Baba made plain that he was "heartily sick" of the reporters and told Lud Dimpfl (a member of Sufism Reoriented) that he would not see any newspaper men or TV representatives in San Francisco. Dimpfl accordingly had to telephone devotees in San Francisco and ensure that all such plans for publicity were cancelled.[287]

Since Baba did not give any charter of "reorientation" to other groupings, e.g. Vedanta, some readers might wonder if this gesture was meaningful in more than the institutional sense which has tended to be given to it. One could certainly point out that in allowing Sufism to be explicitly represented in his following, Baba was leaving room for an esoteric perspective that was sadly lacking amongst his devotees at large – who customarily diminished his emphases to a bare handful of simplistic mottoes favoured by the mawkish. Unfortunately, the superficial nature of much of Murshida Duce's reporting is more aptly described as exoteric. Her style is not mundane, it is true, rather exaggeratedly fantastic in some ways, and does not neglect to promote Baba's supernormal abilities. But all hagiographies do this, and hence one has to view with extreme caution such statements of hers as "it has occurred to me, because it is natural to speculate on these things," that perhaps Baba had been Akhenaten (i.e. was a reincarnation of the Egyptian Pharaoh). Whether it really is natural to indulge in such speculation must be left to the reader's personal appetites; fabulation concerning Akhenaten has always been rife in the popular occult media, and very much represents an indulgence, not wisdom. It can here be observed that the categorical statement of Ivy Duce that one person (Akhenaten) arose in Egypt with the fixed conviction that there was only one God reflects her monotheistic upbringing and preoccupation with the Bible – though possibly facilitated by her reading of "thousands" of psychic and occult books prior to meeting Baba.[288]

Similarly, one has to be wary of such idioms of reporting as: "He (Baba) stopped his pace just long enough to say through Eruch, or I inwardly heard him say: 'This is the way I work.'"[289] What guarantee is there of the difference between fact and fancy in this report? How a "master" works is a delicate subject, no doubt, and should be clearly dissociated from subjective elements.

The reader is always obliged to ascertain context. Even the more tangible reproductions of what Meher Baba said are known to have occasionally been inaccurate; for instance, Eruch, the chief interpreter amongst the *mandali*, once rendered Baba's gestures as communicating to a female devotee that Baba did not want to see her for three days, whereas the truth was that Baba meant he had not seen her for three days.[290]

A pertinent reflection from Duce is that "watching Baba

tackle the devil in people" was like watching a skilled fencing master. "He will set this person against that one so that the thrust, riposte and remise follow each other with bewildering rapidity." Duce adds that it sometimes took months before the lessons involved were faced objectively,[291] though this would seem a chronological contraction in numerous cases. It is arguably more realistic to state that in some cases, the lessons were never objectively assimilated.

An appropriate epistle written by Dr. Ghani in 1948 furnishes useful information on Baba's own definition of a disciple, which was an abused word in general. Ghani states that, according to Baba, the only type of person entitled to call himself or herself a disciple was one who had received "illumination from the master." Until this point of development was reached, all persons were "mere aspirants and nothing more," whether seeming to be high or low in status, whether near or distant from the master's physical proximity.[292] This means that all those casuals, including Duce, who went about calling everybody in the devotional movement disciples, were categorically wrong according to the dictates of their own teacher. This may even be the reason why Baba afterwards began to consistently designate his devotees as "lovers," since their aptitude was anything but illumined. There is certainly no excuse for Murshida Duce, to whom the above-mentioned letter was written, having tagged others of the popular hierarchy (in the devotional movement) as "great disciples,"[293] particularly since these people always denied having received any form of illumination and were notably content with the stylism of "lover," which they employed abundantly. One should not attribute this to modesty, since most of them were very partial to the concept of Baba's "circles," and did not repudiate the common assumption that the presumed great ones had a high place in these.[294] Adi K. Irani went so far as to officially emblazon himself as "Disciple and Secretary," while vociferously denying the validity of any illuminative experience, probably because he himself never had any such experience and was resentful of those who seemed to have anything of the sort – including all other masters and saints of contemporary renown. This zealous devotee was a firm advocate of insularity against all that threatened to compete with his own master's prestige – competition which might, of course, have lessened the level of elevation of the stridently proclaimed disciple.[295]

An example of a disciple in the real sense is more applicably that of Abdullah Pakrawan, alias Chota Baba. This Muslim was never recorded during Baba's lifetime after the Prem Ashram phase. He was not at the ashram, but lived in Iran, quite separate from the subsequently burgeoning devotional movement. During the Prem Ashram phase of the late 1920's, Baba unequivocally stated that Abdullah had gained sixth plane consciousness at his hands. This was at a time when Abdullah experienced a very different state of consciousness to the one he had formerly known; it transformed him, in a way that was evident to his comrades. He remained with Baba for some months after the Prem Ashram was closed, and accompanied Baba on the visit to Iran in 1929. Baba allowed this young man, then only twenty, to stay behind in Isfahan, and so it came about that Abdullah stayed for the rest of his life in Iran after Baba had left for India. Abdullah Pakrawan had put aside his former saintly trappings (a necessary adjustment in the case of many sufi trainees), and instead lived as an ordinary citizen, married, had children, and worked at an ordinary job. There was no correspondence between him and Baba, and it was commonly assumed that he had gone adrift into the world.[296] When he was later contacted in Iran by devotees of Baba in 1975, he denied having had any more spiritual experiences since the Prem Ashram days, but expressed continued respect for Meher Baba.[297] The main point was lost upon the devotional movement, however: here was a disciple whom Baba himself had stated to be on the sixth plane, a person of sufi background who remained aloof from devotee activities and mystical preoccupations of the herd variety. Assumptions based upon the herd instinct clearly have no relevance to persons like Chota Baba (a name meaning "Little Baba").

One does not need to look any further than the case of Meher Baba's parents to find the anomaly of neglected depths displaced in popular thinking by more visible entities.

During Baba's lifetime and after, his father Sheriar never received a sufficiently detailed profile in print. As a consequence, Sheriar was largely unknown, his sufi dimensions limited in popular acquaintance to his obscure early life as a dervish.[298] In contrast, Baba's mother Shirin was well known and much more frequently referred to by devotees. This disparity largely reflects the fact that Sheriar died over a decade earlier, and was more retiring in disposition, and held a different perspective on life to that of his wife. Shirin had strong affinities with the westernized thinking of her Parsi generation in Western India; Sheriar distrusted westernized attitudes, and was much more typically Persian in his disposition. Western devotees did not meet him, and he did not live with the early *mandali* but at his home in Poona. It is rather ironic that the father of Meher Baba had such a pronounced (if unorthodox) sufi background that he was rendered a closed book to most of his son's followers.[299]

NOTES

1. See Shepherd, *A Sufi Matriarch: Hazrat Babajan* (Cambridge: Anthropographia Publications, 1986).
2. For his biography, see Part Two of Shepherd, *Gurus Rediscovered* (Cambridge: Anthropographia Publications, 1986).
3. *Sayings of Shri Meher Baba*, p. 27. I possess Will Backett's personal copy of this early publication, which is unostentatiously bound in a plain blue softcover, and with no photograph inside. Backett had a "Western Sufi" background, though he retained strong Christian traces.
4. *Messages of Meher Baba delivered in the East and West*, p. 94.
5. Ann Powell died in December 1965, and I knew her personally for a year beforehand. In my view, she had learnt much more than many other followers of Meher Baba, and her views differed from general concensus. I was acquainted with the New York group through a regular correspondence with Beryl Williams, an American negro who was also exceptional by comparison with much American devoteeism.
6. Baba's brother Adi S. Irani later confirmed this in London, and graphically related his exasperation with the "Kimco" group owing to their diversionary inclinations at Nasik. I was in personal contact with Adi over a number of years, and he was a rich source of information upon events in which he had been a participant.
7. This detail was related to me by Delia De Leon, one of the "Kimco" group who lived in London. On two occasions in 1966, and another in 1973, I visited her home for lengthy sessions in which she gave me much information about her contact with Baba. (See Bibliography, Oral Sources). Though I could not see eye to eye with her estimation of herself in relation to Baba, she was a useful source of data. I was also in correspondence with Kitty Davy (likewise of "Kimco") at Myrtle Beach during 1965–6, but she was able to add little to her published record.

8. During Baba's lifetime, available published information on this woman was nil. The only substantial reference I could find concerning her was in personal (hand-written) memoranda in my Backett File, and even that was very brief, reporting her burial on Meherabad Hill after observing silence at Baba's instructions, a silence which had lasted twenty years.
9. Gulmai died a number of years before Mehera and others became well known. She moved between Meherabad and her home in Ahmednagar. One of her sons was Adi K. Irani, Baba's secretary who lived at Ahmednagar, with whom I exchanged several letters during 1965–6. Apart from his published articles, Adi was not very informative, and showed a very sectarian approach that seemed unwilling to come to terms with the fact that his mother had simultaneously been a disciple of both Upasni Maharaj and Meher Baba.
10. Donkin was the only Western male to be permanently incorporated amongst the *mandali*, with the exception of the Australian poet Francis Brabazon who arrived much later. Donkin's book was not widely circulated, and passed largely unnoticed in India. I can personally testify to the unfamiliarity with the contents on the part of many Western devotees of Meher Baba. See further Bibliography, no's 20–22.
11. These analyses were based upon personal names, and formed part of my account of the *mast* work in my unpublished biography of Meher Baba (typescript, Vol. 3, pp. 422–3). These analyses were made in 1971–2, and to date have no parallel in the literature on Meher Baba. The percentage calculations relating to *masts* did not extend to the two hundred or so *masts* who lack names in the reports. The *mast* percentages cannot be regarded as definitive owing to the possibility of Muslims and Hindus naming a local figure in accordance with their own descriptive repertories. Nevertheless, these percentages may in fact convey an approximately accurate idea of religious and ethnic componency.
12. This statement was reported by Delia De Leon in *The Awakener*. She was one of those to whom it was addressed, at the time of her brief visit to India in 1948. When I spoke to her much later, it was plain that she could not elaborate upon it.
13. The implications of this chronological stratification were

never taken up during Baba's lifetime in any published material, and nor even by the time of writing this. Much detail relating to the "boys" period was submerged in published accounts, and a misleading picture of it was given in its final years. One of the trio who accompanied Baba from India on his first visit to the West was a Shia Muslim youth; even the detail that he was a Shi'i was never given in published form, and is only ascertainable through colloquialized references in the published material.

14. C.B. Purdom, *The God-Man* (1964), p. 169.
15. *Ibid.*, pp. 187–8.
16. Cf. *ibid.*, p. 202. I was in correspondence with the Meher Center-on-the-Lakes during 1965–6, and no headway had been made in this direction.
17. Ramju Abdulla, "Meher Baba's Fiery Life and External Activities," *The Awakener* (1953) 1 (1): 27.
18. *Life Circular*, No. 9, issued 28–3–1953.
19. *Life Circular*, No. 9, ed. by Adi K. Irani.
20. Purdom, *The God-Man*, pp. 210 ff. This message did not appear in the Life Circulars, but was published separately in a booklet by Adi K. Irani in November 1953.
21. Included in a message Baba gave at Rajahmundry, in Andhra, on Feb. 27th.
22. When I first heard of this theme, I imagined that it was more or less literally intended, but it did not take long for me to conclude otherwise after an inspection of Baba's various statements on the subject. It is quite obvious that he could never have intended it literally. Yet devotees whom I knew accepted the literal dimensions, though occasionally with a vagueness that made it clear they had not given the matter any deep thought.
23. The relevant report was given in an abridged form by Purdom (1964), pp. 216 ff, but was earlier given in full in *The Awakener*, read by Western followers. I found that it did not figure very much in the thinking of devotees at large.
24. Printed in *The Awakener* (1954) 2(2): 2–5.
25. See Life Circulars no's 18 and 27 respectively. This identification was repeated on office stationery.
26. See the note appended to *Life Circular*, No. 22.
27. Baba is known to have used the term "lovers" on rare

occasions prior to the New Life, but it was only after the New Life that he began to make consistent use of it, gradually at first. It seems to have been a rendition of the Persian word *muhibbi* (lover), which was part of the specialized sufi vocabulary dating back to ninth century figures like Somnun Muhibb of Baghdad. But during the 1950's and 1960's Baba used it as a generalized term of reference to all his devotees. Writers of the "old school" like Charles Purdom and Will Backett did not use this term, since it was not in order to copy the idioms of the teacher. Mani overworked it to the extent of providing a literary cliche.

28. C.B. Purdom and M. Schloss, *Three Incredible Weeks with Meher Baba*, bound volume of *The Awakener* (1955) 2(3).
29. Purdom, *The God-Man*, p. 277.
30. See *The Awakener* (1958) 5(3): 2–71 for Purdom's report, which incorporates notes of other devotees that are probably not as accurate, and which are not in Purdom's style. An abridged version was included in *The God-Man*, pp. 297 ff.
31. *The God-Man*, p. 296.
32. I came to such a conclusion very firmly by late 1966, but the number of others that I knew who shared this view was something very close to nil.
33. *The God-Man*, pp. 340–1.
34. *Ibid.*, p. 361.
35. For a complete version of this message, see *The Awakener* (1963), East-West Gathering special issue, pp. 38–40.
36. *Ibid.*, p. 12.
37. Reliably reported by Dr. Ghani in *The Meher Baba Jnl*, in his account of the Manzil.
38. Abdul Karim (Ramju) Abdulla, *Shri Meher Baba: His Philosophy and Teachings* (Ahmednagar, 1933). See Bibliography, no. 5.
39. On *hulul*, see my *Survey of the Sufi Phenomenon*, Vol. 1; *Sufis, Batinis, Scientists and Philosophers of the early Islamic era*, chap. eight.
40. E.g., C.B. Purdom, *The God-Man* (1964), pp. 390 ff., whose Christian interpretation was at variance with the views of the devotional movement. Purdom's interpretation is actually very sophisticated, though it was repudiated by some devotees.

41. Meher Baba, *God Speaks* (2nd edn, New York 1973), p. 307. This description comes from the glossary compiled by L.H. Dimpfl, which was approved by Baba.
42. On Tirmizi, see my *Survey of the Sufi Phenomenon*, Vol. 1 no. 31.
43. A.J. Arberry, *Sufism* (London: George Allen & Unwin, 1950), p. 101. Cf. Shepherd, *Survey*, Vol. 2.
44. Shepherd, *A Sufi Matriarch: Hazrat Babajan*, pp. 48, 50.
45. Shepherd, *Gurus Rediscovered*, Part One, n. 60.
46. See my *Survey of the Sufi Phenomenon Vol. 1*, no. 32.
47. On Hallaj, see Shepherd, *Survey*, Vol. 1, no. 36; *id.*, *Sufis, Batinis*, chapter eight.
48. Cf. e.g. J. Spencer Trimingham, *The Sufi Orders in Islam* (Oxford: Clarendon Press, 1971), p. 162, n. 1.
49. Meher Baba, *God Speaks*, 2nd edn, p. 316, glossary.
50. Probably the most notable instances of the "Indian" theory in studies of Sufism were R. Hartmann, "Zur Frage nach der Herkunft und den Anfangen des Sufitums," *Der Islam* (1916) 6: 31–70; M. Horten, *Indische Stromungen in der Islamischen Mystik* (Heidelberg 1927). Cf. the less edifying argument in R.C. Zaehner, *Hindu and Muslim Mysticism* (London, 1960). For a commentary on Zaehner, see my *The Resurrection of Philosophy*, chap. nine.
51. There is still no translation of this sprawling work which runs to over 2,500 pages in the four-volume Cairo edn of the Arabic text. There are doubts that it could be translated successfully.
52. For a trans., see R.W.J. Austin, *The Bezels of Wisdom* (London: SPCK, 1980).
53. For a trans., see A.J. Arberry, *Discourses of Rumi* (London: John Murray, 1961).
54. See R.A. Nicholson, ed., trans., and commentary, *The Mathnawi of Jalaluddin Rumi* (8 vols, London: Luzac, 1925–40). The commentary should be read with caution.
55. For useful summaries of Shankara texts, see Karl H. Potter, ed., *Advaita Vedanta Up to Samkara and his Pupils* (Princeton, N.J.: Princeton University Press, 1981).
56. See Swami Madhavananda, trans., *The Brihadaranyaka Upanishad with the commentary of Sankaracarya* (4th edn, Calcutta: Advaita Ashrama, 1965).

57. See Swami Madhavananda, text and trans., *Vivekachudamani* (7th edn, Calcutta: Advaita Ashrama, 1966).
58. Swami Jagadananda, trans., *Upadeshasahasri* (3rd edn, Mylapore, Madras: Sri Ramakrishna Math, 1961).
59. Purdom, *The God-Man*, pp. 210 ff, describing this as "the most explicit direct and the fullest public statement made by Baba about himself." Cf. *God Speaks* (first edn), p. 173.
60. Meher Baba, *Discourses Vol. 2* (Bangalore, 1939–40), pp. 7 ff., conceding the necessity for the regulation of population, but effectively supporting Gandhi's policy of birth control, though he does not refer to it as such. In practice, Baba did not impose regulations upon his following. The exceptions were the *mandali* and various pupils and disciples who received special instructions from him concerning a celibate phase.
61. For a translation, see S. Insler, *The Gathas of Zarathustra* (Leiden: E.J. Brill, 1975).
62. For a parallel in variant terminology, see chapter five of Shepherd, *Meaning in Anthropos*.
63. On the eclecticism of Shikoh, see Part Two of Shepherd, *From Oppression to Freedom*.
64. For a more detailed critique of these trends and categories, see Shepherd, *The Resurrection of Philosophy* and *Meaning in Anthropos*.
65. Teilhard De Chardin. *The Phenomenon of Man* (London: Collins, 1959), pp. 324–5. For a comparison of De Chardin and Meher Baba, see *The Resurrection of Philosophy*, chapter seven.
66. Purdom, *The God-Man*, p. 417.
67. *Ibid.*, p. 420.
68. *Ibid.*, pp. 417 ff., esp. p. 422, where the incorrect extrapolation is made that "reincarnation takes place only when the subtle and mental bodies are developed." This is in contradiction to Meher Baba's explicit statements in *God Speaks*, where it is instead asserted that the subtle and mental bodies gain their full development only with the achievement of the human form. See *God Speaks* (first edn, 1955), p. 55.
69. For a description of the transmission involved, see Ivy Duce, *How a Master Works* (1975), pp. 198 ff. Duce also reports that Baba asked Purdom to write a "simplified, layman's version" of *God Speaks*, though he never did, evidently feeling peeved

that the American editors were entrusted with the job of publishing the original. Purdom's version in *The God-Man* was altogether too simplified. Purdom states inaccurately that Dr. Ghani took down the dictation of the main text.

70. Purdom, *op. cit.*, pp. 416–417.
71. On the Upanishads, see Part Three of my *Minds and Sociocultures*.
72. Swami Vireswarananda, text and trans., *Brahma-Sutras* (4th edn, Calcutta: Advaita Ashrama, 1970), pp. v ff.
73. For a trans. of the commentaries of both Shankara and Ramanuja, see G. Thibaut, *The Vedanta-Sutras* (3 vols, Oxford: Clarendon Press, 1890–1904, *Sacred Books of the East*), but with a controversial interpretation.
74. See S. Mackenna, trans., *The Enneads* (third edn, London: Faber, 1962).
75. For a treatment of Eriugena, see Part Four of my *Minds and Sociocultures*. See also I.P. Sheldon-Williams, ed. and trans., *Johannis Scotti Eriugenae: Periphyseon* (3 vols, Dublin Institute for Advanced Studies, 1968–81) for Books I-III.
76. For a convenient trans. of the Ps.-Dionysian treatise *The Mystical Theology*, see F.C. Happold, *Mysticism* (Harmondsworth: Penguin, 1964), pp. 191 ff., who describes this brief treatise as the chief work of Ps.-Dionysius and one of the most important works in the "whole history of speculative Christian mysticism" (p. 190).
77. See E.R. Dodds, ed. and trans., *The Elements of Theology* (second edn, Oxford: Clarendon Press, 1963).
78. Cf. Dean Inge's description of Eckhart as "next to Plotinus the greatest philosopher-mystic," quoted in C. De B. Evans, trans., *Meister Eckhart Vol. 1* (London: Watkins 1956, third imp.,) p. xi. Cf. C. F. Kelley, *Meister Eckhart on Divine Knowledge* (New Haven: Yale University Press, 1977) for a conservative interpretation which rebuts pantheistic interpretations and comparisons with oriental thought. According to Kelley, such mystical forms of thought "were completely foreign to his (Eckhart's) doctrine and actually refuted by him." (*Ibid.*, pp. 47 ff.) Kelley stresses that Eckhart's doctrine is entirely compatible with the Roman Catholic church, to which he was wholly committed. The mystical approach that many others have seen in Eckhart is here denied (p. 51) in

place of "a purely intellectual consideration situated as it were *in divinis*." If this is correct, then Eckhart is of little use to non-Catholics. Kelley's interpretation draws upon the extensive Latin writings of Eckhart which were hitherto little known by comparison with his German sermons and tractates made famous in the Pfeiffer edition. Several of these German works are now considered spurious. The Eckhart corpus is available in J. Quint *et al*, eds., *Meister Eckhart: Die Deutschen Werke*, Vols 1–5; E. Benz *et al*, eds., *Meister Eckhart: Die Lateinischen Werke*, Vols 1–5 (Stuttgart: Kohlhammer, 1938—). The problem for some Eckhart enthusiasts is the context of scholastic theology with which Eckhart is inextricably connected owing to his being a member of the Dominican order in the era of Thomas Aquinas.

79. Gershom Scholem, *Kabbalah* (Jerusalem: Keter Publishing House, 1974), pp. 23 ff., 96 ff.
80. E.g. Scholem, *op.cit.*, pp. 21–2, who contests the theory of Iranian influences and concedes the indigenous nature of early Jewish gnosticism, though suggesting (*ibid.*, p. 27) neo-Pythagorean and Stoic influences upon the doctrine of the *Sefirot* and the language system of the *Sefer Yezirah*.
81. *God Speaks* (first edn), pp. 139–40.
82. Henry Corbin, *Cyclical Time and Ismaili Gnosis* (London: Kegan Paul International, 1983), p. 173.
83. For translations of texts involved, see R.C. Zaehner, *Zurvanism: A Zoroastrian Dilemma* (Oxford: Clarendon Press, 1955), with a very inadequate commentary exhibiting strong Christian bias.
84. On Razi and Hallaj, see chapter eight of my *Sufis, Batinis, Scientists and Philosophers of the early Islamic era*.
85. For a trans. of the *Kitab al-Tawasin*, see L. Massignon, *The Passion of Al-Hallaj Vol. 3* (Princeton, 1982), pp. 282 ff.
86. See G. Bowring, *The Mystical Vision of Existence in Classical Islam: The Quranic Hermeneutics of the Sufi Sahl at-Tustari* (Berlin: Walter de Gruyter, 1980).
87. It is difficult to agree with Dr. Ghani that Jili was the founder of *wahdat al-shuhud* (apparentism), which was in existence before Jili's day. Unless the problem was caused by Ivy Duce, Ghani was incorrect here. Cf. *God Speaks* (first edn, p. 238; second edn, p. 282).

88. For a summary of Jili's treatise, see R.A. Nicholson, *Studies in Islamic Mysticism* (Cambridge University Press, 1921; repr. 1978), pp. 77–142.
89. See T. Izutzu, *Sufism and Taoism: a comparative study of key philosophical concepts* (first edn, 1966–7; rev. edn, Berkeley: University of California Press, 1984).
90. *God Speaks* (first edn, p. 74; second edn, p. 83).
91. *Ibid.* (first edn, p. 242; second edn, p. 286).
92. *Ibid.* (first edn, pp. 208 ff; second edn, pp. 243 ff).
93. This sequence is specified in Meher Baba's statement appearing in F. Brabazon, *Stay With God* (Woombye, Queensland: Garuda Books, 1959), p. 13.
94. *God Speaks* (first edn, p. 105; second edn, pp. 118–119).
95. See Shepherd, *The Resurrection of Philosophy*, chapter two. For a trans. of the *Mahayanasamgraha*, which is attributed to Asanga, see Etienne Lamotte, *La Somme Du Grand Vehicule D'Asanga*, 2 vols (new edn, Institut Orientaliste Louvain-La-Neuve, 1973).
96. *God Speaks* (first edn, pp. 130, 208; second edn, pp. 147, 242).
97. *Ibid.* (first edn, p. 156; second edn, p. 180).
98. *Ibid.*, second edn, p. 288.
99. See Shepherd, *Vivekananda: his life and teaching*, intro., n. 51.
100. Cf. Christmas Humphreys, *Buddhism* (third edn, Harmondsworth: Penguin, 1962), p. 56.
101. Shepherd, *Psychology in Science*, p. 115.
102. Paul Deussen, *Outline of the Vedanta System of Philosophy according to Shankara*, trans. by J.H. Woods and C.B. Runkle (second edn, Cambridge, Mass.: Harvard University Press, 1915), p. 36.
103. Swami Madhavananda, trans., *The Brihadaranyaka Upanishad with commentary of Shankara* (4th edn), pp. 911 ff.
104. *God Speaks* (first edn, pp. 9 ff; second edn, pp. 10 ff.).
105. Specifically mentioned in *ibid.*, p. 32 (first edn).
106. *Ibid.* (first edn) pp. 32–3.
107. Cf. E.R. Dodds, ed. and trans., *The Elements of Theology* (second edn), pp. 313 ff.
108. Cf. H. Corbin, *Spiritual Body and Celestial Earth: From*

Mazdean Iran to Shi'ite Iran, trans. N. Pearson (Princeton University Press, 1977), pp. 90 ff. Cf. *God Speaks* (first edn), pp. 54–5.

109. E.g., James Winston Morris, trans., *The Wisdom of the Throne: An Introduction to the Philosophy of Mulla Sadra* (Princeton University Press, 1981), p. 140.
110. Meher Baba, *Discourses Vol. 4* (1941–2, Bangalore), pp. 48 ff; *God Speaks* (first edn), pp. 33 ff.
111. The main text of *God Speaks* specifies "millions of births and deaths," apparently relating to the human soul (first edn, p. 39). But this may have been a concession to Hindu lore, since Eruch Jessawala's Part 9 reports the Hindu belief that the soul has to pass through eight million four hundred thousand (84 *lakhs*) human forms (*ibid.*, p. 163). The number 84 has an associational significance, and hence one is justified in viewing this number with a due reserve. There is, however, no doubt that Meher Baba was indicating a very large number of human incarnations for each soul.
112. The definitive work on Gurdjieff's system is P.D. Ouspensky, *In Search of the Miraculous* (London: Routledge, 1950). Gurdjieff's insistence upon the mechanical aspect of human psychology resulted in a tapered version of the "astral" and "mental body" (*ibid.*, pp. 31–2, 40 ff), which creates complications for his cosmology if systematically expounded. Gurdjieff himself did not systematize, as his bizarre books attest.
113. For some comments on Hume, see my *Meaning in Anthropos*, chapter nine. Cf. A.J. Ayer, *Hume* (Oxford University Press, 1980).
114. Meher Baba, *Discourses Vol. 4*, pp. 80 ff, 89–90.
115. *God Speaks* (first edn), pp. 40 ff, 108 ff.
116. See W. Donkin, *The Wayfarers* (Ahmednagar, 1948), pp. 1–39, for Meher Baba's explanation concerning spiritually advanced souls, and also a contribution from a Muslim pupil of Meher Baba, namely Ramju Abdulla, on the subject of *masts* (pp. 13–19). Much of the information given is unique insofar as I am aware.
117. *Ibid.*, p. 23. Meher Baba's statement that the God-communed man "never advances beyond the sixth plane"

can be taken to mean that in advancing to higher levels, a different orientation of consciousness becomes operative.

118. Donkin, ed., *The Wayfarers*, pp. 38–9.
119. *Beams from Meher Baba on the Spiritual Panorama* (Sufism Reoriented, 1958), p. 12.
120. For an applicable interpretation, see J. Perez-Remon, *Self and Non-Self in Early Buddhism* (Berlin: Walter de Gruyter, 1980). See also my *The Resurrection of Philosophy*, nn. 179–182.
121. *God Speaks* (first edn), pp. 50 ff., 117 ff.
122. *God Speaks* (first edn), pp. 132 ff; Purdom, *The God-Man*, pp. 364 ff; Meher Baba, *The Everything and the Nothing* (Sydney: Meher House, 1963), pp. 22 ff., which has a superfluous word in the transcription relevant to the Fourth Journey – this word is "forever" (p. 26). On the similarities and differences with earlier Iranian mystical philosophy, see the final chapter of my *Philosophers in Islamic and Jewish Locales* (in preparation).
123. See O. Yahya, ed., *Kitab Khatm al-Awliya* (Beirut, 1965); Shepherd, *Survey of the Sufi Phenomenon Vol. 1*, no. 31.
124. *God Speaks* (first edn, pp. 229 ff; second edn, 271 ff.).
125. N. Mishra, "The Conception of *Samskara* in the *Yoga Sutra*,," *Jnl of Bihar Research Soc.* (1951) 37: 48–60, and finding fault with the definition in S. Dasgupta, *A History of Indian Philosophy Vol. 1* (Cambridge University Press, 1922), p. 263, who described *sanskaras* as "the impressions of the objects experienced."
126. *Ibid.*, pp. 53–4. On the Patanjali text, see also the intro. to my *Vivekananda: his life and teaching*.
127. See S. Pines and T. Gelblum, "Al-Biruni's Arabic Version of Patanjali's Yoga-Sutra," *Bulletin of the School of Oriental and African Studies* (1966) 29: 302–25.
128. *The Complete Works of Swami Vivekananda Vol. 1* (twelfth edn, Calcutta: Advaita Ashrama, 1965), pp. 241–2.
129. Meher Baba, *Discourses Vol. 1*, pp. 36–74.
130. *Discourses Vol. 2*, pp. 66 ff.
131. *Discourses Vol. 5*, pp. 45–7.
132. For Meher Baba's qualified view of occultism, see his *Discourses Vol. 3*, pp. 10–34.
133. *Ibid.*, p. 89.

134. *Ibid.*, pp. 38–9.
135. *Beams from Meher Baba on the Spiritual Panorama*, pp. 13–14.
136. *God Speaks* (first edn, p. 217; second edn, p. 255).
137. A.E. Affifi, *The Mystical Philosophy of Muhyid Din-Ibnul Arabi* (Cambridge University Press, 1939), pp. 143 ff., though the interpretation is inadequate. For an updated version, see Shepherd, *Psychology in Science*, pp. 66 ff.
138. See, e.g., I. Shah, *The Sufis* (1964; repr. London: Octagon, 1977), pp. 394–5; *id.*, *A Perfumed Scorpion* (London: Octabon Press, 1978), pp. 82–4. The *nafs* teaching should not be confused with the "seven men" enumerated in Gurdjieff's teaching, which has clear differences. See P.D. Ouspensky, *In Search of the Miraculous*, pp. 71 ff. Four stages of the *nafs* are mentioned in the supplement to *God Speaks* (first edn, pp. 240–1; second edn, pp. 285–6). Here *nafs-i-lawaama* (the reproachful self) is identified with consciousness of the subtle sphere, while *nafs-i-mutmainna* (the serene self) and *nafs-i-mulhima* (the inspired self) are identified with the fifth and sixth planes respectively.
139. *Messages of Mehor Baba delivered in the East and West* (Ahmednagar: Adi K. Irani, n.d.), pp. 65–6, entitled "God and Religion," read out on 11.11.44 at Nagpur.
140. *Ibid.*, pp. 34–5, entitled "Action and Inaction," given in March 1942. Also in *Discourses Vol. 4*, p. 78.
141. *Messages*, p. 40.
142. *Ibid.*, pp. 47, 42, 44, entitled "Violence and Non-Violence," released in March 1942. Also included in *Discourses Vol. 4*, pp. 27ff.
143. *Ibid.*, pp. 94–5.
144. *Discourses Vol. 3*, pp. 1–9; *Messages*, pp. 13–21.
145. For a treatment of Azar Kaivan, his disciples, and related events, see Shepherd, *From Oppression to Freedom*, Part Two; *id.*, *The Resurrection of Philosophy*, chapters eight and nine.
146. For a biography of Sheriar, see *From Oppression to Freedom*, Part One.
147. I.O. Duce, *How a Master Works*, p. 115, quoting a verse which Baba composed in 1952.

148. See Shepherd, *Gurus Rediscovered*, Part One, for a biography of Sai Baba of Shirdi.
149. For a review of scholarly theories on Zarathushtra, see Part Two of my *Minds and Sociocultures*. See also my *Ancient Cultures in Flux*, final part. In those books I have not referred to Meher Baba's statements on Zarathushtra, though these statements would seem to be as valid (if not more so) as many others on the subject. Meher Baba's reference to 700 years would seem to fit his cyclic framework for events pertaining to the spiritual hierarchy. Though his statements cast doubt upon the first-hand nature of the Gathas, he strongly supports the historicity of the ancient Iranian prophet, and also his moral influence.
150. *The Glow* (Dehra Dun, 1976) 11(2):2, for a verbatim report taken down by one of the *mandali* members present at the time. This report reveals the brief sentence structure typical of Baba's communications via the alphabet board.
151. G. Lanczkowski *Sacred Writings* (English edn, London: Collins Fontana, 1961), pp. 83–4.
152. See further Shepherd, *Minds and Sociocultures*, Appendice 1; *Sufis, Batinis*, chapter eight.
153. On Maqtul, see Shepherd, *Survey of the Sufi Phenomenon*, Vol. 2; *id.*, *Sufis, Batinis*, chapter nine; *id.*, *The Resurrection of Philosophy*, chapter nine.
154. The term *qalandar* became a common one in the thirteenth century, and covers a wide range of dervish types. See Trimingham, *The Sufi Orders in Islam*, pp. 267–8.
155. E.g., K.J. Dastur, ed., *The Meher Message* (1930) 2(1): 12, for an English trans. from Gujerati and Urdu couplets, which include a reference to the execution of Hallaj (Mansur).
156. See L. Massignon, *The Passion of al-Hallaj Vol. 2*, trans. H. Mason (Princeton University Press, 1982).
157. A.K. Abdulla, *Shri Meher Baba: his Philosophy and Teachings* (1933), end of chap. two (*The Awakener*, Vol. 2 no. 2, 1954, p. 31). Abdulla's compilation refers to Hallaj as "Mansoor," actually the name of the father of Hallaj, though this paternal name is commonly used in Eastern sources. The context is one of the "third journey," though prophets are also mentioned.
158. *The Meher Message* (1931) 3 (3): 7–8, being a discourse on

baqa as edited by the Parsi K.J. Dastur. This discourse may have been given as early as 1928. It ends with a comparison of Hallajian and Junaydi *baqa* with equivalent Buddhist perspectives, and also with mystical and orthodox attitudes in Christianity. Baba also observes that the Hindus were more open to gnostic claims as epitomized by the phrase *Aham Brahmasmi* (I am *Brahman*), despite the influence of dualism (Dvaita) and Vishishtadvaita; he adds that, despite this broadness of view, "even amongst the Hindus, those with the true experience of Godhood are but few and far between" (pp. 8–9).

159. R.A. Nicholson, trans., *Kashf al-Mahjub of Al Hujwiri* (second edn, Luzac 1936), pp. 260, 264.
160. Fazlur Rahman, *The Philosophy of Mulla Sadra* (Albany: State University of New York Press, 1975), p. 247.
161. E.g., the Kaivani work *Desatir* includes a reference to the reversion to the mineral stage of evolution, but this reference is too fragmentary to closely compare with Meher Baba's much more graphic insistence upon the dangers of backslide on the fourth plane (cf. Shepherd, *From Oppression to Freedom*, Appendix 1). It is, however, valid to conclude that there was a precedent to Meher Baba's exposition on this otherwise obscure and difficult topic.
162. Gandhi encountered problems in his sanction of rabid dogs being killed. There were vast numbers of stray dogs in India, but many conservative thinkers disagreed with Gandhi on this issue. Gandhi himself was usually a strict upholder of *ahimsa*, having grown up under the influence of Jainism. See L. Fischer, *The Life of Mahatma Gandhi* (1951; repr. London: Granada, 1982), pp. 299 ff.
163. On Abu'l Fazl, see S.A.A. Rizvi, *Religious and Intellectual History of the Muslims in Akbar's Reign* (New Delhi: Munshiram Manoharlal, 1975).
164. On Nagauri, see Shepherd, *Survey of the Sufi Phenomenon*, Vol. 2.
165. See Shepherd, *Survey*, Vol. 2.
166. See M. Mahfuz-Ul-Haq, trans., *Majma'-ul-Bahrain or the Mingling of the Two Oceans* (Calcutta: Asiatic Soc. of Bengal, 1929).
167. D. Shea and A. Troyer, trans., *The Dabistan Vol. 2* (Paris:

Oriental Translation Fund of Great Britain and Ireland, 1843), pp. 114–115.

168. See E.G. Browne, *A Year Amongst the Persians* (third edn, Cambridge University Press, 1950).

169. For these and other early malamatis, see Shepherd, *Survey*, Vol. 1. For a rare reference to Abu Said ibn Abu'l Khair as a *qutub*, see Francis Brabazon, *Stay With God* (1959), p. 162. This reference occurs in Brabazon's notes to his best poetic work, but he does not stipulate whether this was Meher Baba's definition of Abu Said. One tends to assume that it was, however, since elsewhere in his notes Brabazon refers to some famous entities only as "masters," in contradistinction to "Perfect Master." Since Brabazon had met Meher Baba several years before writing this work, and was himself an interested student of Sufism, it is very unlikely that he would have included this definition without basis.

170. There is a fleeting mention of this figure in Ramju Abdulla, *Sobs and Throbs* (1928).

171. R.C. Zaehner, *Concordant Discord* (Oxford: Clarendon Press, 1970), pp. 305 ff. Zaehner comes down in favour of the more "Christian" idioms of Richard of St. Victor, and is preoccupied with the "love of God" to which mysticism is often simplistically reduced.

172. For a treatment of Hafiz, with reference to the scholarly literature, see Shepherd, *Survey of the Sufi Phenomenon*, Vol. 2.

173. On Kabir, see the relevant entry in Shepherd, *Survey*, Vol. 2 (forthcoming).

174. Shepherd, *Gurus Rediscovered*, p. 45.

175. On the wujudi tradition, see Shepherd, *Survey*, Volume Two (forthcoming); *id.*, *Sufis, Batinis*, chapter seven; *id.*, *From Oppression to Freedom*, Part 2. See also S.A.A. Rizvi, *A Hist. of Sufism in India*, Vols 1 and 2 (New Delhi, 1978–83).

176. Purdom, *The Perfect Master*, p. 155, who dismissed Hirsch (Hurst) in a brief footnote, preferring this method to a literary wrangle over misrepresentation.

177. Purdom was accurate in calling him Hurst, though Hirsch was his real name. It has been thought that Hirsch was a Jewish name, though this seems doubtful in the case of

Brunton, who spoke in a thick Cockney accent. Cf. Irene Conybeare, *In Quest of Truth*, pp. 69–70.

178. See the diary of K.J. Dastur in *The Meher Message* (Nasik 1931), the relevant article being compiled before it was known of the defection of Brother Raphael Hurst. On this periodical, see the Bibliography, no. 45.
179. Paul Brunton, *A Search in Secret India* (London: Rider, n.d., but published 1934), p. 253; second edn (London: Rider, 1970), p. 253. There was no change made in the text in the second edition.
180. *Ibid.*
181. To cite an instance personally known to me in 1965, a Western "disciple" planned to go to India for a *sahavas* arranged for December (subsequently cancelled). The person concerned had sufficient money to make the journey, but also intended to go on a tour of India to make the journey "more worthwhile." Upon learning that Baba specifically wished for no attendant tourism, this prospective traveller lost enthusiasm and decided not to go to India at all.
182. Brunton, *op. cit.*, p. 254.
183. *Ibid.*
184. *Ibid.*, p. 257.
185. Purdom, *The God-Man*, pp. 128, 440. The encounter occurred in London, and there is no need to doubt the accuracy of Purdom's brief report. Brunton then felt secure in his new fame, and could divulge details more freely. Purdom always tended to understate, and not to exaggerate, and could have made much more of the matter had he wished, or been told, to do so.
186. Brunton, *op. cit.*, p. 257.
187. Purdom incorrectly gave the date as Feb. 8th (*The Perfect Master*, p. 155), an error which was not corrected in *The God-Man*, p. 94. Yet it was a great improvement upon Brunton's chronological blank.
188. Brunton, *op. cit.*, p. 273.
189. *Ibid.*, p. 278.
190. *Ibid.*, p. 280. For a less clouded view of Maharshi, see Arthur Osborne, *Ramana Maharshi and the Path of Self-Knowledge* (London: Rider, 1954).
191. Brunton, p. 308.

192. *Ibid.*, p. 14.
193. Rather late in the day came a criticism from Irene Conybeare, *In Quest of Truth* (1961), pp. 69 ff., but this is devotionally oriented and does not mention the factual documentation that is more convincing to historians.
194. Brunton, *op. cit.*, pp. 46 ff.
195. *Ibid.*, p. 61.
196. *Ibid.*, p. 62.
197. *Ibid.*, p. 51.
198. *The Awakener* (1959) 6 (3): 21, quoting *The Daily Mirror*.
199. Ramju Abdulla, *Shri Meher Baba: his Philosophy and Teachings* (1933); repr. in *The Awakener* (1959) 6(3): 27. The reported answer includes what is evidently the inserted comment of an editor, since Baba is referred to in the third person.
200. This was apparently recorded by K.J. Dastur during 1928 or soon after. It reappeared in Vol. 1 of *The Meher Baba Jnl*, but was otherwise neglected.
201. Brunton, *op. cit.*, p. 52.
202. Ramju Abdulla, *op. cit.*; repr. *The Awakener* (1959) 6(3): 26–7.
203. E.g., the London reporter for *The Daily Mirror* in 1932 mischievously asked him: "Can you raise the dead?" The good-humoured reply is recorded as: "If necessary . . . but to anybody who has attained the state of consciousness that I have reached, miracles are child's play" (*The Awakener*, 1959, Vol. 6 no. 3, p. 21).
204. Brunton, *op. cit.*, p. 53.
205. Cf. *ibid.*, pp. 61–2.
206. Ramju Abdulla, *Sobs and Throbs* (Ahmednagar, 1929); see further Bibliography no. 16. Cf. Brunton, *op. cit.*, pp. 57–8. Brunton erroneously describes Rustom Irani as Baba's "chief disciple," though not mentioning him by name; he also has a curious story about Meredith Starr being sent back to England from India at Rustom's expense. It would be a charitable inference that Brunton received this tale from Starr after the latter's defection in 1932. The description of the "missionary disciple" Sadhu C. Leik also requires correction.
207. Brunton, pp. 53–4, and reporting that he was told (by devotees) that *darshan* prostration washed away sins. This is the

standard devotional belief in India, and differs from Meher Baba's more complex remarks on the subject.

208. E.g., Osborne, *Ramana Maharshi and the Path of Self-Knowledge*, p. 126.
209. See *Ramjoo's Diaries 1922–1929* (1979), and for comments, see the Bibliography no. 17.
210. Brunton, p. 256.
211. *Ibid.*, p. 255. The "victim" was Adi K. Irani, who provoked Baba by speaking very insolently to him.
212. Cf. *ibid.*, pp. 258 ff., 46. Typically enough, no date is given for the meteorite. Brunton never met Baba after his stay at Nasik. In April 1932, English reporters dubbed Baba in the British newspapers as the "Indian Messiah," which seems to have lent accentuation to the journalism in *Secret India*, since Baba was commonly accepted in India only as a *sadguru*.
213. Paul Brunton, *A Search in Secret Egypt* (London: Rider, 1936), pp. 66 ff.
214. P. Brunton, *A Hermit in the Himalayas* (London: Rider, n.d., published 1937), p. 6.
215. Cf. P. Brunton, *The Secret Path* (London: Rider, 1934).
216. Paul Brunton, *The Hidden Teaching Beyond Yoga* (London: Rider, 1941), pp. 351–2.
217. Paul Brunton, *The Wisdom of the Overself* (London: Rider, 1943; ninth imp., 1955), pp. 7–10.
218. Louis Agostini in "Questions We Answer," *The Glow* (1972) 7(2): 16–18, p. 18. Agostini was Brunton's mail secretary in New York for about three years, attending to the latter's correspondence while he was abroad. He left this employment upon becoming a follower of Meher Baba, having attended the East-West Gathering at Poona in 1962.
219. *A Search in Secret India*, p. 259. This book had gained sixteen reprints by 1955.
220. Rom Landau, *God is My Adventure* (London: Ivor Nicholson and Watson, 1935), pp. 130–148.
221. For a fuller report of this interview, see Purdom, *The Perfect Master*, pp. 162 ff.
222. Most of these details do not emerge in Landau's account, but were later reported in Kitty Davy, *Love Alone Prevails* (1981), p. 63, earlier appearing in *The Awakener*.

223. Bernard Levin, *The Pendulum Years: Britain and the Sixties* (London: Cape, 1970), pp. 46–7. It is more accurate to state that the actress Delia De Leon first met Baba at this performance, and sat silently beside him.
224. See Purdom, *The God-Man*, pp. 94–5. Cf. N. Anzar, *The Beloved: The Life and Work of Meher Baba* (North Myrtle Beach, S.C.: Sheriar Press, 1974), p. 28.
225. R. Landau, *The Philosophy of Ibn Arabi* (London: George Allen & Unwin, 1959), p. 25.
226. Landau preferred the more readily available expositions of Gurdjieff's philosophy as taught by P. D. Ouspensky. See the chapters on Gurdjieff and Ouspensky in *God is My Adventure*. See also Landau's references to these exponents in L. F. Rushbrook Williams, ed., *Sufi Studies: East and West* (London: Octagon Press, 1973), p. 137, stating his preference for scholasticism in a teacher.
227. Christmas Humphreys, "The Man of Love," *Buddhism in England* (London 1941). This periodical was published by the Buddhist Society, and later became *The Middle Way*.
228. *Ibid.* Humphreys quotes from both Purdom and Baba's *Discourses*. He refers to the Meherabad ashram as a "school," though this may represent a confusion with the Prem Ashram.
229. Foreword to Meher Baba, *Life At Its Best* (San Francisco, 1957), p. 8. See the Bibliography no. 12.
230. Purdom, *The Perfect Master*, pp. 126, 154, 160 ff; *The Meher Message* (Nasik, 1931), Vol. 3. See also Bibliography no. 45.
231. This photograph was taken at the Poona *jhopdi* prior to the Manzil phase, and is not particularly flattering to Baba. The photograph was included in a selection which were available upon request to those who wanted them. I purchased a copy in 1966 via Beryl Williams of New York, who supplied me with the relevant information.
232. This photograph can be found in Bal Natu, *Glimpses of the God-Man*, Vol. 2, facing page 372. For written sources on Gustadji, see *Ramjoo's Diaries 1922–1929*, pp. 384–5; C. V. Sampath Aiyangar in *The Meher Gazette* (1935) Vol. 4 no. 6, p. 69; Shepherd, *Gurus Rediscovered*, Part One, pp. 65 ff.
233. Delia De Leon, "An Appreciation of Charles B. Purdom," *The Awakener* (1966) 11(1): 6. De Leon does not include

much information on the League, which had a complex context.

234. For instance, when I later visited a monastery of the Ramakrishna Mission, I found that one of the Swamis regarded Meher Baba disparagingly as the "Parsi messiah" and as a rival to Ramakrishna. This Swami was probably influenced by Paul Brunton's biased portrayal.

235. C. B. Purdom, *Life Over Again* (London: J. M. Dent, 1951), pp. 137 ff.

236. For a confirmation of Purdom's later views on meditation, see *The God-Man*, p. 440, where he says: "That meditation is necessary for spiritual life there can be no doubt."

237. *Life Over Again*, pp. 253 ff. Purdom slightly amplified the details of Brunton's visit in *The God-Man*, p. 125.

238. *Life Over Again*; *The Perfect Master*, p. 157. Cf. Kitty Davy, *Love Alone Prevails*, p. 23, who says that there were no press interviews on this visit. There is much that is missing in Davy's report; this particular confusion probably arose because the newspaper coverage was slight by comparison with 1932.

239. C. B. Purdom, "More about the Perfect Master," *Everyman*, April 21st, 1932.

240. Quoted in Backett's report of Baba's letter to "H. Von F." in *The Meher Baba Jnl* Vol. 1. Some relevant statements on this subject can also be found in *Questions and Answers* (1933), edited by Backett.

241. Cf. K. Davy, *op. cit.*, p. 42, which makes no attempt to qualify the occurrence. This is very typical of the "Kimco" attitude, which in general saw no qualifications at all.

242. Purdom, *Life Over Again*, p. 258.

243. Ivy Duce, *How a Master Works*, p. 163, giving only a few of the details. Delia De Leon mentioned these dresses to me in 1966.

244. Duce, *op. cit.*, p. 163. Cf. Jean Adriel, *Avatar*, p. 143, stating that Starr demanded five hundred pounds and God-realization. I believe that the amount specified by Adriel is the more correct, though the sense of the cable as given by Duce is accurate enough.

245. Duce, *op. cit.*, pp. 163–4. Cf. Adriel, *op. cit.*, pp. 144–5, whose account is misleading in some respects.

246. *Life Over Again*, p. 255. Purdom writes that he did not receive all the information he required for his book, which

probably refers to the inaccessibility of Ramju Abdulla's diaries, which he knew that Brunton had seen. Purdom also says that Baba read his manuscript, which bespeaks a very rare occurrence if accurate. Baba usually read nothing save for the headlines of newspapers.

247. *Ibid.*, pp. 256 ff.
248. C. B. Purdom, ed., *God to Man and Man to God: The Discourses of Meher Baba* (1955), p. 13.
249. C. B. Purdom, "What Meher Baba's Teachings Mean to Me," *The Awakener* (1958) 5(2): 4–7, pp. 6–7.
250. *Ibid.*, p. 6.
251. Purdom, *The God-Man*, p. 414. Purdom includes Baba's reference to speaking the "Primal Oceanic 'M-m-m,' which I will utter through my human mouth." This ambiguous reference appeared in Francis Brabazon's *Stay With God* (1959), p. 66, though the editor is not specified. There is a contradiction apparent in this primal sound being given a physical medium.
252. *Ibid.*, p. 413. No date is given for this episode.
253. *Ibid.*, pp. 410–12. Cf. the review by Don Stevens in *The Awakener* (1965) 10 (4): 39, who minimizes the issue from a more orthodox standpoint. The assertion of Stevens that Baba "corrects minutely all messages given out by him" is misleading.
254. Cf. Purdom, *op. cit.*, pp. 432–3.
255. *Ibid.*, p. 438; *The Perfect Master*, p. 267.
256. *Ibid.*, pp. 433–5.
257. *Ibid.*, p. 442.
258. Will Backett's London Newsletter dated 12th October, 1955; for Kirpal Singh's contact with Meher Baba, see Eruch B. Jessawala, *The Ancient One* (1985), pp. 154 ff.
259. This circular is reproduced in K. Davy, *Love Alone Prevails*, pp. 712–14. See also "On Following Baba," *The Awakener*, Vol. 7 no. 2, pp. 8–9. The original was contained in a communication from Bili Eaton dated March 10th 1956, and stated that "Mani felt confident that these explanations are Baba's expressed wishes."
260. Jean Adriel, *Avatar* (1947), p. vii. See also my Bibliography no. 19.
261. In 1966 Delia De Leon told me details of her meeting with

Adriel in 1948, when they both stayed with Baba for some weeks in India. According to De Leon, Adriel had entertained big ideas about her own significance as a consequence of writing *Avatar*, and expected a due prominence that was not in fact given. De Leon was one of those who felt that Adriel made a big mistake in 1955.

262. K. Davy, *Love Alone Prevails*, p. 23.
263. This detail I learnt from Delia De Leon in 1966. There is a confusing interpretation in Duce, *How a Master Works*, p. 725.
264. His definitive statement is contained in the discourse on "The Circle" in *The Awakener* (1955), Vol. 3 no. 1, which specifies nine outer circles.
265. Cf. Duce, *op. cit.*, p. 456, who states the belief that Mehera and Mani were the two female appendages to Baba's inner circle, though Baba himself is not known to have stipulated this. In other respects, Duce was more critical of the tendency amongst the Western women to ascribe themselves a high place in Baba's work via loose references to the Circle (*ibid.*, pp. 449 ff.). She aptly quotes Mani's observation that people often drew conclusions from what Baba said that could not be definitely deduced from his statements (*ibid.*, p. 454).
266. Related to me in 1966. Tolhurst later reappeared in the London group during the 1970's.
267. M. Craske, *The Dance of Love*, pp. 22–3, who names Aminta and Norina Matchabelli as purchasers of the "God-realization" dresses. Both of these women were actresses by profession.
268. Adriel, *Avatar*, p. 142.
269. A fragmentary report is to be found in Bal Natu, *Glimpses of the God-Man, Meher Baba Vol. 1* (1977), pp. 375–7.
270. This visit was only briefly referred to in her article "Sufism," *The Awakener*, Vol. 7 no. 4, pp. 30–6. More detail appeared in *The Awakener* (1966) Vol. 11 no. 3, pp. 24–6. See also Duce, *How a Master Works*, pp. 24 ff.
271. Duce, *How a Master Works*, pp. 42–3.
272. *Ibid.*, p. 82.
273. *Ibid.*, p. 85.
274. *Ibid.*

275. Brabazon wrote: "This meeting was the culmination of ten years of spiritual study and search . . . I had studied the methods and practices of the great Sufi schools and had read fairly widely in Vedanta, Buddhism and other systems, including Taoism and Confucianism. In Meher Baba I found that person who not merely *knew* these things, but was the living embodiment of all these systems and knowledges." This comes from the introduction to Brabazon's *Journey With God* (Beacon Hill, N.S.W., Australia: Beacon Hill Publishing Co., 1954), p. 3.
276. Duce, *How a Master Works*, p. 105.
277. *Ibid.*, p. 123.
278. *Ibid.*
279. *Ibid.*, p. 124.
280. *Ibid*, p. 168, stating that on November 16th, 1952, Duce's grouping legally reincorporated as Sufism Reoriented.
281. *Ibid.*, p. 263.
282. *Ibid.*, p. 264.
283. *Ibid.*, pp. 238 ff. Duce was enthusiastic over advertising Baba's book *God Speaks*, but took this job much too far.
284. *Ibid.*, p. 266.
285. *Ibid.*
286. *Ibid.*
287. *Ibid.*, p. 270. *Cf. ibid.*, pp. 639–40, which evidences how Murshida Duce was given equal ranking with Baba by members of Sufism Reoriented.
288. *Ibid.*, pp. 438, 18.
289. *Ibid.*, p. 275.
290. *Ibid.*, p. 248.
291. *Ibid.*, p. 243.
292. Ghani's letter is reproduced in *ibid.*, pp. 718–19, and is dated September 10th, 1948.
293. E.g., *ibid.*, p.4.
294. Delia De Leon, for instance, insisted to me that she was one of Baba's "nearest and dearest," and felt that she had been one of Krishna's gopis.
295. It is relevant here to observe that Adi K. Irani was nominated as the secretary of the "Sufi Circle" at Poona in 1948. His familiarity with sufi teachings appears to have been slight. He can be considered to have been in a similar

position of testing to other devotees who were given prominence in the movement.

296. E.g., the version of Meherji Karkaria reported by Duce, *op. cit.*, pp. 38 ff. Karkaria was a Parsi devotee and encountered Abdullah Pakrawan in Iran in 1943, who was then working in a customs office. There is a fragmentary narration of Abdullah's parting with Baba in 1929, though the date is erroneously given as 1930 or 1931. Abdullah's sixth plane status is included in Karkaria's version.

297. See the interview reported in *The Glow* (May 1976) Vol. 11 no. 2, pp. 12–14. The interview occurred at Bundar Abbas.

298. Duce does not make much mention of Sheriar, and does not evidence any knowledge of the Kaivani tradition.

299. I have attempted to remedy this lacuna in my biography of Sheriar incorporated in *From Oppression to Freedom: A Study of the Kaivani Gnostics.*

A SELECTED AND ANNOTATED BIBLIOGRAPHY

Much of the current literature available on Meher Baba falls into two basic categories: selections from his teachings, and highly personal records of contact with him by devotees. The former are often very selective, and the latter are often markedly non-objective. In this bibliography therefore, I propose to focus upon primary source material, and also some of the more distinctive and longer books in the secondary literature concerning the subject. There has to date been no critical bibliography apart from Purdom's very brief list in *The God-Man*.

TEACHING:

1. Meher Baba, *God Speaks: The Theme of Creation and Its Purpose*. First edition (New York: Dodd, Mead & Co., 1955), 255 + xxix pp. Second edn (New York: Dodd, Mead & Co., 1973), 334 + xxxv pp. Edited by Ivy O. Duce and Don E. Stevens. With charts.

The major text, distinctly original. The main part differs negligibly in the two editions. The supplement, largely Dr. Ghani's work in collaboration with Meher Baba, was revised at Baba's direction for the first edition, and has been amplified in the second edition. A glossary by Lud Dimpfl was also added in the second edition, and which states that it was approved by Meher Baba prior to his death.

There is a devotional introduction to the first edition written by Don Stevens, which was retained in the later edition. A new devotional introduction to the second edition was contributed jointly by the American editors, who conclude with the sentiment that all of life amounts to the "game of watching Meher Baba deal with Meher Baba" (p. xxxv). This curious extrapolation misrepresents the text, like other editorial statements. One could point out that the editors have correctly stated that no publicity was given to Baba's 1958 visit to America (p. xxxii), but neglect to state that the prodigious attempts to publicize him during his preceding visit to America in 1956 were the outcome of the enthusiasm of the editors of *God Speaks*, and not at the instruction of Meher Baba.

The first edition was favourably reviewed by the Tibetological scholar W.Y. Evans-Wentz, but in general was neglected. For further remarks, see Part Two of the present work.

2. Meher Baba, *Discourses*, 5 volumes (Ahmednagar-Bangalore: Meher Baba Universal Spiritual Centre Publication Committee, 1938–43; repr. Ahmednagar: Adi K. Irani, 1943–55, culminating in fifth edition).

Averaging 100 pages per volume, these discourses originally appeared on a monthly basis in *The Meher Baba Journal*. They were dictated on the alphabet board, a procedure which involved a tightly abbreviated sentence structure of simple words and expressions. (This characteristic sentence structure appears in diaries and other reports). Dr. Chakradar D. Deshmukh of Morris College, Nagpur, a Professor of Philosophy who took his Ph.D. at London University, was requested to put these discourses into a more rounded English, which he did without, for the most part, distorting the sense of the original. Deshmukh's English was very good by Indian standards, though with the occasional tendency to colloquialism. There were subsequent disagreements amongst Western pupils as to whether Deshmukh's version was adequate. Charles Purdom did not think so, but Will Backett of Kent was one of those who thought it best to leave the text as it was.

With praiseworthy humility, Deshmukh preferred not to have his name given in any of the Indian editions, though he was urged to do so by some of the *mandali*. Deshmukh felt that his version reflected Baba too closely for there to be any additional credits. But this anonymity of editorship does have its drawbacks, since it was subsequently discovered that there were several errors in Deshmukh's text. Some Indian devotees in Andhra drew the attention of Eruch Jessawalla to those inconsistencies, and when the matter was aired before Baba, he agreed that the wrong sense had been given and duly supplied corrections (see *The Awakener*, 1955, Vol. 3 no. 1, pp. 44–5, which refers to "several important errors" and gives two corrected explanations). The errors relate to technical points such as the number of *sadgurus* in the world; these errors are very minimal by comparison with the total extent of editing, and do not affect the contour of any of the discourses.

Nevertheless, this matter effectively illustrates the hazards of edited material, which was the norm with Baba's published dictations. Baba seems to have regarded errors as inevitable; he allowed much free rein to some editors, though with Deshmukh he is known to have rigorously dictated parts of the exposition word by word. The extent of his checking seems to have varied with different editors, though he generally left the finished version to their own discretion.

Wherever cited in the present work, the *Discourses* have been used in the original edition. The "fifth edition" differs imperceptibly.

3. Charles B. Purdom, ed., *God to Man and Man to God: The Discourses of Meher Baba* (London: Gollancz, 1955), 272 pp.

In his introduction, Purdom states that he had edited the *Discourses* for a wider public at Baba's request. "What seemed to be redundant words or phrases have been eliminated to reduce their length and to make them clearer." The idea of a compact single volume edition was sensible enough, and the introduction is refreshingly sane by comparison with the rather exaggerated stylisms of many devotees. Some partisans of Meher Baba queried the very tight editing, particularly since it seems an arbitrary matter as to what words or phrases were deleted. The discrepancy in pagination is misleading, since Purdom's book has a much more compact print and dispensed with the paragraph inset captions of the original. There are no colloquialisms in Purdom's version.

4. Ivy O. Duce and Don E. Stevens, eds., *The Discourses of Meher Baba*, 3 vols (San Francisco: Sufism Reoriented Inc., 1967).

This version is very much closer to the original edited by Deshmukh. It describes itself as the sixth edition, and was concerned with grammatical improvement rather than alterations in format. Duce is correct in stating: "Baba himself made certain changes" (*How a Master Works*, p. 410). These corrections were duly incorporated. Baba gave his permission for this edition. The editors chose to alter the arrangement of chapters.

5. Abdul Karim (Ramju) Abdulla, *Shri Meher Baba; his philosophy and teachings* (Ahmednagar: Circle Publications, 1933), 120 pp., with charts.

An early version of Baba's cosmology and evolutionism as recorded by a Muslim pupil. It can be described as an embryonic form of *God Speaks*. The originality of Baba's teaching is quite evident at this early date. There are many words of Sufi and Vedantic association which testify to Baba's close familiarity with the terminologies of these traditions.

The sub-title reads "Compiled from his own dictations," indicating the firsthand nature of the exposition. "Almost the whole of the subject matter of this compilation was personally dictated to me by the master during the last five or six years," records Ramju, who was writing in 1933. The foreword is dated 21st September, 1933. The dictations can therefore be dated back, in part, to the Prem Ashram period of 1928–9, and indicate the substance of the discourses to which Ramju refers in his account of the Prem Ashram (see below, no. 16). Ramju acknowledges assistance from K.J. Dastur in some literary changes made in his editing. This apparently refers to the fact that K.J. Dastur included a version of these dictations in his periodical *The Meher Message*.

There are various statements and nuances in these dictations which do not appear in later publications, despite the fact that much of the material was superceded by *God Speaks*. Ramju's compilation was long out of print by the 1950's, when it was reproduced in serialized form in *The Awakener* (1954) 2 (2): 17–31, *et seq*.

Ramju's compilation also includes a selection of "questions and answers," some taken from interviews, other questions being framed around selected portions of messages, while yet other answers represent the interpretations of editors, as the style discloses.

6. *Shri Meher Baba: Questions and Answers* (London: Circle Editorial Committee, 1933).

A collection of answers dictated by Baba in response to questions put to him in the West. It was compiled (anonymously) by Will Backett, who had formerly been a pupil of Inayat Khan. Some of the "answers" were taken from general messages Baba had given. This compilation achieved translations into German and French.

7. *The Sayings of Shri Meher Baba* (London: Circle Editorial Committee, 1933), 48 pp.

Compiled anonymously by Will Backett. The editorial preface is markedly non-sensational. The contents are of good quality, and reflect a predominance of Vedantic terminology. Many of these statements were dictated in India during the 1920's. The Parsi K.J. Dastur recorded a large number of early sayings in his magazine *The Meher Message* (see below, no. 45). Backett's compilation was subsequently translated into German.

8. *Shri Meher Baba on Meditation, with the Divine Theme for Meditation: Journey of the Soul to the Over-Soul* (Ahmednagar: F.H. Dadachanji, n.d.).

Published in the mid-1930's, this was in the form of two fold-out sheets each having four large pages. The first was a statement on meditation, distinguishing between meditation and concentration (as in the later *Discourses*, Vol. 3), and advising on "intelligent meditation," for which purpose was given a concise exposition of the evolutionary theme. The latter was presented in the second fold-out, and was a very synoptic form of his teaching.

The emphasis upon meditation throws into relief a later misunderstanding of influential Parsi devotees amongst the *mandali* in the post-New Life phase. They were averse to meditation, preferring a simplified *bhakti*, and confused various apparently conflicting statements of Baba. For instance, in the first fold-out he says: "For those who are in contact with a God-realized master, meditation is unnecessary." But it is here quite obvious (as in the *Discourses*) that he meant by this the laborious and inferior forms of visualization. Concentration remained the ideal, and should not be confused with devotionalism. Meher Baba's purpose in his expositions on meditation was quite definitely one of encouraging people to meditate, though in a controlled manner, and on a theme that was not harmful to them (as some visualization techniques can be). His brevity was without doubt intentional. There is no doubt that some people are ill-suited to any form of meditation, though this temperamental discrepancy should not be regarded as proof of advancement.

These two fold-outs were reproduced in normal page-size in Purdom's *The Perfect Master*, pp. 305 ff. Dadachanji's editing was retained; at least one necessary correction was not made.

9. Meher Baba, *The Divine Theme: evolution, reincarnation, realization* (Ahmednagar: Adi K. Irani, 1943), 16 pp. + two fold-out charts.

An early statement of cosmology and evolution, later superceded by *God Speaks*. The two large colour charts were of good quality.

10. *Messages of Meher Baba delivered in the East and West* (Ahmednagar: Adi K. Irani, n.d.), 101 pp.

Compiled by Adi K. Irani, with a foreword by Dr. William Donkin dated October 1945. These messages date from 1932 to 1944, and afford insights into Baba's perspective on current affairs. Both political and religious issues are represented.

11. *Meher Baba on the Fiery Free Life and Seven Other Messages* (Ahmednagar: Adi K. Irani, 1952), 24 pp.

Dictated in November 1952. There were numerous messages published over the years, often singly, and often comprising only a few pages or less. Most of these were reproduced in the journals listed below, and in some of the biographical works. Different interpretations can be given to those messages relating to his "work."

12. Meher Baba, *Life at its Best*, ed. by Ivy O. Duce (San Francisco: Sufism Reoriented, Inc., 1957), 73 pp.

A collection of short discourses, statements, and sayings dictated by gestures during the summer of 1956, as Baba travelled across America. There is a foreword by Dr. W.Y. Evans-Wentz, the scholar of Tibetan Buddhism who was partial to Meher Baba.

13. *Beams from Meher Baba on the Spiritual Panorama*, ed. by Dr. C.D. Deshmukh (San Francisco: Sufism Reoriented, Inc., 1958), 88 pp.

A collection of explanations given in response to questions from Ivy Duce arising from the contents of *God Speaks*. Baba dictated these explanations via his new repertory of gesture language, and Deshmukh gave them an essay form. The English is of good standard. When Baba gave the manuscript to Duce, he characteristically dismissed further responsibility for it with the remark that it could either be destroyed or printed (Duce, *How a Master Works*, pp. 310–11).

14. Meher Baba, *The Everything and the Nothing* (Beacon Hill, N.S.W., Australia: Meher House Publications, 1963), 115 + x pp.

A collection of discourses and statements made during the years

1959–62, compiled by Francis Brabazon. Many of the statements are brief, and have an off-the-cuff stamp frequently attended by a sense of humour, which also makes itself apparent in some of the discourses. Meher Baba's "gnostic humour" was here expressed via gesture language, and the style is different to the earlier alphabet board idioms, bearing in mind that Eruch Jessawala was the major interpreter of the new gesture language implemented from 1954 onwards.

An introduction by Francis Brabazon, the Australian poet, is rather verbose, and attempts to use some of the gnostic terminology of Baba. This was a mistake of several writers, since the relevant idioms do not sound in context when copied, however well-intentioned the reproduction.

BIOGRAPHICAL:

15. Khaikhushru Afseri, *Kashf ul-Haqaiq* (Ahmednager, 1928).

A short work in Persian by a Zoroastrian pupil of Meher Baba which included a record of the experiences of Abdulla Pakrawan, alias Chota Baba, a Muslim youth who gained prominence at the Meher Ashram in 1927–8. It is one of the most important reminiscences in the whole of the Meher Baba literature, and amongst other things, serves to attest the difference between disciples and devotees. A translation into English was made by Farhad Shafa, and appeared in *The Glow Quarterly* (1976) 11(2): 3–11. This is reproduced in *Ramjoo's Diaries*, pp. 532 ff.

16. Abdul Karim (Ramju) Abdulla, *Sobs and Throbs* (Ahmednagar: N.N. Satha, 1929). Illus.

An account in English of the Meher and Prem Ashram by a Sunni Muslim participant. Comprising nearly two hundred pages, it is an important source, though marred by pronounced colloquialisms. However, the grammar does not affect the documentary value. Ramju focusses upon the experiences of Sayed Ali, the son of Sayed Haji Muhammad, though many of the Prem Ashram inmates gain cameo appearances. The mystical quality of the experiences reported is pronounced, and should be regarded as part of the twentieth century sufi tradition.

The sub-title refers to Hazrat Qibla Meher Baba, bespeaking the Muslim associations of the subject. There is a significant foreword by Maulana Mazhar ul-Haque, who had been President of the All-India Muslim league in 1915, a prominent Indian Muslim who showed an interest in Prem Ashram events and was well disposed to Meher Baba, whom he respected highly. The Maulana wrote: "To appreciate the book fully, it is necessary to read it with the eye of a Sufi."

This book was largely unknown to Meher Baba's later following in the post-New Life phase. During the mid-1960's, some American devotees had it mimeographed in a very plain edition minus the photographs. Beryl Williams of New York sent me a copy, and was surprised to find that I possessed the original edition, bequeathed to me by Ann Powell. I found that the significance of the Muslim element had been lost. Some influential Parsi devotees at Meherazad repudiated the importance of meditation in preference for a simplified *bhakti*, quite contrary to Meher Baba's own emphases during the pre-New Life years.

17. *Ramjoo's Diaries 1922–1929*, ed. by Ira G. Deitrick (Walnut Creek, California: Sufism Reoriented, 1979), 585 pp. Illus.

The diaries of Abdul Karim Abdulla, nicknamed Ramju owing to his birth during the Ramadan fast. Part of this work consists of an abridged version of *Sobs and Throbs*. There is a useful supplement to this comprising interviews with some of the Prem Ashram participants who could be located during the 1970's. But these reports leave problems for the more diligent readers, since various factors are left unexplained.

The major portion of this work presents the diaries kept by Ramju during the years 1922–5, and varies between important source material and the more external preoccupations of diarists.

Also included (pp. 380 ff.) is a collection of short biographies of the *mandali* from K.J. Dastur's unpublished *Life of Shri Meher Baba*, written at Meherabad in 1928. Dastur was a Parsi devotee of erratic tendencies.

18. Charles B. Purdom, *The Perfect Master* (London: Williams & Norgate, 1937), 330 pp. Illus.

A biography up to 1936. The first published biography, and impressive for its attempt at objective reporting. There is no devotionalism, no sentiment, but a concern to arrange the facts in due sequence. In his preface, the author says he had written the book at the request of some of Baba's Indian followers, though in his autobiography he relates that Baba suggested the project to him.

Purdom's account of the 1920's events was based upon the unpublished biography of K.J. Dastur abovementioned, and improved greatly upon the sentimental stylisms of his predecessor. He also had access to the diary of Behli J. Irani, a Parsi of lesser literary talent than Dastur but with less pretentious merits.

It is typical of Purdom's detached air to have stated in the preface that his study did not pretend "to be anything but a preliminary and tentative account of Baba for Western readers." To date, no other published report save that of Dr. Donkin has approached the objectivity of Purdom's preliminary version. The literati of his time would not give his biography a review, and one suspects that an ethnocentric bias must have been at work – unless it were the influence of Paul Brunton and Rom Landau.

Part Three (pp. 229 ff.) consists of an interpretation of the subject, which incorporated a substantial amount of factual data, including a lengthy report of interviews given by Baba at Zurich in 1934. Purdom did not shift from his basic (though independent) Christian viewpoint, and parried the question of "messiahship" that many found a barrier. Baba himself never insisted upon this issue dogmatically, and many of his remarks upon it were oblique. These remarks were furthermore of a consistently private, and not a public, nature.

I am not a Christian, and could wish that many Christians were as liberal as Charles Purdom, though I am sceptical of his rather generous crediting to Nietzche of a saintly illumination (p. 298). I was more impressed by Purdom's unbiased talk on Ramakrishna of Dakshineswar in 1965. At his death soon after, I was in correspondence with his wife Antonia (Lilian Cutlar), who gifted me with Purdom's own copy of *The Perfect Master*.

19. Jean Adriel, *Avatar: The Life Story of the Perfect Master Meher Baba; A Narrative of Spiritual Experience* (Santa Barbara, California: J.F. Rowney Press, 1947; repr. Berkeley: John F. Kennedy University Press, 1971), 284 + x pp.

This is a mixture of biography and autobiography, with a strong accent on personal experiences. The biographical treatment extends to the early 1940's, and much information was drawn from the *Meher Baba Jnl.* More original data relates to the author's meetings with Baba in America during the early 1930's, and as an inmate of the Nasik ashram in 1937.

Purdom described this book as "a highly coloured personal account" (*The God-Man*, p. 449). It is indeed emotional in tone by comparison with Purdom's reporting. But it differs quite pronouncedly from most of the "devotee" books that have been published. A careful investigation reveals that Jean Adriel (Jean Schloss) had learnt something of psychology through her contact with Baba, though not in any clearly verbalized sense. The verbalization was created as a result of her association with the psychiatrist Dr. Fritz Kunkel during the 1940's. As a consequence, she was able to describe the basics of an advanced psychology, though frequently in an inadequate form. Ivy Duce later adopted Adriel's perspective, but likewise without achieving total objectivity. The majority of devotees, including the influential mouthpieces, never came to grips with this more demanding dimension.

From the purely biographical point of view, the book is inadequate, since events prior to 1931 receive very scant coverage, and events of the 1930's are very unevenly described. There are some errors in interpretation.

20. William Donkin, *The Wayfarers: An Account of the Work of Meher Baba with the God-intoxicated, and also with Advanced Souls, Sadhus, and the Poor* (Ahmednagar: Adi K. Irani, 1948), 405 + ix pp. Illus., with maps.

This is a unique book. It is a study of one of the most important and least understood of Baba's activities. Purdom aptly wrote of it as "a scientific study at first hand by a qualified medical man" (*The God-Man*, p. 449). It is indeed scientific; there is an entire absence of the distracting devotional preoccupations found in other books. Dr. Donkin set out to present as much direct information as was available to him concerning the *masts* and other categories of saints and holy men contacted by Meher Baba over a period of many years. The extensive supplement (pp. 183–369) assembled a mass of data on the hundreds of contacts made in India and Pakistan. Quite often the individuals described are classified in accordance with definitions provided by Meher

Baba, but since many of these individuals were famous in their own right (though locally for the most part), this feature gains additional gazetteer interest. This supplement, with its accompanying maps, also gives statistics of Meher Baba's humanitarian work with the poor, an aspect of his activity that went notably unpublicized.

The earlier part of the book deals in more detail with entities who gained a longer association with Meher Baba, notably the "five favourites." There is also a coverage of the "*mast* ashrams" operative intermittently since 1939. The "Mad ashram" of Rahuri is also documented. Donkin himself was an eyewitness of many events described.

Despite the fact that this is a critical bibliography, I have no criticisms to make of Donkin's work, and regret that it was not longer. There was some additional information that he did not include, though omissions are pardonable in such an original work. *The Wayfarers* remains a remarkable testament to dimensions of the Muslim and Hindu populations of India and Pakistan that are generally unsuspected, far less documented. I have never encountered its like in any other work. Donkin himself did not draw all the relevant conclusions from his study, as I have attempted to indicate in the present book and also in my unpublished study (see below no. 35).

An additional feature of *The Wayfarers* are the explanations of *masts* and other categories. The book commences with two explanations by Meher Baba, and one by Abdul Karim Abdulla, who was understandably interested in the phenomenon. There follows (pp. 21–39) a detailed categorization which represents Donkin's (reliable) editing of Meher Baba's dictations specially given in the interests of clarification. There is a notable preponderance of Sufi terms in this distinctive exposition, which are given a clear elucidation in English. The only error (if it is one) that I can find is Donkin's attribution of an ode, translated by the Cambridge scholar R.A. Nicholson, to Shams-i Tabriz, an ode which is scholastically attributed to Rumi.

21. W. Donkin, *The Work of Meher Baba with Advanced Souls and Sadhus* (Ahmednagar: Adi K. Irani, 1948), 15 pp.

A supplement to *The Wayfarers* covering the period 15th March to 14th May 1948.

22. W. Donkin, *The Work of Meher Baba with Advanced Souls, Sadhus, the Mad and the Poor* (Ahmednagar: Adi K. Irani, 1949), 57 pp. Illus.

A further supplement, covering the period 8th June 1948 to 1st August 1949. Donkin enlivens his dairy with a distinctive sense of humour, a polished use of English, and a good command of Latin.

23. Ramju Abdulla and C.D. Deshmukh, *Meher Baba in the Great Seclusion* (Ahmednagar: Adi K. Irani, 1949), 28 pp.

An account of the seclusion of forty days lasting from 22nd June to 31st July, 1949. It was based on the diary of Jal D. Kerawala, who was one of the few pupils allowed access to the seclusion precincts at Meherazad. This diary was published in full in *The Glow Quarterly* (May 1977), pp. 3–16, 23–25, 29–32. The same issue of *The Glow* includes the diary of Dr. Abdul Ghani Munsiff on Baba's visit to Poona during this seclusion (pp 16–23). Read in conjunction with Donkin's second supplement, this phase achieves considerable detail. It became known as the "Great Seclusion," though it was by no means the longest of Baba's numerous seclusions, which were such a regular feature of his life.

24. *The New Life of Avatar Meher Baba and his Companions*, ed. Swami Satya Prakash Udaseen (Hyderabad, Andhra Pradesh: Meher Vihar Trust, 1967), 285 + xxix pp.

Despite the title gloss, this is a valuable documentary source, being a compilation of all the 34 New Life Circulars issued between October 1949 and February 1952. Some of these Circulars were quite lengthy, and include diary notes by Dr. Nilu, one of the companions of this phase. The object was to provide up to date information on Baba's activities for his followers, most of whom had no hope of seeing him during this period. An Appendix is provided which gives Ramju Abdulla's account of the introductory stages of the New Life. The data notably focusses in detail upon the various material and economic arrangements made by Baba in connection with his ashrams, followers, and activities.

Supplementary material exists in the diary of Dr. Abdul Ghani Munsiff, which did not achieve publication until after Baba's death. This diary covers the period Oct. 15th – Nov. 23rd, 1949. See *The Glow* (May 1973) 8 (2): 1–29.

25. D.E. Stevens *et al*, eds., *Tales from the New Life with Meher Baba* (Berkeley, California: Beguine Library, 1976), 191 + x pp.

Though a relevant source, this book significantly attests the inconsistencies of reporting that occur in retrospect. Shortly after Baba's death, Stevens taped the reminiscences of four of the Parsi *mandali* concerning the New Life. These four were Eruch B. Jessawala, Mehera J. Irani, Mani S. Irani, and Meheru Irani. Stevens notes the inconsistencies in his Preface, but commendably decided to reproduce the original reports rather than rewrite them. While these reports are of value, the conscientious historian will give precedence to the earlier sources.

I can add here a word of caution to investigators who find reports of events purporting to be factually authentic that were taped or transcribed after Baba's death. The words of the *mandali* were regarded as infallible by most devotees, and there was very seldom any attempt made to analyze discrepancies. It is my conclusion that these later reports, not always first-hand, represent only a partial view of events, an incompleteness that can be more serious at psychological levels of interpretation than in the purely factual dimensions.

26. Charles Purdom and Malcolm Schloss, *Three Incredible Weeks with Meher Baba: A Diary* (Seattle, Washington: W.C. Healy Press, 1955), 86 pp. Illus.

This appeared as a special issue of *The Awakener* (Vol. 2 no. 3) and gained the status of a bound volume, which no other issue of that magazine did. The diary covers the period September 11th–30th 1954, at the time when a group of Western male pupils were invited to Meherabad ashram. The diary includes a number of discourses given by Baba to the visitors, using much Sufi and Vedantic terminology, and an account of a rare visit to the Sakori ashram of the deceased Upasni Maharaj.

A slightly abridged version was included in Purdom's *The God-Man*, pp. 219 ff. Complementary material from the diary of Kishan Singh can be found in *The Glow Quarterly* (May 1975) 10(2): 1–20, and particularly relevant is the entry on Sakori. In addition, my acquaintance with the late Fred Marks of London, one of the men invited to Meherabad, furnished some additional data not recorded elsewhere. Marks was one of those who briefly contributed to the article "Facets of the Diamond" in *The Awakener* (1955) 2(4): 25–48, which recorded the impressions of other Westerners invited to the Meherabad sessions. Marks was one of those devotees very reverential in tone, and never flippant, though he tended to be inarticulate in his written statements. He wanted me to write his biography, which I did, though I was only sixteen at the time; it was only of monograph length, and was never published, aptly enough in view of its immature style.

27. D.E. Stevens, ed., *Listen, Humanity* (New York: Dodd, Mead & Co., 1957), 262 + xvi pp.

A substantial portion of this book (pp. 93–196), appearing as Part Two, consists of an edited version of various discourses and messages of Meher Baba which can be found in earlier publications. Its original contribution lies principally in Part One (pp. 3–90), which gives an account of the *sahavas* programmes held at Meherabad in November, 1955. Stevens attended this *sahavas* and made use of material recorded by the diarists Faram and Kishan Singh, material which was later collated by Ramju Abdulla. Stevens adopted the recourse of describing various events and statements occurring during the four weeks of the *sahavas* in terms of one week only. This assisted compact reporting no doubt, but has disadvantages from a rigorous historical perspective. The editor included many "original on-the-spot translations of Baba's gestures made by Eruch," which he admits to having "modified in the interest of continuity and greater ease of perusal" (p. v). With these reservations, the account is still of documentary value, particularly when collated with other extant material.

Also of value is the appendix (pp. 244–62) which assembled various autobiographical reminiscences made by Baba during the month of *sahavas*. Stevens conscientiously observes (p. 244) that Baba's gestures conveyed an essential idea put into words by one of the *mandali* (usually Eruch), and that "therefore the words are not always Baba's very own – unless he chooses tediously to have a word spelled out – but the sense is his."

Part Three (pp. 199–237) reflects the preoccupation of the editor with the issue of avatarhood, and largely reflects his personal views. Like many devotees, Stevens was concerned to push this point and to finalize it more or less as a credo. I personally view this tendency with acute reserve, since it seems to me to verge far too closely upon dogmatism. This preoccupation had already made itself felt in the editorial introduction to *God Speaks*, and with due losses in impact. Stevens stops short of the point of actual dogmatism, though others were less restrained. In relation to his query as to whether Meher Baba was really the *avatar*, he comments, "I believe that I cannot *know* until the day I too have finally achieved the Godhood within me, for only perfection can know Perfection" (p. 203). This seems a very sensible statement, but on the very same page he tends to negate the value of this perspective by insisting that it (the question of avatarhood) "is the most supremely important question which anyone can ask." I disagree; there are more important questions, such as: "Am I functioning correctly?" Particularly in relation to the sufi interests of Don Stevens and others, there is also the question of the total balance of factors in the sufi work which can never be allowed to crystallize into anything resembling dogmatism by those with sufficient perception and ability.

To his credit, Stevens wrote in his preface that although the contents of *Listen, Humanity* had been "approved" by Meher Baba, this did not mean that Baba "necessarily agrees completely with certain expressions of opinion which have inevitably been the narrator's (p. vi)." This honesty was not always forthcoming from other writers, who tended to think that every word they wrote was a faithful representation of Baba. Such people were in ignorance of his method of "approval," and sadly overestimated imagined personal accomplishments.

Part Two of this work occasionally rolls several messages and/or discourses into one, under one heading. An example is the section entitled "Origins and Effects of War" (pp. 128–141), which includes part of the 1940 discourse on *The New Humanity* with other messages. Yet there is no specification given as to the sources, and the reader might well imagine that the whole section was given out by Baba in one intact piece. This questionable format received further pronunciation in the distribution of a booklet entitled *Meher Baba on War* (Poona, 1963), which reproduced the "Origins and Effects of War," and again without mentioning the sources and respective dates of dictation. This was rather unfortunate owing to confusion that resulted amongst certain readers of this booklet, which carried an introduction by Francis Brabazon. The latter was a poet who wrote verse of very varying quality; he resided with the *mandali* at Meherazad for some years. Brabazon mentioned the Chinese invasion of India which was then a topic of grave political concern, and advised his readers to study the discourse contained in the booklet. In not stating the historical background of this "discourse," he misled some readers into thinking that Baba delivered this "discourse" at the time of the Chinese aggression on the Indian frontier. Such are the hazards of poetry.

It is incumbent to add that there are a number of booklets (and larger publications) giving potted versions of various discourses and messages, and which are of negligible value for the serious student in proportion to their truncated characteristics.

28. Irene Conybeare, *In Quest of Truth or How I Came to Meher Baba* (Kakinada, Andhra Pradesh: Swami Satya Prakash Udaseen, n.d., but published 1961), 311 pp.

An autobiography by one of the more literate persons amongst Baba's Western following. She was the daughter of the Oxford scholar F.C. Conybeare, a specialist in Patristic and Armenian literature. Irene Conybeare furnishes some relevant data on Meher Baba in addition to the more personal details of her book. Some of her insights are above average in the literature, though she was one of those who felt the need to stress the issue of avatarhood. This she had already done in a book entitled *Civilization or Chaos?* (London, 1955), which discussed the world crisis and religious theories.

A commendable feature of the autobiography is the "Special Note" at the beginning of the work which states that it should "clearly be understood that the Master (i.e. Meher Baba) does not necessarily agree with the views expressed by the author." Conybeare was one of those who had perceived Baba's distinctive strategy of allowing devotees to say their piece. "Meher Baba has always allowed full freedom of thought and expression to his followers," she adds. One could wish that many others had understood this aspect of his method, but perceptiveness is not a hereditary feature in the human race.

Conybeare met Baba briefly in India in 1941, and later in 1952 at Hamirpur and Meherazad. There were new explanations from

Baba which appeared in the appendices, including the distinctive "Aura and the Halo," which was reproduced in *The Awakener*, a repository of much miscellaneous material.

29. C.B. Purdom, *The God-Man: The Life, Journeys and Work of Meher Baba with an interpretation of his silence and spiritual teaching* (London: George Allen & Unwin, 1964), 463 pp. Illus.

This was the major biographical work published during the lifetime of the subject, and takes the record up to 1962. An abridged and corrected version of *The Perfect Master* constitutes the account of the early years up to 1936. The remainder of the book continues Purdom's commitment to detached reporting, though there are some errors discernible. The account of the *masts* (pp. 136 ff.) was disappointingly brief, and some factual mistakes crept in. However, it should be said that little comprehension was shown in general of this important period, and that Purdom wrote more on it than anyone else except Donkin and Adi K. Irani during Baba's lifetime. He commented that the *mast* work "has no parallel so far as I know in the life of any other man," (p. 136) and one can second this judgment a quarter century later.

After giving a very compact account of the New Life, Purdom opens up with more space on the *sahavas* programmes of the 1950's, culminating in the East–West Gathering of 1962. He had been present at some of these events, and was a leading diarist in this respect. Some supplementary material to the May 1958 *sahavas* at Myrtle Beach can be found in his account earlier appearing in *The Awakener* (1958) 5(3): 2–71, which comprises his own notes mixed with those of some other writers.

In retrospective analysis, it now seems worthwhile to observe that Purdom's account of the pre-New Life phase takes up less than half of his biographical section. This disproportionate reporting does not seem to have been intentional, but rather a consequence of his own full diaries kept during his later meetings with Baba. However, this anomaly does throw into relief the comparative obscurity befalling the pre-New Life years that came to prevail amongst the less studious. This was not Purdom's fault; he was the only writer at that time, apart from Donkin, to compile material to an extensive degree outside the channels of purely personal reminiscences.

Turning to the interpretative section at the end of the book (pp. 373 ff.), it is to find an expanded version of the corresponding portion of *The Perfect Master*. His Christian conditioning is still very much in evidence, and he lamentably failed to understand the evolutionism in *God Speaks*. But in addition to the defects, there are some very sound points expressed, particularly in his exposition of Baba's silence and method. He surpassed most of the devotees in this respect, to the extent that some of them expressed irritation with his views on such matters. Cf. the reviews by Don Stevens and Phyllis Frederick in *The Awakener* (1965) 10(4): 38–40.

30. Adi K. Irani, *The Life Circulars of Avatar Meher Baba*, ed. Swami Satya Prakash Udaseen (Hyderabad, Andhra Pradesh: Meher Vihar Trust, 1968), 140 + v pp.

A compilation of the sixty-seven "Life Circulars" issued (and edited) by Adi K. Irani from Ahmednagar between Feb. 1952 and Feb. 1968. They are of a documentary value, though one that is mitigated by their brevity and extreme formal style. By comparison with the New Life Circulars, they are markedly inferior. They relayed messages and instructions from Baba, but without the background information supplied by the earlier circulars. The editorial touches are pompous. In 1954 Adi K. Irani began to insert Baba's identity as "Avatar Meher Baba," a stylism which came to be widely copied by devotees in both East and West. This was a result of Adi K. Irani's preference, and not the instructions of Baba. In 1956 Adi K. Irani began to style his own identity as that of "Disciple and Secretary," and was careful to insert "Avatar Meher Baba" immediately below this rather pronounced statement of honours. These credentials were reproduced on Adi K. Irani's office stationery, and all correspondents were thus made aware of his distinction. I was in intermittent correspondence with him during 1965–6, but his letters were always brief. One person of my acquaintance received a letter from him which made it explicitly clear that as a disciple of over forty years standing, he (Adi K. Irani) must know sufficiently about all matters connected with Meher Baba to be able to pronounce upon them with due authority. I was not impressed by his humility, though devotees rated him very highly, believing him to be an infallible mouthpiece of Meher Baba.

What devotees did not know until after Baba's death was that the latter had expressed acute dissatisfaction with Adi K. Irani during the last few years of his (Baba's) life. This was so pronounced that the secretary would feel under strain when visiting the ashram at Meherazad. Baba does not appear to have stipulated the cause of the disapproval, but this was a typical method of his. Brief references appeared in *The Awakener* amongst the miscellaneous data culled from the reminiscences of the *mandali*. The Ahmednager elite were quick to squash such incongruous details however, and the status of Adi K. Irani subsequently became apostolic owing to the uncritical mentality of devotees. Baba himself had consistently stressed the need for critical acumen, but devotees rarely took the hint in practice.

In circulars dating before 1954, Baba is never referred to as *avatar*, but always as Meher Baba, Shri Meher Baba, or more simply, as Baba. There is a useful circular of 1946 written by Adi K. Irani which is both lengthy and informative, giving details of Baba's *mast* tours. It is lacking in the pompousity of his later news-sheets (I possess the original, given to me by Ann Powell). My conclusion is that something happened in the psychology of Adi K. Irani over the next ten years which caused him to feel unduly important and censorious. When Baba gave him the position of secretary, it doubtless constituted as much of a test in the intrinsic teaching situation as it did for others who fawned upon status roles.

31. Mani S. Irani, The "Family" Newsletters, Meherazad 1956–69, repr. as *82 Family Letters* (North Myrtle Beach, South Carolina: Sheriar Press, 1976), 366 pp.

These newsletters were written by Baba's sister at his request, and were sent out to his Western following, which was referred to as part of his "family." The purpose was to keep the Westerners informed of his activities and messages. There were several of these newsletters per year, usually several pages in length. They have been inaccurately described as the only continuous record of Baba's last years, and their importance has been overestimated.

There are many expressions of praise for these newsletters in the devotional literature. During Baba's lifetime, various writers praised the author's style of diction and descriptive ability, though to critics the general context of these remarks seems to be one of maintaining the mutual admiration society common in human groupings of all kinds. This flattery continued after Baba's death, and any unacquainted reader might be forgiven for thinking that the contents of the "family" newsletters must be revelatory. These remarks have never received critical treatment in any of the literature on Meher Baba, which currently appears to dislike innovations. But when one finds assertions that Mani's "flawless expression is nonpareil," (*The Glow*, May 1977, p. 28) one is justified in attempting to ascertain the reasons for this lavish praise.

An examination of these newsletters reveals that only the earlier ones consistently narrate Baba's activities in any detail. During the 1960's an increasing preoccupation with secondary events is evident. Baba largely recedes into seclusion, save for the occasional message or quip. The lion's share of attention instead falls to events within the "movement" at large, e.g. birthday celebrations, the activities of various devotees, and a new wave of publicity for "Avatar Meher Baba" in America as launched by devotees during the late 1960's. One is left with the dominant impression that secondary, and even irrelevant, news items are the stuff of description, particularly since the flora and fauna of Meherazad are given noticeable space. All this may or may not reflect the author's repute as one of those "closest to Baba," but it is a fact that the mode of description employed strikes critical readers as pronouncedly sentimental.

While these newsletters are of documentary relevance, that relevance is very uneven. The coverage of the 1960's largely documents the peculiarities of the "movement," and not the activities of Meher Baba, who very often appears as a sort of appendage to the environment rather glibly taken for granted. Even if information in seclusion was minimal, there was much unpublished data concerning Baba that could have been dwelt upon instead of the secondary matters.

It is my conclusion that the reason why Meher Baba gave Mani the task of writing newsletters for the West was because of her greater inclination to literacy in English than other members of the Indian *mandali* then living, both male and female. One could wonder what newsletters by Dr. Donkin would have been like, but possibly one relevant factor here was that Donkin had already received his exposure to status, whereas Mani had not. In terms of grammar, her writing is well above average by Indian standards, and is free of the colloquialisms apparent even in Dr. Deshmukh's work. Her writing is not pompous in the manner of Adi K. Irani, but it does tend to trivia and sentiment. It set what was, in many ways, an unfortunate model for Western devotees, who copied Mani's idioms concerning "the Beloved" to very monotonous effect.

In conversations with Baba's brother Adi S. Irani, who lived in London, I found a curious anomaly. He deferred to his sister Mani in terms of an elevated personage, but it was evident enough that the reason for this was because she lived at the ashram and was considered to relay the words of Baba. By comparison with the residents at the ashram, even former members of the *mandali* were demoted (by devotees) to roles of lesser significance. I found this reasoning rather pathetic, and totally illogical. It is my conclusion that "out-station" members of the *mandali* (and persons of other categories) were often of greater significance than the nominal elite. A person like Ramju Abdulla, for instance, never had his praises sung for his literary talents, writing in a very colloquial vein; yet his affinity with both Sufi and Vedantic concepts perhaps lent him deeper perceptions than some of the resident *mandali*. Ramju lived a very plain role in ordinary life far distant from the ashram, and died outside the ashram, gaining only brief notice at his decease in 1967.

32. H.P. Bharucha, *Meher Baba's Last Sahavas* (Navsari: Dr. H.P. Bharucha, 1969), 48 pp.

This account by a Parsi devotee is of interest owing to its coverage of Baba's death and the events of the following week. It was written very close in time to the events described, and notably reflects the feelings of shock and uncertainty that prevailed amongst the *mandali* and others. This gives the account an especial value, providing a description of what happened prior to the rationalizations that soon afterwards gained currency. On the debit side, there are several statements reflecting the highly crystallized devotional attitudes of reverence for authority figures in the "movement" other than Baba. I do not here implicate Mehera, whom I do credit as being an exceptional entity, as the facts attest. The same considerations apply to the exceptional entity Kaikobad Dastur, who remained in low profile through the years.

33. Tom and Dorothy Hopkinson, *Much Silence: Meher Baba, his life and work* (London: Victor Gollancz, 1974), 191 pp.

The declared aim of this book, written by two English devotees, was to provide a short record covering the whole period of the subject's life "written in language the man in the Western street can readily understand" (p. 7). A biography is followed (pp. 145 ff.) by an interpretation of the teaching. This book does not totally dispense with devotional stylisms. Though stressing Baba's emphasis against mounting a new religion (p. 42), it still shows strong traces of deference to the elite that the *mandali* were felt to comprise, and certain of whom were dogmatic. It is not surprising, therefore, to find that Baba is here stressed as the *avatar*.

In respect of biography, such books have only a curiosity value to a scholar of the subject, unless they can effectively bring out some trend or aspect left in amorphous profile in the sources. There are now several such books, not all of them as restrained as the Hopkinsons' version.

34. Ivy Oneita Duce, *How a Master Works* (Walnut Creek, California: Sufism Reoriented, Inc., 1975), 766 + xxiii pp. Illus.

This autobiographical account by the Murshida of Sufism Reoriented is of a problematic nature. To its credit, it does contain some psychological insights which are difficult to find elsewhere in the literature, and can be regarded as an extension of Jean Adriel's reporting. The author's account of her meetings with Baba in 1948, 1952, and 1956 are particularly detailed. But taken as a whole, the book strongly reflects the interpretations of the devotional movement, and more particularly, interpretations supplied by this movement that came into circulation after Baba's death. This is also abundantly evident in the extensive supplement (pp. 483 ff.) of more than 250 pages, which comprises a diversity of material that requires due evaluation. An example is the deference shown to the interpretations of Adi K. Irani, who was typically strident in such assertions as that declaring Meher Baba had no chargeman (p. 431). This statement, and many others, represents Adi K. Irani's own view and preference, but such statements were treated as gospel truth by Duce and numerous others. It obviated the need to look elsewhere than amongst the "elite" of the movement for fresh directives.

It is pertinent here to give the information that in 1962, at the

East–West Gathering, Charles Purdom asked Baba about the matter of the latter's chargeman. There were already some devotees who thought that Baba would not have any chargeman (i.e. spiritual successor). Baba told Purdom that there *would* be a chargeman, but did not divulge the identity of this individual. (This detail was related to me in 1973 by Delia De Leon, who had known Purdom well. See Oral Sources *infra*).

The title of Ivy Duce's book seems ambitious, and one suspects that the author has only very partially succeeded in describing how a "master" works. In some respects, her Christian conditioning is apparent, though in a different direction to that of Purdom's. But her conditioning to the devotional movement is obviously a much stronger influence, and her continual emphasis upon Baba as Avatar is not original. These considerations make critics wary of her interpretation of "Sufism Reoriented," a phrase associated with Meher Baba, though unclarified in formerly published literature. Duce interpreted this in terms of an organization, but other interpretations are possible.

Duce's interpretation of Baba's last years is unsatisfying. She frequently quotes from Mani's newsletters, but perhaps more revealing of distractions is the plate entitled "Typewriter Doodles by Mani" (facing p. 507). I do not know the significance of these doodles, unless it be that they reflect the uneven scale of attention which elevated some devotees to paragon status. It is perhaps worth noting in respect of this otherwise puzzling insertion in the plates that regular correspondence with Mani was believed to confer an elite status upon those few who were the recipients of this privilege, recipients who included Ivy Duce. Even some of the uncritical devotees would have preferred a photograph of Meher Baba rather than the substitute.

A further word of caution as to the contents of some reports in the supplement. Many of the reminiscences of the *mandali* recorded after Baba's death are dependent for accuracy upon the transcriber and/or the memory of the person being interviewed. For instance, certain of the statements of Adi K. Irani concerning Mahatma Gandhi (pp. 572–3) should be read with due reserve, particularly since Gandhi is represented as being of little importance and as being in error. This does not reflect the content of the many sympathetic references to Gandhi made by Meher Baba.

35. K.R.D. Shepherd, *The Life of Meher Baba* (four vols, unpublished. The first three vols are in typescript and total over 1700 single-spaced quarto pages. The last vol. is mainly in manuscript).

This unpublished work was written during the years 1967–77. It covers the whole period of the subject's life. To the best of my knowledge, it was the first multi-volume biography of the subject to have been written. Ivy Duce knew of its existence in 1979, and asked to see it, but I declined this request via an intermediary. It was never sent to any prospective publisher. My reasons for withholding it were as follows:

(a) It had no appropriate audience – the devotional movement desired only straitjacket idioms, and there had been so much misrepresentation of Meher Baba that non-partisan audiences were (understandably) averse to the subject.

(b) I had sufficient knowledge of the tactics of commercial publishers to know that the typescript would be considered far too long. I accordingly kept it as a work of personal reference, and reached the conclusion that it was unnecessarily lengthy owing to the fact that I had incorporated many messages and discourses verbatim from copyright sources. I also concluded that it was unnecessary for me to have rewritten the whole of Donkin's supplement to *The Wayfarers*, though my additional data was relevant.

(c) The style is not devotional but on many pages is immature, more markedly so in the first two volumes. It could be much better expressed, though the conclusions I still agree with. There was a highly idiosyncratic appendage to the first volume, an appendage entitled "The Cosmic Cycle," written when I was only seventeen; this section attested my interest in world history, which I later studied extensively. Later to receive addition and correction were my inchoate biographies of Hazrat Babajan, Sai Baba, Upasni Maharaj, and Sheriar Irani, which commenced the first volume.

(d) I had adopted a quite rigorous method of investigation and compilation in writing these volumes, but had not always been certain of the factual correctness of some data. I acquired a distrust of certain types of devotional reporting, and was often exasperated at the conflicting versions of events as recorded by different writers. I sometimes attempted to conflate different versions, but this I would no longer do. My early attempts at historicity stem from this biographical pursuit of mine – I "cut my teeth," as it were, on non-objective partisan accounts.

Having stated these reasons, it is now an intention of mine to at some time produce a condensed one-volume version incorporating some data from more recent sources. The original drew from most of the source material available to me up until 1977, including what I term the "Backett file." This latter consists of material bequeathed to me by Ann Powell at her death in December 1965, and some of which had formerly been in the possession of Will and Mary Backett. This bequeathal included old and rare periodicals, many letters, old news-sheets and circulars, and other diverse memoranda. Some of this represents unique material, though more unique was much of the oral data accessible to me, of which I made notes very close in time to hearing it.

To sum up, this biography attempted to achieve an etic version of events as distinct from the prevalent emicism of the devotional movement. It was commenced in June 1967 soon after Meher Baba's last cablegram to me, and was completed just prior to my new research commitments which resulted in the formulation of anthropography. During the lengthy interim, the only persons belonging to the "movement" with whom I had personal contact were Adi S. Irani and his wife Freiny, Fred Marks, and also, more briefly, Delia De Leon. All of these people I met at their private homes. On three other occasions I went (anonymously) to the London group meeting, and found my misgivings confirmed as to the mentality operative there. My writing of such a lengthy biography without being a member of the "movement" was an attempt to ascertain historical events and to distil the significance of an exceptional life without being distracted by the conditioning imposed by devoteeism and mouthpieces who were conflated with Meher Baba by the uncritical. There are many sociological and psychological implications in the biography of Meher Baba which have not yet been assimilated in general.

36. Bal Natu, *Glimpses of the God-Man Meher Baba Vol. 1* (1943–1948) (Walnut Creek, California: Sufism Reoriented, 1977), 431 pp.

An account by a Hindu devotee who first met Baba in 1944. It is a compilation of articles which appeared some years earlier in *Divya Vani*. Some of the material was new, but other published sources are used, notably Donkin's work. Natu commenced to write his memoirs in 1969, after Baba's death, and was able to utilize notes earlier made by him.

The style is devotional. The Preface includes some refreshingly honest remarks. "I claim no authority, and I do not profess to teach anything to anyone" (p. 17), Natu emphasizes. Also admirable is his comment that: "I have frankly recorded my interpretations, but these inferences are personal and open to correction" (p. 18). This makes it much more difficult for a critic to object to devotional insistences, and I am disposed to pass over whatever deficiencies I might personally be able to find. Further, one does not always discover such statements as: "Anyone is free to have his or her own outlook. What Meher Baba expects of everyone is purity of heart and honesty in life" (p. 18). This represents the best in the Hindu contingent, an attitude which I have always admired.

One has somewhat different feelings in reading the introduction by Adi K. Irani, which is verbose in tone and insistent upon Baba's avataric status.

37. Bal Natu, *Glimpses of the God-Man Meher Baba Vol. 2* (Jan. 1949–Jan. 1952) (Bombay: Meher House Publications, 1979), 406 + xvii pp.

This consolidated the first published multi-volume work on the subject. In his Preface, the author comments in relation to the phrases "Old Life" and "New Life" used by Baba: "To be frank, it is beyond my ability to explain, even remotely, the significance of these two terms" (p. xii). This attractive honesty makes it easier to respect his attempt to present a factual account of the New Life phase. He draws heavily upon the New Life Circulars and other publications, but there is some data not found elsewhere. His account of the *Manonash* phase (pp. 353 ff.) utilizes the diary of Pendu (A.R. Irani), one of the participants. This important phase was formerly in low profile.

Natu shows conscience in reporting. With regard to the discourse on *manonash* given in June 1951 at Hyderabad, he observes that a few persons, including himself, attempted to note down Baba's words from the alphabet board "to the extent that we could." He stresses that he was not a professional stenographer. "But from whatever I scribbled in long hand and with the gaps filled in from my memory," he reconstructs this discourse (pp. 338–347). He observes that the notes on this discourse were edited close to the time of occurrence by Ramju Abdulla, who included his version in the booklet *Meher Baba and the God-determined Step* (Ahmednagar, 1951). This serves to emphasize the provisional nature of reporting in some instances, or perhaps a better word would be fragmentary.

38. Bal Natu, *Glimpses of the God-Man Meher Baba Vol. 3* (Feb. 1952–Feb. 1953) (North Myrtle Beach, South Carolina: Sheriar Press, 1982), 327 + xv pp.

This account of a single year is not all new material, since the author also includes information from earlier publications. The style is devotional. The period covered is referred to as the "Life" phase, in deference to Baba's statement that: "The union of the Old and New Life states has given birth to Life." Natu adds in his earlier spirit of modesty: "To be frank, the literal and real meaning of these three specific terms that Meher Baba used is far beyond my comprehension" (p. x). But he does give his views and interpretations of various events, though he is again honest in his Preface with the reflection: "On some factual accounts, I have expressed my personal views which are open to correction" (p. ix). The present author is much less happy about Natu's statement that: "My chronological account of Avatar Meher Baba's life in *Glimpses* is not primarily intended as a 'history,' but is meant to glorify 'His story'" (pp. viii–ix). I am not certain as to what this means, but in the interests of clarity, I must state that my own chronological account of Meher Baba's life was intended throughout as history, and eschewed the glorificatory glosses found in many of the sources.

In view of the abovementioned statement, it is relevant to note what Natu says he is sharing with others in the volumes of *Glimpses*: "what I was privileged to absorb and gather during my long and short stays with Meher Baba, and also from my association with his close disciples" (p. ix). One might conclude that what he absorbed from some of the "close disciples" has unduly influenced his historical acumen. Natu's views would appear to reflect those of the surviving *mandali*, with whom he has been living at Meherazad.

39. Bal Natu, *Glimpses of the God-Man Meher Baba Vol. 4* (Feb.–Dec. 1953) (Myrtle Beach, South Carolina: Sheriar Press, 1984) 200 + xv pp.

An account of Baba's nine-month stay at Dehra Dun in 1953, utilizing the diary of Kishan Singh and some other new material. This period was formerly very sparsely documented in published works.

At the time of writing, Vol. 5 is not yet available. Bal Natu is also the author of *Avatar Meher Baba Bibliography 1928 to February 1978.*

40. Margaret Craske, *The Dance of Love: My Life with Meher Baba* (Myrtle Beach, South Carolina: Sheriar Press, 1980), 193 + xii pp.

A collection of stories told by one of the "Kimco" group of English devotees. The title implies the author's commitment to dancing, in which capacity she had a professional career in ballet. The episodes recounted date from 1931 onwards, but were told many years after the events of the pre-New Life phase. The narrations were recorded in America after Baba's death. In her foreword, Craske makes a very pertinent comment: "after being told the same story usually returns to the teller mutilated and trimmed up so that it has quite a different meaning" (p. ix). This is one reason why caution is required in relation to many written versions of oral reports. Craske says that she has tried to keep to those stories "with which I was personally associated or am fairly certain of their exactness and origin" (p. ix).

This book does give some indication of psychological frictions and processes which occurred during the 1930's and 1940's, at the ashrams and elsewhere. The problem is: how much of the context is missing? In the foreword, the author relates that the "differences in social structure in the different places" (i.e. the West and India) were faced and finally accepted, but did "at first cause much surface trouble" (p. ix). My own investigations revealed that the trouble was much deeper than in mere surface layers, and furthermore, that other differences in social structure were rarely faced and transformed. A person who is not mentioned in Craske's book was Ann Powell, who similarly met Baba in 1931, and who was another oral source on the 1930's. But Powell reaped almost complete oblivion in the literature devoted to Meher Baba; an entry in *The Meher Baba Jnl* attests her existence, but otherwise "Welsh Ann" was ignored. Even the significant cable from Baba at the time of her death (sent to Fred Marks of London) achieved only a very partial exposure. Accordingly, very few people knew that she served "Kimco" as a domestic servant during the early 1930's; they treated her as inferior, assuming that their more privileged and affluent middle-class background meant that they were more "elect." This dubious attitude was at its worst in Princess Norina Matchabelli, as even some members of "Kimco" found to their frustration. Powell gave me to understand that Margaret Craske had less class sense than the other women who comprised "Kimco," and they were accordingly on better terms. Indeed, Craske was in correspondence with Powell during the 1940's while the former was in India; I have some of the correspondence, which gives additional dimensions lacking elsewhere. Craske does briefly mention (pp. 147–8) the friction that existed between her and Rano Gayley, an American woman who was another resident at the ashram during the war years. This gives a sense of realism to relationships, though these tensions were customarily, in retrospect, glossed under the auspices of the "Love" paradigm currently in favour amongst devotees. Cf. Rano Gayley, *Because of Love: My Life and Art with Meher Baba* (Myrtle Beach, South Carolina, 1983). Gayley was an artist who was the only one of the Western women who stayed as a permanent resident at Meherazad.

It can be suggested here that one of the actual possessors of the much-vaunted "Love" was Ann Powell, who lived in comparative oblivion, her praises never sung in print, though Fred Marks revered her as a virtual saint. I can vouch for the fact that Powell was totally self-effacing in her attitude. To the best of my knowledge she did not receive one letter from Mani, unlike "Kimco" members, though it would be unwise to take this as an indication of inferiority.

41. Kitty Davy, *Love Alone Prevails: A Story of Life with Meher Baba* (Myrtle Beach, South Carolina: Sheriar Press, 1981), 727 + xv pp. Illus.

The author was another of the "Kimco" group of English female devotees. The book is divided into two parts. Part One (pp. 1–407) presents the author's reminiscences relating to the period 1931–52, a substantial part of which appeared in articles contributed to *The*

Awakener during the 1950's and 1960's. This record has a documentary value, but also has pronounced drawbacks. The reporting is disappointingly flat, and there is little of psychological intricacy. When compared with the total body of extant data, it is evident that much is missing, and indeed, some descriptions in this book are quite misleading. The interpretation of events is frequently rather banal, and the uninformed reader might be forgiven for thinking that Meher Baba was taking European holidays in the early 1930's with a group of leisurely society women addicted to frivolous pursuits and sightseeing. In brief, it is a typically "Kimco" account that is represented, minus certain touches in Craske's narrations.

The account has a little more psychological depth in the chapter on the Nasik ashram (pp. 139 ff.), but this would be very difficult to avoid, since that phase was particularly obvious for the intricacies and undercurrents attendant upon physical events. The much "tougher" reminiscences from Adi S. Irani and other sources leave one feeling that the kernel has been mistaken for the essence in the "Kimco" version.

The account of the Blue Bus Tours (pp. 249 ff.) could have been fuller, particularly since there are extant letters from Davy used as news-sheets by Will Backett (in my Backett file) which give additional information. However, more important is the interpretation given to the general contour of events, which has unfortunately to date been insipid in nearly all post-New Life literature. Revealing data is sometimes given, but with an accompanying failure to digest its implications. Despite the adulation showered upon members of "Kimco" by the latter-day movement, it is worth pointing out that Davy's own report contains the information that in 1941 she had not graduated beyond the stage of throwing an orange at Baba when criticized by him for anomalies in housekeeping (pp. 303–4). This was after he had repeatedly flattered her, saying (or rather dictating): "Kitty tries only to please me." Davy very aptly comments: "Sometimes Baba holds up to us an ideal" (p. 303). This point was sorely neglected in later years, since various people assumed that they were an ideal as a consequence of flattery. Devotees too rarely make good psychologists, as an examination of much literature will show.

In 1952 Kitty Davy was instructed by Baba to live at the new Center-on-the-Lakes at Myrtle Beach, South Carolina. The author makes much of this place as Baba's "Home in the West" in a separate chapter (pp. 361 ff.). But one fears that there is some distortion, since noticeable space is devoted to praise of Elizabeth Patterson and Norina Matchabelli as founders of this allegedly unique centre. What Meher Baba actually specified was an egalitarian venue for his followers, "for one and all," but elitist history has typically diminished the proportions of such an emphasis from the real "founder" (or rather instigator). It was not particularly difficult for Patterson to establish such a property, since she was a wealthy businesswoman, and the land was owned by her very wealthy father. Matchabelli's role was very largely verbal, and in no sense to be construed as any qualification of spiritual greatness. Ideals have to be realized, otherwise they will remain at the level of mere mouthing, which is particularly reprehensible in supposedly elite personages.

Part Two of Miss Davy's book includes over 250 pages of correspondence dating to the period 1952–68, largely between herself and Mani, Baba's sister at Meherazad. Davy expresses a high estimation of this correspondence (pp. 412–14). These letters are indeed revealing, though not perhaps in the way that "close disciples" liked to think. Mani includes some descriptions of Baba, and there is the occasional message or cable from him that is reproduced, but there is also much small talk that reads insipidly. In view of this, it is not altogether surprising that Baba sometimes imposed restrictions on this correspondence, which Mani described in 1962 as "cozy chats," to which she was evidently very partial (p. 598). During Baba's last years, his personal communications were notably rare, and usually impersonal; the substitute strikes some readers as a distraction. The distinctions that were believed to be conferred by this type of correspondence seem extremely dubious, to say the least, but myths were created that have become strongly rooted. Davy also quotes from the ubiqitous newsletters written by Mani, which are here described as containing an "incredible beauty of expression and matchless love for Baba" (p. 414). Even some devotees can find fault with this unrestrained praise, since Baba himself stated that it was Mehera who had the most love for him amongst the female contingent.

In view of such considerations supplied by the evidence, it seems particularly incumbent here to stress the egalitarian dimensions of Baba's teaching that were sometimes neglected by persons commonly deemed his "close disciples." Elizabeth Patterson, Norina Matchabelli, and Kitty Davy gained an elite prestige amongst the commonalty as a result of being correspondents with Mani, whose newsletters were originally addressed to "EliNori-Kit," an abbreviation for the names of the three women abovementioned. None of their writings prove any elite status. Patterson never wrote very much; Ann Powell bequeathed me a brief notebook written by Patterson on Meherabad Hill in 1938, but it is only a very factual description of events that is represented. Davy was a much better annalist than Princess Matchabelli, whose extravagant style some readers have found nauseating. The revelatory innuendoes of Matchabelli's *Fragments of a Spiritual Diary* may have unduly mystified the more gullible devotees unable to perceive what was really happening.

For complementary data upon how one of the less elite females in this movement fared at the hands of the elite ministers of "Baba's love and compassion," see Kate Thomas, *Beloved Executioner* (Cambridge: Roseking Publications, 1986), pp. 230–2, briefly detailing a persecution and excommunication perpetrated by some of the influential mouthpieces (all of them Parsis) in 1966–7. The author here abbreviated events in order to cause as little offence as possible. As a personal witness of events described, I can add that there was very much more which I have recorded in unpublished notes. The name of the persecuted was not literally circulated "amongst the whole of Baba's following," but only amongst certain elite members of the movement who had substantial influence in various countries. The commonalty knew nothing of the complexities involved. One of the punishments meted out in this case was non-access to Mani's newsletter, an indication of the mentality involved. One of the expurgated portions of Kitty Davy's published correspondence with Mani relates to this matter. Davy was not responsible for the vindictiveness; she was merely one of the uncritical spectators of this non-egalitarian gesture by Mani and one of her brothers (not Meher Baba). With typical ingenuity, Baba had washed his hands of the matter, and delegated it to those who did not always demonstrate the ideal of which they were considered the infallible representatives. But uncritical assenters render any demonstration soporific, which is what Meher Baba may have felt behind his increasing wall of secluded silence.

42. Bhau Kalchuri, *While the World Slept* (North Myrtle Beach, S.C.: Manifestation, Inc., 1984), 72 pp.

Reminiscences by one of the *mandali* who lived at the ashram from 1953 onwards. Veer Singh (Bhau) Kalchuri was given the job of a night watchman at Meherazad, and the episodes narrated accordingly reflect nocturnal events, giving them an unusual documentary accent, despite their brevity. A very sentimental introduction by a Western devotee is misleading.

43. Bhau Kalchuri, *Let's Go to Meherabad!* (Berkeley, California: Beguine Library, 1985), 147 + xii pp. Illus., with maps.

A devotional work of very mixed content. Numerous details of Meherabad pertaining to the period 1923–1930 are given, and do have a documentary value. These details were gleaned from the memories of two of the early *mandali* still living after Baba's death, namely Pendu (Aspandiar R. Irani) and Padri (Faredun N. Driver), and were written down by 1972. Three detailed maps of Meherabad also have a historical value. More disconcerting for the historian is that the facts are presented in a dialogue format, relating to the Indian genre of *Hari-katha* ("stories of God"), a form of devotional drama. Poems and songs are included.

44. Eruch B. Jessawala, *The Ancient One: A Disciple's Memoirs of Meher Baba*, ed. by Naosherwan Anzar (Englishtown, N.J.: Beloved Books, 1985), 245 + xxix pp. Illus.

Eruch Jessawala was one of the Parsi *mandali*, and was highly esteemed at Meherazad after Baba's death. Some of the material in this book comes from Eruch's diaries, notes, and letters, though much of it consists of narrations recorded after Baba's death. The editor observes that many accounts narrated by Eruch "contain material he identified as having been obtained from Meher Baba and are not to be taken as direct quotes from Meher Baba" (p. xi). Not all of the material is new, since some of it appears in earlier publications. The pre-New Life phase gains only brief exposure, which is a disappointing feature, since Eruch joined the *mandali* in 1938. The general atmosphere of the book reflects the post-New Life phase and some dominant devotional interpretations.

The style is devotional and occasionally dogmatic. For instance, Eruch is reported as saying after Baba's death: "The only guru in the proper sense is our Lord, Avatar Meher Baba" (p. 9). One finds it strange that the transcriber of *God Speaks* should have become so exclusivist. He urges that it is unnecessary for followers of Meher Baba to search for a living Perfect Master (i.e. *qutub, sadguru*), an emphasis strongly reminiscent of Adi K. Irani. This emphasis is arguably folly in view of Baba's own statements on the importance of qutubs and sadgurus, and the impossibility of gaining the ultimate realization without the assistance of such a rare entity. Eruch instead favours continual visits to Baba's tomb at Meherabad (pp. 10–12). While the present author would not wish to detract from the value of associations in this respect, it seems incumbent to point out that there is a blatant distortion in Eruch's reported statement that "many Sufi masters . . . relinquished their hold on intermediaries once they got into the orbit of the Avatar" (p. 10). Inspection of the relevant sources would soon dispel this misunderstanding, since there was no tradition more consistent than Sufism in stressing the essential factor of a living teacher of high grade. The Sufi trend was actually in the reverse direction to that insisted upon by Eruch, since dogmatic insistences upon Islamic literalisms caused trainees in Sufism to seek the contemporary reality instead of reliance upon the religious establishment which cited the *Quran* and *hadith* unperceptively. Also extremely questionable is Eruch's attendant statement that the Hindu saint Mira left her living spiritual teacher to devote herself exclusively to the long-dead *avatar* Krishna (p. 10). This represents an extreme devotional emphasis extrapolated from hagiography that has no basis in known fact. Eruch's similar reflection upon Francis of Assisi (p. 10) is contradicted by an extant statement of Meher Baba to the effect that it was not Jesus, but Khizr, who transformed the Christian saint (see Ivy Duce, *How a Master Works*, p. 426, which includes an inaccurate gloss by Duce). Khizr is the name given in Sufi lore to the human teacher who appears when the candidate is ready for advancement; the symbolic entity of Khizr has sometimes been interpreted literally in popular Sufism, but such interpretations could scarcely be more literal than those currently in fashion in the devotional movement associated with the name of Meher Baba.

Periodicals:

45. *The Meher Message*, ed. Khaikhushru J. Dastur (Ahmednagar-Nasik, Jan. 1929 to Nov. 1931). A monthly magazine promoted by

the editor, and not by Meher Baba, who here typically allowed an admirer to express what he wanted to. Dastur was a Parsi devotee who had lived with the *mandali* at Meherabad; he had written an unpublished biography of Baba, and industriously collected and edited a substantial number of his "sayings" and discourses. This seems to have gone very much to Dastur's head. The articles in this magazine are mediocre. Its major value lies in the editor's diary of Baba's activities, and the publication of the "sayings" and discourses. There is also some additional documentary value in relation to entities like H. Raphael Hurst, alias Paul Brunton. Dastur's enthusiasm eventually waned, even though he had taken great satisfaction in styling himself as "The Disciple of His Divine Majesty," the latter term referring to Baba. It was a graphic instance of an egocentric individual seeking to promote his "master" in extravagant terms in order to gain himself a corresponding degree of salience. This has occurred rather frequently since. This was one "close disciple" who experienced the indigestion of a deflated admirer, but there have been others who have made an equal exhibition of themselves, and who are even better documented in some instances. It is currently much easier to pose as a "close disciple" in the absence of any restraining factor represented by the teacher, who is conveniently considered to posthumously sanction any caprice of "discipleship" in his supposed intimates.

46. *The Meher Gazette*, ed. C.V. Sampath Aiyengar (Madras, June 1930–Sept. 1938). Another magazine of indifferent merits, though lacking the pompous stylisms of its predecessor. Sampath Aiyengar was a Hindu devotee, a retired Judge who presided at Saidapet ashram. He published this bi-monthly magazine upon his own initiative. A number of his editorial entries and the regular instalments from the diary of F.H. Dadachanji are of documentary value. The editor's "Biography of Shri Meher Baba" was serialized.

47. *The Meher Baba Journal*, ed. Elizabeth C. Patterson (Meherabad, Ahmednager – Bangalore, Nov. 1938 to Oct. 1942). This monthly, unlike the two preceding periodicals, was sanctioned by Baba, though due consideration should be extended in this respect to the complexities of sanction. To start with, the editorial

committee consisted of a superfluity of persons, far more than was actually necessary for the tasks involved. This committee initially consisted of C.V. Sampath Aiyengar, Dr. Abdul Ghani Munsiff, F.H. Dadachanji, Ramju Abdulla, Adi K. Irani, the managing editor Elizabeth Patterson, Estelle Gayley, and Princess Norina Matchabelli. Not all of these persons were of equal literary ability by any means. The quality of this journal was superior to the two preceding ones, but comprises very mixed contents. The *Meher Baba Jnl* demonstrates Baba's typical open-handed policy with devotees – he allowed them free rein in their expression, but discerning readers could see at once who really knew anything and who was shallow.

The contents of this Journal vary from Baba's regular discourse commissioned on a monthly basis to Princess Matchabelli's extremely idiosyncratic expressions of "revelation from the master." There were occasionally some valuable articles from contributors like Dr. Deshmukh, who penned his biography of Upasni Maharaj at this time. Several of Dr. Ghani's articles on Sufi subjects are also well above average. F.H. Dadachanji's diary of Baba's activities was entered on a regular basis, and is of a documentary value, though written in a very devotional style. There was also an editorial series entitled "Those who met the Master," referring to brief biographies of various devotees; these are of some relevance, though they sometimes tend to be glorifying. Noticeable is the absence of contributions from Charles Purdom and Dr. Donkin, but both of these men were very retiring when it came to devotional expression; Purdom would doubtless have been horrified at the prospect of his literary image being juxtaposed with that of Matchabelli.

The title of this Journal is misleading, and gives no idea of the underlying emphases that were initially made by Baba. He made three broad stipulations as to the content of this periodical: (1) it was to reflect his work and philosophy (2) it was to be interreligious in emphasis, and in this manner avoid any sectarian overtones (3) not only religion, but science, literature, and the arts were to be represented, since his teaching stressed the spiritual application of all these departments when correctly oriented. These emphases were duly, though briefly, reflected in the editorial (pp. 9–10) of the first issue of *The Meher Baba Journal*. As it transpired, the third emphasis proved very difficult for the editorial committee, and it is evident that views differed as to what his work and philosophy really comprised. Baba's "work" has in general been so poorly represented in extravagant cliches that analysis of what he meant by it is crucially necessary.

Some attempt was genuinely made by the editors (or some of them) to balance the devotional contents with other topics. Dr Ghani's Sufism, Sampath Aiyengar's articles on Hindu saints, and Will Backett's efforts with Western traditions all helped to give a non-sectarian flavour to this periodical. These and other writers achieved the inter-religious requirements well enough, but the polymathic requirements in science and literature were not met. Baba's polymathic "ideal" was too demanding even for Dr. Ghani. Having stated his requirements, he did not (characteristically) reiterate, but instead left the writers concerned to get on with their assignments. The mixed responses, and the resultant deficiencies, were probably the real reason why he allowed the Journal to terminate after a few years, whatever various persons may have assumed. He never again instigated any such project. To this date, the devotional movement associated with him has lamentably failed to implement this ideal. The *mandali* have been rather conspicuous for their lack of interest in this direction. Ivy Duce grasped that there were implications for the physical sciences in Baba's teaching, but was unable to extricate the necessary guidelines from the morass of devotional sentiment with which she and others were encumbered. Cf. *God Speaks*, second edn, editorial introduction, p. xxxv. Some other, and very atypical, partisans of Meher Baba of a scientific background, were aware of the lack of practical expertise in this direction, but have been vastly outnumbered by the disposition for "poetry and art" that tends to typify the devotional movement. It is very easy to write simplified verse that does not even have to rhyme.

The devotional movement has published selections from *The Meher Baba Jnl*, but has missed the point of that project.

48. *The Awakener*, ed. Phyllis Frederick (New York, 1953——). This was a very informative quarterly during Baba's lifetime. It described itself as "A Journal Devoted to Meher Baba," though for the most part it focussed upon documentary material and not sentimental expression. It was much superior to the first two "Meher" periodicals, but lacks the expansiveness of *The Meher*

Baba Jnl. Purdom became an editorial adviser, but with one or two brief exceptions, did not contribute any new articles save for his diary notes on the 1954 and 1958 *sahavas*. Most of the *sahavas* events of the 1950's were well covered, and some coverage was given to sequels in the 1960's, as in "Guruprasad Glimpses, 1963" by H.P. Bharucha, a serialized record of Baba's discourses and remarks during the 1963 assemblies at Poona. In addition, there were various experiences and views of devotees represented, and more consistently useful, numerous messages of Baba that were then recent. There was some flashback material relating to the pre-New Life, though it is mainly the post-New Life period that is documented. It is a rich source for this period. The editorial versions of Baba's statements were often taken from context, with no sources listed; it is very difficult to check some of them.

The Awakener is a major source of factual information, and maintained its primary value for some fourteen years, before deteriorating in the late 1960's, when the new wave of "hip" expression made its appearance. It has continued as a bi-annual.

49. *Divya Vani*, ed. Swami Satya Prakash Udaseen (Nicadavole, Andhra – Hyderabad, Andhra, 1961——). A quarterly in English that found it hard to compete with *The Awakener* for primary material. There is much space given during the 1960's to the activities of devotees in India, e.g. birthday celebrations. Some of the articles were more relevant to Baba's life and teaching, notably those of Bal Natu, which appeared after Baba's death. One article that did relate to Baba's life, but which was of a very poor quality, was H.P. Bharucha's contribution in 1966. This Parsi devotee did much better in his abovementioned report of 1963 events at Guruprasad, where he was content to record Baba's words without interpretation. But his later article proffered a very primitive view of "obedience," a theme often stressed in devotional literature, though frequently distorted. Bharucha cited factual episodes, or rather partial versions of these, and gave his own (or Adi K. Irani's) interpretation of these episodes. I can remember feeling great surprise that this kind of interpretation was uncritically accepted by a large number of Eastern and Western devotees as authoritative, as if it were Baba's words that were represented. I may add that the spirit of Bharucha's article was quite foreign to the liberal thought of Hinduism, both popular

and philosophical. The interpretation in question represents Baba as the agency of wrath and dire retribution whenever his orders were disobeyed. It can be pointed out here that this is a symptom of hagiography, and is akin to some of the less enlightened anecdotes in Persian hagiographies of Sufi shaikhs.

50. *The Glow*, ed. Naosherwan Anzar (Dehra Dun – Bombay, 1966——). A quarterly subsequently entitled *Glow International*. The early issues were poor, but during the 1970's some valuable diary material was published, both in full and in extract. There are also some interviews with the *mandali* and other persons recorded in the 1970's; these are of very varying degrees of relevance. This magazine as a whole reflects the views and sentiments of the devotional movement which crystallized after Baba's death, and more particularly, the views of the surviving *mandali* at Meherazad. The editor, a Parsi devotee, has shown some concern with repudiating insinuations of the movement constituting a sect, but unfortunately has demonstrated sectarian characteristics. Certain editorial features have rather stridently cried down other sects and teachers (though anonymously) in favour of the "Avatar" theme of exclusive adherence and sole importance. It is unfortunate that it is not so much Meher Baba that is being represented as the views of persons purporting to represent Meher Baba, persons who are glorified out of all proportion.

Diaries:

Many diaries relating to Meher Baba have been published, either fully or in part. These vary considerably in detail, and some writers show a greater sensitivity than others. There are some diaries treating the same period which afford an insight into the disparities of reporting. Some diaries are rather frequently disconnected in their contents, and there is much trivia in some of them, e.g. lengthy reports of the weather. Constant cross-referencing is necessary where possible. In the more detailed coverages, many external events receive a disproportionate emphasis, e.g., even the times at which Baba urinated are recorded, and the length of time he snored. However, sufficient detail is often crucially important in relation to psychological events, but this aspect is very often lop-sided, or even ignored. There are other drawbacks in entries. F.H. Dadachanji, one of the early Parsi *mandali*, kept regular diaries prior to his death in 1943, some of which were published in Gujerati and in early periodicals, but these are often very devotionally coloured, which limits their psychological insights.

Correspondence:

Much extant correspondence is not of primary value, and some writers are unreliable. There has been a recent tendency in the devotional movement to treat the letters of the *mandali* (written after Baba's death) on a par with communications from Meher Baba, a graphic indication of the lop-sided sense of priorities that has occurred. Cf. J. Mistry, ed., *Letters from the Mandali of Avatar Meher Baba*, 2 vols (Myrtle Beach, S.C.: Sheriar Press, 1981–5). Baba himself never wrote letters after 1926; he only appended his signature, "M.S. Irani," to epistles and postcards written by *mandali* members on his behalf. Most of these communications were very brief. F.H. Dadachanji ("Chanji") was the writer of most such letters during the 1930's. but extended his prerogative in this secretarial capacity to letters written at his own personal volition, embellishing these with misleading phrases which gave the impression that they came from Baba. (This is well known to the devotional movement, or should be, having been clearly stated in *The Glow Quarterly* in 1974, a commendably accurate statement from the editor). Later amanuenses included Dr. Donkin (briefly), Adi K. Irani, and Eruch Jessawala. Of these, there is some reason to believe that Adi K. Irani adopted the tactics of Dadachanji, though this has never been recognized or acknowledged by the movement. To the best of my knowledge, Eruch was a very faithful reporter of Baba's statements in epistles written during Baba's lifetime, though he did of course use his own wording. Donkin also seems to have been very accurate, though letters written by him are comparatively rare.

Baba sent many cablegrams to numerous followers over the years. These were dictated word for word, and vary prodigiously from mere greetings and expressions of blessing to much more intricate messages, sometimes to individuals, and sometimes to groups. A great deal depends upon the context in the interpretation of the more intricate cablegrams, and it is necessary to be in full possession of the facts before attempting interpretations.

This leaves the investigator with extant epistles written about Baba, or to Baba. The factual relevance of these varies enormously, as published examples amply reveal, and many are mediocre in quality. I possess unpublished letters by Dr. Donkin in my Backett file which are disappointing from the historian's point of view, since they detail only surface events at Meherabad during 1940, such as games of cricket with the *mandali* in leisure hours. Donkin was then newly arrived in India, and he makes very little mention of the *masts*, with whom his name was later to be closely associated. There is no devotional sentiment in these letters, and much more than most others, Donkin later came to realize that it was individuals like Chatti Baba who were the really important cogs in Baba's "work," and not devotees or *mandali*. Donkin is known to have acquired an eccentric and introverted sense of humour which few understood, and which does not emerge fully even in his accounts of the *masts*.

There are idiosyncrasies exhibited by some letter-writers. Will Backett (d. 1963) wrote his letters to Baba in an archaic "Biblical" style that strangely contrasts with his newsletters to the English devotees. These private letters were usually written jointly with his wife Mary, and I was never able to ascertain which of the two was most responsible for the archaisms (though I think it was Mary). Cf. Kitty Davy, "Thirty Years in the Service of Meher Baba, 1932–1962," *The Awakener* (1964) 9(3): 1–18, for a commemorative article on the Backetts which has important details missing. Will Backett showed more intellectual tendencies than his wife, though he was not an academic; from the early 1930's until the mid-1950's he relayed information from India in regular letters and news bulletins to English (and other) followers, and demonstrated a rare dedication and efficiency. He used much correspondence in these newsletters, which reveal a notable absence of sentiment, quite unlike the later "Family newsletters" of Mani and the mawkish London circulars of the Hopkinsons written after Baba's death. Backett never used the *avatar* tag, even when Adi K. Irani had commenced to bombastically air this as an "official" credential. (I have a substantial, though incomplete, collection of Backett's news bulletins in my Backett file).

During the mid-1950's Mani became an increasing correspondent with Western devotees, and often relayed brief statements and hints from Baba, together with her own comments. She frequently made it clear what the difference was, though devotees were occasionally misled when due distinctions were not made. A major problem here was that many devotees already accepted Mani's words as being somehow an invariably accurate reflection of Baba's meaning and wishes. A letter from Mani that was printed in *The Awakener* during Baba's lifetime was extracted from an epistle of Bili Eaton dated March 10th, 1956. Some devotees had recently appealed to Mani over some issue, and she replied of her own accord, basing her explanation upon former statements of Baba given in earlier years. Eaton remarks that "therefore Mani felt confident that these explanations are Baba's expressed wishes" (*The Awakener*, Vol. 7 no. 2, p. 8). But it is obvious that context may change over the years.

In his news bulletin dated 12th October 1955, Will Backett incorporated a letter from Mani which he himself described as "an explanation by Baba." But it is quite evident from the wording of this letter that it is very largely Mani's comments that are represented, interspersed with some remarks of Baba. The subject was potentially very misleading (as indeed it proved to be), since it was treated as "the path of love versus meditation," to use Backett's uncritical heading. It is apparent that Baba did make fleeting cautionary references to the episode of Jean Adriel seceding from the "movement" while receiving instructions in meditation from Kirpal Singh, whom Baba defined as a fifth plane *wali*. Devotees of Baba, including the *mandali*, were anxious to criticize this allegiance, but certain confusions resulted. Mani briefly described the Prem Ashram in very inadequate terms of a decline from "love" to "meditation," an interpretation that does not fit the facts of the late 1920's. She described Chota Baba as a fifth plane *wali*, whereas nearly thirty years before, Ramju Abdulla had described the same individual (on Meher Baba's authority) as a sixth plane saint. One suspects that this "decline" had become inordinately confused with Kirpal Singh, though neither he nor Chota Baba were condemned. But the intricacies of the demanding Prem Ashram phase were forgotten in preference for a simplified devotionalism that was amenable to persons of lesser capacity than the inmates of the Prem Ashram. This same letter of Mani's was quoted in *The Awakener* without adequate indication as to its authorship – it was misleadingly entitled "Baba on Meditation, from a disciple's notes." See *The Awakener*

(1956) 3(4): 31–2. It was consequently regarded as the literal statement of Meher Baba in its entirety, and was reproduced as such in Bal Natu, *Glimpses of the God-Man Meher Baba Vol. 2* (1979), p. 345, who refers to it as "a discourse which Meher Baba gave," and quotes excerpts from it.

It is worth noting here that Backett was amongst those who believed that Deshmukh's version of *The Discourses* amounted to a word for word exposition from Baba. Mani was one of those who had to dispel this illusion at the time of Purdom's edition, but it was too seldom acknowledged by the *mandali* that their own words rarely represented Baba in any verbatim context.

Some correspondence gives details of events not reported in published material by the same author. For example, in 1966 I received a generous nineteen-page letter from Irwin Luck of America which supplies additional information to that recorded in his article "How I met Baba," *The Awakener*, Vol. 7 no. 4, pp. 21–30. This article was not written but tape-recorded after his return trip from India in 1960. This article included one of the very few references to Dr. Donkin that appeared in print during Baba's lifetime, and indicates how different Donkin's disposition was from several other members of the *mandali*. Donkin preferred to laugh instead of talk, and often avoided answering questions; he had evidently learnt some wisdom from the *masts* and other entities. Luck believed that his association with Donkin at the same hotel in Poona was carefully, though unproclaimedly, arranged by Baba for his (Luck's) psychological needs. Though there have been many glorifying references to the *mandali* that are uncalled for, this particular reference can be credited by the present author.

During my early researches into the history of Meher Baba and his followers, I found that the American negroes in the movement were much more helpful than most of the other Westerners. I was impressed with their very genuine regard for Baba, and the way in which they actually demonstrated certain of his ideals – quite unlike some of the other followers. A good example of this contingent was Beryl Williams of New York, my closest correspondent during 1965–6, who was very helpful with both literature and reminiscences. She never made the slightest pretence of being a "close disciple," though she had met Baba in 1952, earlier than numerous other Western devotees. On the contrary, she treated me as an equal, even though I was very young. She was very reticent about her ethnic identity, and it was some time before she sent me a photograph which proved her colour. She was delighted with my reactions, and indicated that she had been so reticent on this point because she had formerly been rebuffed by white devotees, though she was reluctant to state any identities. She died in 1968. If more people were like her, the world would be a much better place.

Oral Sources:

Oral sources are of particular relevance where there is a sufficient diversity of contrasting material and levels of interpretation to be analyzed and compared. A premium is to be set on oral sources pertaining to early phases of Meher Baba's life, since these are less well represented in the literature. My own biographical investigations were able to draw upon a number of contrasting oral sources during the lifetime of Meher Baba, when there was no need felt to "justify" facts. Informants gave information very freely in some cases, and I made copious notes very close to the time of hearing the details. Much of this information has never appeared in print, but it serves to throw light upon various phases and aspects of method. My principal oral sources were as follows:
1) Adi S. Irani, the younger brother of Meher Baba, often known as Adi Jnr in order to distinguish him from Adi K. Irani (Adi Snr), who was a decade older. He lived in London from 1956 onwards, though he had formerly been resident at various ashrams of Baba since the late 1920's. His reminiscences stretched back to Upasni Maharaj in the earliest years of the Sakori ashram, which he visited as a boy with his mother c. 1919. Adi Jnr was, during his London phase, a hard-headed business man, and often critical of Western devotees, though adroitly. A few of his reminiscences of earlier years were recorded in the literature during Baba's lifetime, but he had a fund of memories that were never tapped in published form. Some of his recountings of 1920's and 1930's events had a realistic flavour very seldom found in the literature. This perspective tallied with Inder Sen's version, though there were differences in outlook between these two sources. I first met Adi in 1965, and was invited to his home in 1966. In his later years in London, Adi was difficult to contact, partly owing to

illness. After Baba's death, he was known to express a low opinion of the "movement" in the West, of which he was strongly critical. In 1973, he expressed to me a critique of certain Western devotees, which, in its pointedness, almost matched my own. I found him very talkative at that time, and we got on much better than formerly, when there had been differences of view between us.

2) Inder Sen, a Hindu, and another who was unusually independent in his thinking. He had taken his degree in physics at London University, was highly intelligent, and in his capacity as an electronics designer he invented a new "musical link" at Pye Telecommunications, Cambridge, with the collaboration of another scientist personally known to me. His contact with Baba dated from 1946, and he had thereafter lived during his early teens at Meherazad ashram during its incipient phase until the New Life. He was an important source of information on both the pre-New Life and post-New Life periods, and also expressed many unusual insights of his own in relation to these periods. He had known the early *mandali* surviving in the late 1940's, including Dr. Ghani, and liked to quote from the latter's poetry in Urdu entitled *Hosh-e-Madhosh.* He remained on excellent terms with Muslims, living with the family of Hoshang Patel, the Muslim follower of Meher Baba, for some years in Nottingham during the late 1950's. Sen never expressed himself devotionally, but gave an "inside" view of Baba's activity that was remarkably graphic. In the early 1960's he studied for his D.Sc., which he had delayed, but abandoned this academic course owing to pressures of overwork – he had continued a full-time job as an electronics designer in order to help maintain Meherazad ashram in India as Baba had wished. Nearly all of his wage packet was sent regularly to the ashram, and both this and his demonstration of the "non-status" ideal were particularly impressive. He returned to India in 1964 under circumstances that were grossly misinterpreted by Adi K. Irani and others, who were amongst the beneficiaries of Sen's financing. I met him on numerous occasions in 1965, when he returned briefly to England, and also recorded his earlier statements as relayed by my mother, who had known him well during the years 1962–4.

3) Ann Powell, of Welsh blood, and hence known as "Welsh Ann." She had first met Baba in 1931, and was a valuable source on his

visits to England in the early 1930's, particularly in relation to events at East Challacombe, Devon. She had kept only very minimal notes of these years, but her vivid report had the flavour of an exceptionally realistic authenticity. She was also a revealing source on later events, particularly since she was the closest friend of Mary and Will Backett, the pivots of the "English group." I knew her during the last year of her life in 1965, and visited her home in London on several occasions with my mother, usually staying overnight. She bequeathed to me her literature and photographs. She died in December 1965, aged seventy-six, and remained largely unknown. I found her unique amongst the female followers of Meher Baba. She had known much hardship in her varied life, and at one period had lived a gypsy-like existence in a caravan; her last years were easier, and spent at the home of her sister in Hornsea, a pleasant and spacious Victorian dwelling. Her approach was intuitive; she used very little devotional terminology.

4) Delia De Leon, a member of the Kimco group of English women who met Baba in 1931. During Baba's lifetime, only fragmentary reminiscences of hers appeared in published form. In 1974 *The Glow* magazine devoted one of its issues to her report of her contact with Baba, though without stating whether the material was written or tape-recorded. A former actress, she gained a star role amongst the devotional movement in England after Baba's death, being the only one of the early followers in England to have survived on native soil. I had met her in 1965, and was invited to her home in Richmond in 1966. There was a lengthy session during which she showed me her extensive photograph albums, containing very numerous snapshots of Baba from 1931 onwards. She gave a running commentary on this pictorial collection, and reviewed in some detail her contacts with Meher Baba. Quite frequently I would interpose a question to draw out amplifications of the record. In this way she reviewed all the events accessible to her immediate memory in which she had been in Baba's physical proximity, the last being at the East–West Gathering in 1962. She also showed me several letters she had received from Baba, mainly via Dadachanji. In 1973 I again visited her home for another such session. The details tallied very closely with my notes of the earlier occasion, though there was some supplementary information; the 1973 session was not as long as the

precedent, and there was proportionally less data. The overall details agree with those in *The Glow* report, though the latter report is rather flat and lacking in a good number of facts which I was told. Substantial space is given in *The Glow* article to reproducing a number of De Leon's letters from India, some of which I did not see, and of which I was unable to take a verbatim report. But *The Glow* is almost entirely lacking in the interpretations of events which the informant offered quite frequently. These interpretations differed very markedly from those of Ann Powell and other informants. One of her insistences was that she was one of Baba's "nearest and dearest," which many others accepted more uncritically than I did, though I did not mention any reservations to her. Baba did indeed send extravagant-sounding encouragements in epistles to members of "Kimco" (amplified by Dadachanji), but the sense was sometimes one of stating an ideal which had to be lived up to (for one letter in which this is evident, see p. 18 of *The Glow*; the letter is dated Feb. 10th, 1940).

Factually, De Leon was a relevant and helpful source on the early and mid-1930's, and also 1948. I believe that her memory was reasonably good. She was rarely devotional in speech, retaining much of what seems to have been the "Kimco" speech style – the British middle class accents of the 1930's. These accents had their own drawbacks and clipped much of the discernible content of events described. Recently, De Leon has gone to the opposite extreme and described "Kimco" and other early followers in mystical terms. This does not agree with her earlier statements, and nor with other data. An attempt at glorification seems visible. Cf. De Leon, "The Early English Scene," (Pt 1) *Meher Baba Association Newsletter*, London 1984, pp. 6–8. Ann Powell is notably missing from the honours list. Though I have stated above that I believe De Leon's memory to have been reliable in earlier reports, I cannot extend this consideration to recent statements. She says that Fred Marks went to the Charing Cross office directed by Will Backett in the early 1930's, and implies that Marks was thus amongst the earliest English followers who met Baba. This is definitely an error. Marks did not meet Baba until 1952, and did not contact him by letter until 1946. Cf. De Leon, "The Early English Scene" (Pt 2), *Meher Baba Association Newsletter*, London 1985, p. 4. It is possible to see why this error occurred. Marks first met Baba at the Charing Cross Hotel in 1952, and hence the geographical associations with the Charing Cross office used by Backett many years before. The conflation is therefore explainable, but does not inspire confidence in slipshod reporting. There is a chronological error of lesser proportions in De Leon's memoirs in *The Glow* (*supra*), where she includes (p. 3) the first encounter of the Backetts with Baba under 1931. The correct date is 1932, as proven in an extant diary of Will Backett. Further, in the same report De Leon incorrectly names the Backetts as being amongst the group who assembled at the East Challacombe retreat in 1932 (*art. cit.*, p. 5). I suggest that this error occurred as a result of confusion with Ann Powell, a very close friend of the Backetts in subsequent years, but who is totally neglected by De Leon in her published memoirs. In her talks with me, De Leon similarly ignored Powell, and it was only when I specifically questioned her concerning the latter that she briefly said that Powell "would not have fitted in with us," meaning with Kimco. This was a reference to the greater amount of time which the Kimco group spent with Baba in Europe. Ann Powell was indeed a much less superficial type than her middle class superiors, and would have been quite uninterested in much of the frivolous activity they were so intent upon.

5) Fred Marks, another English devotee, a close friend of the Backetts and Ann Powell, though he lacked the intuitive discernment of Powell. Factually, he had comparatively little to add to details supplied by other informants. He had first met Baba in 1952, and had thereafter met him in 1954, 1956, 1958, and 1962 on various *sahavas* occasions in India, America, and England. His value chiefly lay in a study of his disposition and views, and the contrasts afforded with other informants. I knew him quite well during 1965–6, and had further contact with him during 1973–5. He had a much closer contact with Adi S. Irani than other English devotees, but like most devotees in general, received only very infrequent and brief communications from Baba. He gained little or no eminence during Baba's lifetime, though after Baba's death, he gradually acquired a greater exposure. However, unlike other devotees, his tendency was always to zero-rate himself. His lifestyle was also notable. Like Inder Sen, he lived in a simple bed-sittingroom in an unelevated area, though he lacked the insights of Sen. Though Marks had been an antique dealer of the

more humble type, and was now retired, he had no material assets worth speaking of. The furniture in his room in Putney was worthless, and he lived on a pension that did little more than supply his needs. He treasured an old shirt once worn by Baba that he hung on the wall as if it were a priceless relic. He also possessed an old pair of Baba's sandals (bequeathed by Will Backett) which he devotedly guarded in an unostentatious box. A visit to his room was rather like meeting someone out of a dervish *khanaqah* or tomb-shrine, though he did understand the difference between relics and more underlying realities. His mode of speech was not of the modern devotee variety, but much more in the reverential idiom of Backett, who seems to have been a major influence upon him. Marks spoke very slowly, and had a habit of sagely nodding his head at appropriate junctures of conversation. He was always dignified, never flippant. Amongst his books was the original two volume edition of Lt. Col. Wilberforce Clarke's translation of the *Diwan* of Hafiz; Marks had industriously rephrased the whole of it in pencil between the printed lines. He told me that an updated correction was needed, with which I agreed, though the new version still read a little anachronistically perhaps. The sincerity of Marks was very tangible. His interpretations of Baba's methods were not always very objective, and he had (to me at least) a disconcerting tendency to attempt conversions to the movement. He is known to have distributed pamphlets on street corners, and to have tried to get newspaper offices interested in Meher Baba. These things he did entirely of his own accord, not from any instruction to do so. Yet to him, this was "Baba's wish." He contrasted with Backett in this respect, who seems to have been much less demonstrative (and more widely-read). Marks died in 1985, aged eighty-five.

N.B. Some researchers may wonder why I did not use a tape recorder in my oral investigations. The fact is that I never used one, and more to the point perhaps, I never liked these machines. The conditions under which many of the details were related were not compatible with the "forced" nature of talking into a machine. De Leon's almost non-stop recounting was the most suited to on-the-spot recording, though even here, appropriate questioning on different occasions could be crucial. Many of the best details from informants 1–3 were given at sporadic, unexpected moments, in flashes of clarity. Sen did not talk deeply with "outsiders," though he was nothing of an elitist. Adi Jnr had to be very much in the mood in order to recount in any detail. Contrary to the views of those who believe that they have all the data on tape, experience teaches that this is not so. In fact, in the interests of documentation, I would like here to stress that much has been lost in diverse taped and written sources that are over-rounded and over-finalized, amounting to potted versions eschewing essentials and subtleties.

INDEX

About the Author:

Kevin R.D. Shepherd was born in 1950, and has been engaged in an extensive private research project since 1977. He is the founder of the Intercultural Research Centre of Anthropography, a non-political educational project which was initiated in November 1984 upon completion of his manuscript *Meaning in Anthropos: Anthropography as an interdisciplinary science of culture*, which now awaits publication. Anthropography is a new science of culture conceived and promoted by the author in a polymathic sense of commitment.

Anthropography covers philosophy, the social sciences, the human sciences, natural science, and the history of religions. It is both scientific and humanistic. Anthropography here extends well beyond current dictionary definitions; the geographical distribution of mankind is given a polymathic focus that does not obscure intrinsic evolutionary dimensions.

Anthropography does not stress mere polymathy as an antidote to over-specialized studies, but is concerned to indicate the priorities that should govern a comprehensive curriculum.

The interdisciplinary strategy of anthropography takes particular account of the heritages of non-Western peoples. The European heritage is also covered, but not at the expense of Asiatic contributions. The author is currently working upon a series of books which has a cross-cultural relevance to Western, Islamic, Jewish, Indian, Chinese, and other culture-groups.